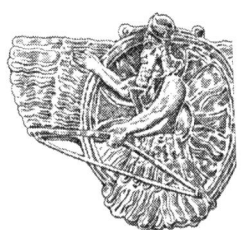 

Anunnaki Series

In 2010, Maximillien de Lafayette, for personal and security/safety reasons wrote and published several books under the pseudonym of Germain Lumiere. A so-called trusted friend betrayed the oath of friendship, and maliciously revealed this secret.

Thus, the pseudonym cannot be used any longer! So, in order to set the record straight, all previous books that appeared under that pseudonym, are currently re-published under the name of Maximillien de Lafayette.

The present volume is one of those books.

Copyright ©2010 by Maximillien de Lafayette. All rights reserved. No part of this book may be used or reproduced by any means, graphic, electronic, or mechanical, including photocopying, recording, taping or by any information storage retrieval system without the written permission of the author except in the case of brief quotations embodied in critical articles and reviews.

The Anunnaki Final Warning to Earth, and their Return in 2022.

The Grays' creation of a hybrid-human race, and the final clash between extraterrestrials and Earth. 5th Edition

Maximillien de Lafayette
Commentaries and teaching by
Ulema Mordachai ben Zvi
Ulema Penjabi Tien Utan
Ulema Yira Kerma
Ulema Meli Po
Master O. Kanazawa

From the Mouzakraat of Sinhar Marduchk*
Announcing the return of the Anunnaki to Earth

From Ana'kh, the Anunnaki language:
1. Michrachk Sinhar Anunna Ila Erdu Ina Kitbani Nouru Ilmu
2. Wa Tahiriim kiblah-ra Michrachki
3. Ana mia "Maiyaa" inaduu nisa khalkah

Translation
1. [The] Return of the Lords Anunnaki to Earth is written in the Light of Knowledge
2. And the Purified shall prepare my return
3. In the waters shall cast a new creation

Translated from Ana'kh to English by Germain Lumiere/Maximillien de Lafayette, Cairo, 1962.

***   ***   ***

Linguistic notes:
a-Mouzakraat means records, notes or diary in Ana'kh, the language of the Anunnaki. In ancient and modern Arabic, the word Mouzakaraat means memoirs. And the word "Zikr" means memory or remembrance.
b-Sinhar means lord.
c-Anunna means Anunnaki. It is a linguistic variation of the words "Anunnaki" and "Anaki", in their archaic use by the ancient Semites, Arwadians and Phoenicians. The Hebrew word Anakim and the ancient Hyksos term/name Anuramkim mean the same thing.
Other names of the Anunnaki:

---

* Mouzakraat of Sinhar Marduchk shall be published soon. It is the world's first authentic Anunnaki's manuscript provided by an Anunnaki Sinhar.

From the Mouzakraat of Sinhar Marduchk

The Anunnaki were known to many neighboring countries in the Near East, Middle East, and Anatolia. Because of the languages' differences, the Anunnaki were called differently.

For instance:
- 1-The Habiru (Early Hebrews/Israelites) called them Nephilim, meaning to fall down to earth, as well as Anakim.
- 2-Some passages in the Old Testament refer to them as Elohim.
- 3-In Ashuric (Assyrian-Chaldean), and Syriac-Aramaic, they are called Jabaariyn, meaning the mighty ones.
- 4-In Aramaic, Chaldean and Hebrew, the Anunnaki as Gibborim mean the mighty or majestic ones.
- 5-In literary Arabic, it is Jababira. The early Arabs called them Al Jababira; sometimes Amalika.
- 6-The Egyptians called them Neteru.
- 7-The early Phoenicians called them An.Na Kim, meaning the god or heaven who sent them to us.
- 8-The early inhabitants of Arwad called then Anu.ki, meaning the subjects or followers of Anu. Sometimes, they were called Anu. Ki.ram. (Ram means people, persons, community, tribes, group)
- 9-The early Hyskos (Ancestors of the Armenians) who invaded and ruled Egypt for more than 300 years, called them the Anuramkir and Anuramkim, meaning the people of Anu on earth. It is composed of three words: Anu + ram (People) + Ki (Earth). The primitive form of Ki was kir or kiim.
- 10-The Greeks called them the Annodoti.
- 11-In the Book of Enoch, they are called The Nephilim, "The Sons of God," or the "Watchers".
- 12-The Ulema call them Annakh or Al Annaki, meaning the people from above.
- 13-In other parts of Anatolia, and especially in the lands of the Hittites, the Anunnaki were also called Anunnaku, and Ananaki.

d-Erdu means planet Earth. Ard in Arabic. Heretz in Hebrew. Erda, Irdi in proto-Phoenician, Ugaritic.
e-Kitbani means written. Kitaba is a document or a book (Conic Inscriptions) in Ana'kh.

Kitab in Arabic, and a variation of Ketab in ancient Turkish, Farsi and Urdu. All these words were directly derived from the Anunnaki language.

f-Nouru means light. From this Anunnaki's word derived numerous words included in the languages of the ancient and modern Near East and Middle East. For instance the word Nour appears in Arabic, Urdu, Turkish, Farsi and several ancient languages. Even the Judaic/Hebrew word Menora is closely related to Nouru.

g-Tahiriim means the Purified Ones, sometime it refers to the Ascended Masters, which are one of the two highest categories of the Anunnaki-Ulema.

h-Mia "Maiyaa" means water. Mia or Mie appeared in the ancient Assyrian texts, as well as in the Akkadian/Sumerian inscriptions of Tiglath Pileser. In Pre-Islamic and modern Arabic, it is Maii or Ma'. In Phoenician it is Mem.

i-Khalkah means the Creation of Man. Khalikah in Arabic.

*** *** ***

Kitab in Arabic, and a variation of Ketab in ancient Turkish, Farsi and Urdu. All these words were directly derived from the Anunnaki language.

f-Nouru means light. From this Anunnaki's word derived numerous words included in the languages of the ancient and modern Near East and Middle East. For instance the word Nour appears in Arabic, Urdu, Turkish, Farsi and several ancient languages. Even the Judaic/Hebrew word Menora is closely related to Nouru.

g-Tahiriim means the Purified Ones, sometime it refers to the Ascended Masters, which are one of the two highest categories of the Anunnaki-Ulema.

h-Mia "Maiyaa" means water. Mia or Mie appeared in the ancient Assyrian texts, as well as in the Akkadian/Sumerian inscriptions of Tiglath Pileser. In Pre-Islamic and modern Arabic, it is Maii or Ma'. In Phoenician it is Mem.

i-Khalkah means the Creation of Man. Khalikah in Arabic.

*** *** ***

The day, the Anunnaki will return to Earth!

Wednesday, November 30th, 2022:
Indications and signs of the Anunnaki's return will appear.

Thursday, December 1st, 2022:
Date of the return of the Anunnaki.

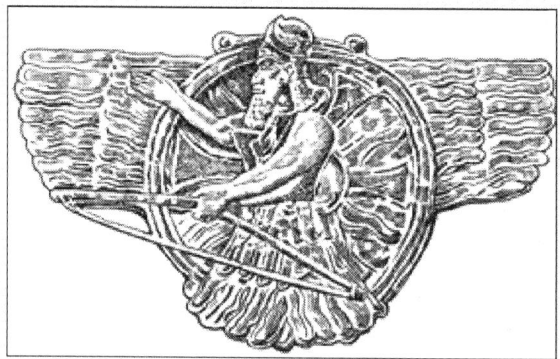

Acknowledgements

For their enormous contributions to this book, and especially for their guidance, I am extremely grateful to:

Ulema Mordachai ben Zvi
Ulema Penjabi Tien Utan,
Ulema, Grand Master Master W. Li,
Master Sorenztein,
Master Oppenhemier,
Master O. Kanazawa,
Master Ghandar,
Master Govinda,
Ulema Cheik Al Mutawalli,

A special thank you note goes to:
Dr. Mary Ann Ghafurrian, administrator of the United States Chapter of the Anunnaki Ulema Ramadosh Society for revealing the truth.
Author Laura Lebron for translating major manuscripts and books on the Anunnaki from English to Spanish, and for enlightening the international Latin/Spanish speaking communities.
My loyal friends Peggy Sulin, Indra Sulln, Colonel Petrit Demaliaj, and Melinda Pomerleau for their constant encouragement and support.

*** *** ***

The Revised, Indexed and Complete Book of the Anunnaki-Ulema Final Warning to Humanity, the End of Time, and the Return of the Anunnaki in 2022. 5th Edition

The Grays' creation of a hybrid-human race, and the final clash between extraterrestrials and Earth.

Based upon the writings, Kira'at (Readings) and books of Ulema Maximillien de Lafayette (Dirasat/Work1960-2010)

Maximillien de Lafayette

Commentaries and teaching by
Ulema Mordachai ben Zvi
Ulema Penjabi Tien Utan
Ulema Kira Yerma
Ulema Meli Po
Master O. Kanazawa

Contribution by
Ulema Nathaliyi ben Yacov
Ulema Mordachai ben Zvi
Ulema Kira Yerma

*** *** ***

Times Square Press. Elite Associates International

Notes by
Jamiya Ramadosh Al-Ulema Al-Anunnaki

London New York Paris Marseille Benares Cairo Alexandria Baalbeck Damascus Tokyo

*** *** ***

2010

Table of Contents

From the Mouzakraat of Sinhar Marduchk...5
Announcing the return of the Anunnaki to Earth...5
Table of illustrations...37
Introduction...41

PART ONE
The Return of the Anunnaki...43

Final warning and the Apocalypse
- The Mayan Calendar and other return's dates...49

Table of contents

- How about the 2022 scenario? ...49
- What contact? What return??...51
- Why the Anunnaki contact or Anunnaki return is so different and so important on many levels?...52
- Identified cities in India for the return of the Anunnaki...55
- Earth's designated landing areas for the Anunnaki's return to our planet in 2022...56
- Will you be there when the Anunnaki return to earth? Find out! ...57
- What are you chances of meeting an Anunnaki? ...57 Here is the formula! Do your math! ...57
- The following is an excerpt from a dialogue between a student and an Ulema...57
- Is it true that their return will seal the fate of Planet Earth and all humanity?...59
- Did the Anunnaki plan on returning to Earth to clean house?...59
- Ambar Anati's story and revelations...59
- Sinhar Ambar Anati in her own words...60
- Three members of the NSA were waiting for me...61
- The Grays attended the meeting...61
- Holographic pictures that showed them the entire sequence of the Roswell crash...62
- At the Dulce Base...64
- We were joined by a Gray...66
- The First Level...66
- The Second Level...67
- The Third Level...67
- The Fourth Level...68
- The Fifth, Sixth and Seventh Levels...68
- The Eighth Level...69
- The Ninth Level...69
- The Tenth Level...70

Table of contents

- Grays in shape-shifted form...70
- The Grays and their slaves, the Hybrids, have invaded the world...71
- The Grays and their slaves, the Hybrids, have invaded the world...70
- The Anunnaki Council...73
- The United States military authorities would not cooperate...73
- The Anunnaki needed a planet-sized laboratory...76
- The Anunnaki fostered the evolutionary process...76
- Humanity is divided into three groups, regarding their level of contamination...77
- The first group...77
- The second group...79
- The third group...80
- A cataclysmic event...81
- The Anunnaki's Bubble...81
- Anunnaki guides will be there for the humans...82
- Ba'abs (Star Gates) exist everywhere...83
- The final stage...87
- The final clash...94

Coding and decoding the significance of the year 2022...103
- First interpretation of the Code...103
- Second interpretation of the Code...104
- Characteristics of the number 6...104
- The number 6, carbon and the creation of mankind...104
- The number 6 is one of the six major extraterrestrial hot spots on Earth...105

Table of contents

- Statue of a Phoenician goddess found in Malta...106
- Photo of the ruins of ancient Malta, which is one of the six major extraterrestrial hot spots on Earth...107
- Photo of the ancient walls of Malta...108
- Photo of the ruins of Baalbeck, one of the earliest colonies of the Anunnaki on Earth...109
- Photo of the Trilithon of Baalbeck, part of the early space centers of the Anunnaki in the Near East...109
- Another view of the legendary Trilithon of Baalbeck...110
- Photo of the tomb of Hiram, king of Tyre, founder of the first Freemasonry Rite in the world, and an offspring of the remnants of the Anunnaki in the Near East...111
- Photo of the ruins of the ancient city of Tyre in Phoenicia (Modern day Lebanon). ...111
- Tyre was one of the six major esoteric cities of the Anunnaki on Earth...112
- Photo of Tyre (Sour) today; a Shiite Muslim city in Southern Lebanon...113
- Photo of the Ziggurat of Nippur. ..114
- The ancient city of Nippur in Iraq was one of the six major extraterrestrial hot spots on Earth...114
- Photo of a tower toward the heavens in Nippur...115
- Ur Nammu atop the Ziggurat (Tower of Babel) at Ur...115
- The Phoenician "Hook"...116
- Meaning of the number 6 in Anunnaki-Phoenician Alphabets...116
- Facts...116

In 1947, a Grays' spacecraft crashed in Roswell...119

- Statement by Ambar Anati on record...120
- On the night of February 20, the President of the United States disappeared...123
- A Cover-up!...124
- It was a cover-up for the President's real business...124
- Photo of Muroc Field/ Edwards Air Force Base...126
- Eisenhower was actually taken to Muroc Airfield, which was later renamed Edwards Air Force Base. There, he met with the Grays...126
- How was this meeting arranged, in the first place?...127
- Before the meetings: Two major black projects...127
- Second meeting in 1954...128
- United States "Protocol on Extraterrestrials' visit to Earth in 2022"...129
- Master Kanazawa's Kira'at (An excerpt)...130
- United States Government publications on extraterrestrial invasions...132
- 1-Government alien invasion plan...133
- 2-Government publications on aliens and security...133
- 3-The US government's plan with Aliens...133
- 4-United States National Defense Against Aliens' Invasion...133
- 5-Aliens' attack plan...133
- 6-What to do in case of an alien attack...134
- United States government major concerns...134
- Xenotransplantation and aliens-cross-species infections...134

Table of contents

- United States Government Official Statement...134
  "Extraterrestrials could seek to unravel the inner secrets of mankind." ...135
- United States Government Findings: In case of extraterrestrial invasion, the power supply known a electricity would most likely be a high value target for hostile parties...135
- Recently discovered publications by the United States Government pertaining to alien invasion...136
- 1-Likely Defense Against Alien Invasion...136
- 2-Surviving Extraterrestrials Invasion...136
- 3-Aliens and Government Preparation...136
- 4-US Emergency Plan for Extraterrestrial Invasion...136
- 5-Extraterrestrial Alien Invasion Government Procedure...136
- United States current intelligence about the mode of transportation of beings of other worlds...136
- Department of Defense Briefings: Area 51, a location often believed to contain materials of extraterrestrial origin...137

*** *** ***

PART TWO
The Return of the Anunnaki: Q&A...139

Questions answered by Maximillien de Lafayette.

Outlook for mankind after the year 2022...147
- Question: What is the outlook for mankind after the year 2022? ...147

- You have explained this in some detail in your books but will we live in peace or does humankind still pose a threat to one another if challenges and greed are proposed like they always have been?...147
- Answer...147

Another extraterrestrial threat other than the Gray's aliens...150
- Question: After the Anunnaki's job is finished here on earth through decontamination will we ever have to deal with another extraterrestrial threat other than the Gray's aliens?...150
- Answer...150

On aliens competing with the Anunnaki to rule our planet...152
- Question: Are there any other alien races in this galaxy or another that could compete with the superstar status of the Anunnaki and rule our planet?...152
- Answer...152

Would the Anunnaki come to aid the planet if another alien threat happens?...155
- Question: You have said that the Anunnaki feel responsible for the hybrid contamination between the humans and the Gray's, would the Anunnaki ever come to the aid of the planet again if this threat would happen?...155
- Answer...155
- Question: Has the planet ever come close to another threat as serious as the Gray's and will it be a possibility?...155

Table of contents

- Answer...155

Hybrid Grays: Adoption and DNA contamination...156
- Question: Have there been a large number of ones that were disease free and human enough to be adopted?...156
- Answer...156
- Question: Could someone have a relative hybrid or be a child of a hybrid and not know it?...156
- Answer...156
- Question: I always wonder how people with no compassion what-so-ever are the same species. It seems that living as a loving and compassionate being is what our natural instinct wants us to do, so I wonder if hybrids have any connection to emotionless behavior? ...156
- Answer...156
- Question: I have read the discussions about contaminated DNA and am curious to know if it is to the point where large amounts of people have some connection to hybrids?...157
- Answer...157
- Question: Is it true that hybrid human/grey babies and children are being created and raised in secret bases?...157
- What of the stories of horrific experiments being performed on abducted humans in labs by the Greys as part of their breeding/tissue harvesting programs?...157
- Answer...157
- Question: What is the reason behind the Greys interbreeding program with humans?...176

Table of contents

- Answer…176
- Question: Is one of these Anunnaki Gods going to take over the earth after the pole shift?…184
- Answer…184
- Questions: I am very worried by what you have written on the subject of the return of the Anunnaki in 2022? Is it for real?…184
- Are they going to change the way we look?…184
- Are they going to get rid of us and replace us with a new human race?
- What kind?…186
- Answer…186
- Questions: Is it true that a massive Russian underwater base exists one mile deep in the Marianas trench in the Pacific ocean?…187
- If so, what activities/research/experiments are going on there?…187
- Do the Chinese have one too?…187
- Answer…187
- Question: Will the Anunnaki intervene to prevent possible use of atomic/thermonuclear weapons prior to, or during their return in 2022?…193
- Answer…193

Who will survive the return of the Anunnaki?
- Question: What percentage of the world's population will survive the return of the Anunnaki to become part of the new human race after 2022?…196
- Answer…196

How many other Anunnaki will be part of the return? …197

Table of contents

- Question: Though the return will be led by Sinhars Marduchk and Inannaschamra, how many other Anunnaki will be part of the return? …197
- And how many Anunnaki guides will there be, for humans who will be saved and returned to earth after the cleansing?…197
- Answer…197

Efficient energy systems of the Anunnaki…200
- Question: What kind of clean and efficient energy systems, and modes of transportation will the Anunnaki introduce after 2022?…200
- Answer…200

Stargate over Chicago…201
- Question: Is there a stargate/ba'ab in Chicago?…201
- Where exactly is it located, and what does it look like? How would you jump into a ba'ab?…201
- Terminal of Grand Central Station in downtown Chicago…201
- Answer…202

Signs before the return of the Anunnaki…204
- Question: What are the signs that people will see in the skies the day before the Anunnaki return, and where will they be seen?…204
- Answer…204

Anunnaki's "tool of annihilation"…205
- Questions: Who/what created the "tool of annihilation" that the Anunnaki will use when they return?…205
- Answer…205

Table of contents

PART THREE
The World of the Anunnaki and Ulema: Q&A...207

On divination and Tarot reading...221
- Question: Do the Ulema believe in divination and Tarot card reading? At the beginning I was skeptical but after having consulted a Tarot reader, I became a believer. She predicted things nobody knew or heard about. Sometimes her predictions touched on a very personal note. So my question to you is this: Is the Tarot something your people accept? Is it a game or the real thing?...221
- Answer...221
- Question: If your answer is yes, then would you please explain the difference between regular Tarot cards and Ulema Tarot cards?...222
- Answer...222
- Question: OK, would I be able to learn about my future if I use the Ulema Tarot cards?...223
- Answer...223
- Question: Is there a particular book on the Anunnaki-Ulema Tarot? If so, who wrote it? Is it about the past, present or the future? What did the Ulema say about the future? Is it already written for us? Can we change our future?...223
- Answer...223

On inner bio-rhythm, bad luck, good luck and Anunnaki...229
- Question: Is it true what some mediums have said that some people are conditioned by a bio-rhythm that creates good luck and bad luck?...229

25

Table of contents

- If so, can we change this rhythm and become luckier, if we were not so lucky in the first place?...229
- Was this rhythm created by the Anunnaki when they manipulated our DNA?...229
- Answer...229

On ghosts, entities, holographic projections, and the 40 days period after death...235
- Question: I know you don't believe in ghost stories, but what about the idea that sometimes people see themselves like a ghost. I read about this in a Celtic story where a prince saw himself getting killed. Is it a hallucination or a prediction?...235
- By the way, the prince saw himself like a ghost, and in fact he got killed short after. So, if seeing ourselves as a ghost, is it an indication that something bad is going to happen to us?...235
- Could it be holographic projection, such as those images projected by aliens to impress or frighten abductees?...235
- Answer...235

Living continuously in 3 different time-space zones and Anunnaki...239
- Question: On the Science Channel, Dr Michio Kaku said the universe is expanding, and there are many universes he called multiverses where people live in different time and space zones...239
- Is this something the Ulema can do?...239
- Answer...239

On Anunnaki purification and a new identity...241

- Question: You wrote somewhere about Anunnaki purification, and the new identity a young Anunnaki receives after a purification ceremony on Nibiru. What do you mean by purification?...241
- Since you do not believe in the existence of SOUL, what are you talking about? Purify what? Dirty laundry?...241
- Assuming what you have said is true – I don't believe a bit of it– can you tell me in plain English how does this purification stuff happen and for what purpose?...241
- Answer...241
- I. Definition...241
- II. Annunaki purification and its relation to water in Judaism, Essene's sect, and Christianity...242
- III. Anunnaki's "Nif-Malka-Roo'h-Dosh"...243
- IV. Creation of the mental "Conduit"...244

Were dinosaurs created by extraterrestrials?...247

- Answer...247

The lost continent of MU's connection with the Anunnaki...249

- Question: This is the most important question for me. In any of the books I read, I haven't come across any information about the lost continent of MU's connection with the Anunnaki. I assume you know lots of things about it. According to James Churchward's books, MU was even older than Atlantis and home of human civilization. Humans migrated from MU to all over the world. But we already know that Anunnaki were in Mesopotamia.

Table of contents

- So what about it? What can you tell me about the lost continent of MU? ...249
- Answer...249
- I. Introduction/Mythological backgound...249
- II. Scientific/geological facts...250
- III. Anunnaki-Ulema views...252
- IV. So, what did we learn from all this?...253

Where are the Anunnaki now and why don't they interfere in our planet?...257
- Question: Where is the Anunnaki race right now and why don't they interfere in our planet anymore? ...257
- Answer...257

Don't ever underestimate the power of your mind!...261
- Question: I can't understand how you could write so many books in a such a short time? Do you use some sort of magic or a supernatural power?...261
- You know what, some are spreading rumors that the overwhelming number of your books you wrote were made by a machine and because of this you are a machine...261
- Answer...261

Scanning brilliant minds to create a "Super-Baby"!...263
- Question: I am not sure who has said aliens can scan our brains and create a new species of babies for their hybrid program. Is it true? ...263
- Can they do that? And how it is done?...263
- Answer...263

On the Ulema-Anunnaki group administration...265
- Question: Is the Ulema-Anunnaki group administered by men or a matriarch woman as I have heard?...265
- Answer...265

The relationship between our mind, body and cellular memory...269
- Question: What is the relationship between our mind, body and cellular memory?...269
- Answer...269

Anunnaki-Phoenician Chavad nitrin and the immortality of the gods...273
- Question: I am originally from Byblos(Jbeil) in Lebanon, and we Lebanese are descendants of the Crusaders who have learned some of the secrets of the Anunnaki in Lebanon and Jerusalem. I have heard that my ancestors the Phoenicians have used a product similar to athletes' steroids. This product I was told was also used by the Egyptian Pharaohs. Could you please tell me more about it?...273
- Answer...274

Hidden entrances to other worlds and dimensions, right here on Earth...277
- Question: Do UFOs and extraterrestrials use galactic entrances and space-time corridors to enter and exit our world? How many are there? Are they visible to the naked eye?...277
- Answer...277
- a-Entrance to the next-life...277

- b-Entrance to the fourth dimension...278
- c-Entrance to the parallel dimension...279

Paranormal mirror and extraterrestrials: Mirrors that remember their previous owners...281
- Question: I read a small article on a mysterious antique mirror that caused the death of it's owner, because, as it was explained in the articles, the mirror had a vengeful memory against one owner. There are people who believe that the mirrors had an extraterrestrial origin and were contaminated by aliens. Logically, they said the contamination killed people. What is your personal opinion?...281
- Answer...281
- I. Introduction...281
- II. The story...282
- III. Italian philosopher Tommaso Campanella's explanation...282
- IV. Paris Academy of Science...283
- V. Parapsychology...283
- VI. Psychology and metalogic...284
- VII. Extraterrestrial influence...285

Anunnaki type of civilization...287
- Question: What type of civilization are the Anunnaki at this moment in time?...287
- A Type One, Two, Three, or other type of civilization?...287
- Type One, according to Professor Michio Kaku, a theoretical physicist from New York University, is a civilization that gets their energy from all planets. Type Two Civilization is getting energy from their, Mother Sun only! Type Three Civilization gets their

energy from all the suns in our universe and the next...287
- Answer...287

Anunnaki's immaturity, emotional control, sin, jealousy?...289
- Question: Have the Anunnaki matured away from their immaturity in emotional control, past stories of jealousy, power, etc., sin?...289
- Answer...289
- 1-The Akkadian clay tablets texts...289
- 2-The Bible...291
- 3- Phoenicia/Anatolia texts and archeological finds...292

Anunnaki management skills...293
- Question: Have they learned to manage their emotions and improve their management skills?...293
- Answer...293

The Anunnaki's God: A critical God?...295
Question: Is the Anunnaki a Critical God?...295
No forgiveness, no exceptions, as in an eye for an eye and a tooth for a tooth?...295
- Answer...295

Benevolent and malevolent Anunnaki gods...297
- Question: Is there a benevolent and a malevolent faction of Anunnaki Gods?...297
- Answer...297

Clairvoyance; Telepathy between members of the same family...299

Table of contents

- Question: Is there clairvoyance (Telepathy) between members of the same family...299
- Answer...299

On the Anunnaki's creation of early humans and Earth original species...301

- Question: Were the quasi-humans the Anunnaki encountered (when they first came to earth), a natural product of evolution, or genetically manipulated by the Igigi /prior E.T. ?...301
- Answer...301
- Question: Have we ever found skeletons and bones of them and what do we call them? (Australopithecus, Afarensis, Homo habilis, Erectus, Cro-magnon?)...302
- Answer...302

All human beings do not come from the same origin...303

- Question: Have the Anunnaki created/genetically upgraded species on other planets? If so, what has been the outcome?...303
- Answer...303
- Question: Page 138 of book one of the three books of Ramadosh mentions that though we are all human beings, we do not come from the same origin. Some were born here on Earth, others were born somewhere else, in some other dimensions and far different spheres. Can you please explain in further detail what do you mean by that, and by us being created according to different specifications?...304
- Answer...304

- I. Introduction...
- II. First category of humans...305
- Man (Humans) created on Earth from clay...305
- III. Second category of humans...306
- Akama-ra...306
- IV. An'th-Khalka...307
- V. The Earth-made human creatures created from a cell...308
- VI. The space-made human creatures...308
- VII. The Basharma early creatures...308
- VIII. Metabolism created an early human-like form...309
- IX. Bashar category...309
- XI. The Shula with programmed brains...311
- At the time we were created, three things happened to us...313
- a-The Brain Motor...313
- b- The vibrational dimension...314
- c-The Conduit=Health/Youth/ Longevity...314
- XII. The Shula species...316
- XIII. The Emim...316
- XIV. Ezakarerdi, "E-zakar-erdi "Azakar.Ki"...317
- XV. Ezeridim...318
- XVI. Fari-narif "Fari-Hanif"...318
- XVII. The Anunnaki-Ulema from Ashtari...319

Anunnaki-Ulema esoteric and mind-power techniques...321
- Question: What techniques and practices can help us become more spiritual and more open to the 'paranormal' such as seeing auras, ghosts or spirits, seeing into the future etc?...321

- What effect can this awakening have on our lives?...321
- Answer...321
- 1-Gomari "Gumaridu" technique...321
- 2-Gomatirach-Minzari technique...322
- From Ulema Mordechai's Kira'at (Reading)...322
- 3-Gubada-Ari technique...322
- Synopsis of the Theory...323
- 4-Cadari-Rou'yaa technique...324
- 5-Chabariduri technique...324
- 6-Daemat-Afnah technique...324
- 7-Da-Irat technique...325
- 8-Dudurisar technique...326
- 9-Arawadi technique...326
- 10-Baaniradu technique...326
- 11-Baridu technique...327
- 12-Bisho-barkadari "Bukadari" technique...327

On the old way of thinking...329
- Question: A lot of spiritual teachers tell us that the mind with all its conditioning, becomes a barrier to growth and enlightenment. When will mankind be able to move on from the old way of thinking to a new paradigm?...329
- Einstein says that "problems cannot be solved by the same level of thinking that created them." What might this new way of thinking look like?...329
- Thinking and judging obessively itself may be a large part of the problem...329
- Answer...329

Esoteric/secret calendar of your lucky days and hours...331

- Question: One person who has read your books told me about a technique the Ulema sorcerers used to read the future. As I understood, it is a calendar of the good days, and the bad days in the life of each one of us. I would be grateful if you could explain to me what it is about and see the calendar. I promise I will use it for a good cause. ..331
- Answer...331
- I. Synopsis of the concept...332
- II. The Ulema-Anunnaki days are...332
- III. The calendar's grids...333
- IV. The use of a language...333
- Grid 1: Calendar of the week...334
- Grid 2: Calendar of your name...335
- Calendar of your lucky hour...335
- Grid 3: Calendar of your lucky hour...336

On different dimensions and multidimensional beings...339
- Question: What dimensions lie beyond the 4th, that we can experience?...339
- Question: Do other beings exist in these dimensions?...341
- Answer...341
- Question: Can we ever contact them, and would there be negative repercussions from doing so?...341
- Answer...341

*** *** ***

Table of contents

Miscellaneous...342

Are Earth Governments controlled by aliens?
- Question: Is it true that lots of Earth governments including the U.S. are controlled or ruled by an Alien race called the Reptilians?...342
- Answer...342

Insignia or logo of the Anunnaki...342
- Question: What is the royal insignia or logo of the Anunnaki? The winged disk? Do they use banners or flags like us?...342
- Answer ...342

The Face on Mars...342
- Question: In the Lost Book of Enki (written by Zecharia Sitchin) he wrote that the mysterious face on Mars (which is still unaccepted by NASA) was the Anunnaki Alalu's graveyard. Do you know if it is true?...342
- Answer...342

Question: Are Enlil, Enki, Anu etc. still alive?...342
- Answer...342

On eating meat...343
- Question: Must we stop eating meat for our preparation for 2022 or will we prepare ourselves mentally only? Because I love eating meat!...343
- Answer...343

Table of Illustrations

- Statue of a Phoenician goddess found in Malta...106
- Ruins of ancient Malta, which is one of the six major extraterrestrial hot spots on Earth...107
- The ancient walls of Malta...108
- Ruins of Baalbeck, one of the earliest Anunnaki's cities/colonies on Earth...109
- The Trilithon of Baalbeck, part of the early space centers of the Anunnaki in the Near East...109
- Another view of the legendary Trilithon of Baalbeck...110
- Tomb of Hiram, king of Tyre, founder of the first Freemasonry Rite in the world, and an offspring of the remnants of the Anunnaki in the Near East...111
- Ruins of the ancient city of Tyre in Phoenicia (Modern day Lebanon). Tyre was one of the six major esoteric cities of the Anunnaki on Earth...112
- Tyre (Sour) today; a Shiite Muslim city in Lebanon...113

- Ziggurat of Nippur. The ancient city of Nippur in Iraq was one of the six major extraterrestrial hot spots on Earth...114
- A tower toward the heavens in Nippur. Ur Nammu atop the Ziggurat (Tower of Babel) at Ur...115
- Eisenhower was the first American President to sign a treaty with the extraterrestrials...125
- Muroc Field/ Edwards Air Force Base. Eisenhower was actually taken to Muroc Airfield, which was later renamed Edwards Air Force Base. There, he met with the Grays...126
- NASA's ring of hydrogen particles...147
- Jesse "The Body" Ventura...190
- Photo of Benazir Bhutto...193
- Photo of Nikola Tesla in his lab...195
- Terminal of Grand Central Station in downtown Chicago...201
- Madison Square Garden...202
- Tammuz and Ishtar (Sumerian Inanna)...207
- Ulema-Anunnaki, Alain "Allan" Cardec...230
- Baalbeck, one of the Anunnaki earliest cities of on Earth..251
- Map of Pangaea...253
- Map of Santorini...254
- Map of Crete...255
- Marduk fighting the dragon Tiamat...266
- Marduk chasing and fighting Tiamat...267
- Roman pillars leading up to the temple of Balaat Gebal...273
- God Osiris...274
- Ruins of the ancient city of Ugarit...275

Introduction

The great Babylonian king Hammurabi, the sixth monarch of the first Babylonian dynasty. Hammurabi received his Code from the Anunnaki.

Introduction

Earlier this year, Maximillien de Lafayette's book "Anunnaki Final Warning" was sold out and no longer available.
We approached him with the idea of updating and rewriting a new edition of this book, with the intention of bringing to the reader, knowledge and information never before released to the public, and source material directly from Maximillien de Lafayette's work and the Ulema Anunnaki Kira'at.

This book contains brand new material as well as new questions and answers and revelations on the return of the Anunnaki in meticulous detail.
Please note that the ideas and information within these pages are strictly and solely that of Maximillien de Lafayette and the Ulema, as previously published in his books.
No bibliography has been used or recommended, as no other authors have disserted on this subject.

Introduction

This book, and all subsequent publications will exclusively contain the original work of Maximillien de Lafayette and the Ulema.

> No reference to any other author's book, or use of any other source material will ever be included in our publications, except for short inclusions of governmental data when is permitted and part of the public domain, such as government press releases and information obtained through Freedom of information Act requests.

*** *** ***

PART ONE

The Return of the Anunnaki

Final warning and the Apocalypse

PART ONE

The Return of the Anunnaki

Final warning and the Apocalypse
- The Mayan Calendar and other return's dates...49
- How about the 2022 scenario? ...49
- What contact? What return??...51
- Why the Anunnaki contact or Anunnaki return is so different and so important on many levels?...52
- Identified cities in India for the return of the Anunnaki...55
- Earth's designated landing areas for the Anunnaki's return to our planet in 2022...56
- Will you be there when the Anunnaki return to earth? Find out! ...57
- What are you chances of meeting an Anunnaki? ...57 Here is the formula! Do your math! ...57
- The following is an excerpt from a dialogue between a student and an Ulema...57
- Is it true that their return will seal the fate of Planet Earth and all humanity?...59
- Did the Anunnaki plan on returning to Earth to clean house?...59
- Ambar Anati's story and revelations...59
- Sinhar Ambar Anati in her own words...60
- Three members of the NSA were waiting for me...61
- The Grays attended the meeting...61
- Holographic pictures that showed them the entire sequence of the Roswell crash...62
- At the Dulce Base...64

Table of contents

- We were joined by a Gray...66
- The First Level...66
- The Second Level...67
- The Third Level...67
- The Fourth Level...68
- The Fifth, Sixth and Seventh Levels...68
- The Eighth Level...69
- The Ninth Level...69
- The Tenth Level...70
- Grays in shape-shifted form...70
- The Grays and their slaves, the Hybrids, have invaded the world...71
- The Grays and their slaves, the Hybrids, have invaded the world...70
- The Anunnaki Council...73
- The United States military authorities would not cooperate...73
- The Anunnaki needed a planet-sized laboratory...76
- The Anunnaki fostered the evolutionary process...76
- Humanity is divided into three groups, regarding their level of contamination...77
- The first group...77
- The second group...79
- The third group...80
- A cataclysmic event...81
- The Anunnaki's Bubble...81
- Anunnaki guides will be there for the humans...82
- Ba'abs (Star Gates) exist everywhere...83
- The final stage...87
- The final clash...94

Table of contents

Coding and Decoding the Significance of the Year 2022...103

- First interpretation of the Code...103
- Second interpretation of the Code...104
- Characteristics of the number 6...104
- The number 6, carbon and the creation of mankind...104
- The number 6 is one of the six major extraterrestrial hot spots on Earth...105
- Statue of a Phoenician goddess found in Malta...106
- Photo of the ruins of ancient Malta, which is one of the six major extraterrestrial hot spots on Earth...107
- Photo of the ancient walls of Malta...108
- Photo of the ruins of Baalbeck, one of the earliest
- Photo of the Trilithon of Baalbeck, part of the early space centers of the Anunnaki in the Near East...109
- Another view of the legendary Trilithon of Baalbeck...110
- Photo of the tomb of Hiram, king of Tyre, founder of the first Freemasonry Rite in the world, and an offspring of the remnants of the Anunnaki in the Near East...111
- Photo of the ruins of the ancient city of Tyre in Phoenicia (Modern day Lebanon). Tyre was one of the six major esoteric cities of the Anunnaki on Earth...112
- Photo of Tyre (Sour) today; a Shiite Muslim city in Southern Lebanon...113
- Photo of the Ziggurat of Nippur. The ancient city of Nippur in Iraq was one of the six major extraterrestrial hot spots on Earth...114

Table of contents

- Photo of a tower toward the heavens in Nippur. Ur Nammu atop the Ziggurat (Tower of Babel) at Ur...115
- The Phoenician "Hook"...116
- Meaning of the number 6 in Anunnaki-Phoenician Alphabets...116
- Facts...116

In 1947, a Grays' spacecraft crashed in Roswell...119
- Statement by Ambar Anati on record...120
- On the night of February 20, the President of the United States disappeared...123
- A Cover-up!...124
- It was a cover-up for the President's real business...124
- Photo of Muroc Field/ Edwards Air Force Base. Eisenhower was actually taken to Muroc Airfield, which was later renamed Edwards Air Force Base. There, he met with the Grays...126
- How was this meeting arranged, in the first place?...127
- Before the meetings: Two major black projects...127
- Second meeting in 1954...128
- United States "Protocol on Extraterrestrials' visit to Earth in 2022"...129
- Master Kanazawa's Kira'at (An excerpt)...130
- United States Government publications on extraterrestrial invasions...132
- 1-Government alien invasion plan...133
- 2-Government publications on aliens and security...133

Table of contents

- 3-The United States government's plan with Aliens...133
- 4-United States National Defense Against Aliens' Invasion...133
- 5-Aliens' attack plan...133
- 6-What to do in case of an alien attack...134
- United States government major concerns...134
- Xenotransplantation and aliens-cross-species infections...134
- United States Government Official Statement...134 "Extraterrestrials could seek to unravel the inner secrets of mankind." ...135
- United States Government Findings: In case of extraterrestrial invasion, the power supply known a electricity would most likely be a high value target for hostile parties...135
- Recently discovered publications by the United States Government pertaining to alien invasion...136
- 1-Likely Defense Against Alien Invasion...136
- 2-Surviving Extraterrestrials Invasion...136
- 3-Aliens and Government Preparation...136
- 4-US Emergency Plan for Extraterrestrial Invasion...136
- 5-Extraterrestrial Alien Invasion Government Procedure...136
- United States current intelligence about the mode of transportation of beings of other worlds...136
- Department of Defense Briefings: Area 51, a location often believed to contain materials of extraterrestrial origin...137

*** *** ***

The Return of the Anunnaki
Final warning and the Apocalypse

The Mayan Calendar and other return dates

2012 marks the end of the Mayan calendar. It has no relation whatsoever to the return of the Anunnaki. Any advanced theory pertaining to this date is not backed up by science.
Such assumption is pseudoscience.
Mr. Burak Eldem was the first writer to suggest that the Anunnaki will return in 2012. Again, this "assigned" date could not be backed by astronomy or any other science. It is evident that people are confusing the Mayan calendar that ends in 2012 with the Anunnaki return or intention to return.
Some authors have suggested that the Mayas and the Incas have some sort of link to the Anunnaki, because of their extensive knowledge of astronomy and cosmology. The same thing was said about the Sumerians who mapped the heavens. Yet, there is no date for their return to earth in the Sumerian texts.
According to Mr. Sitchin, the next passage of Nibiru will occur in the year 2085. This means that the Anunnaki will show up in 2085.
Any scientific data to substantiate this idea?
No.
However, Mr. Sitchin must have his own reasons and logic for advancing such a theory. On what foundation did he cement his assumption? We don't know. We respect the man and admire his pioneering work. But, we have no clues as to how Mr. Sitchin came up with this date.

*** *** ***

How about the 2022 scenario?
The only reference made to the date 2022 was found in the Ulema manuscript called "The Book of Ramadosh."

Part one: The return of the Anunnaki

> In essence, the Book of RamaDosh is a cosmological-metaphysical-philosophical work based upon science, astronomy and quantum physics.
> Yet, at the time it was written or compiled, quantum physics theories did not exist.
> How the Ulema knew about quantum physics, and anti-gravity laws, remains an unsolved mystery, unless you are one of their adepts.
> The "Book of Ramadosh" and the book "Ilmu Al Donia" described *ad infinitum* the return of the Anunnaki to Earth, and their plan for humanity.
> According to two Anunnaki-Ulema, Masters, Ambar Anati, and Maximillien de Lafayette, the Anunnaki's return has already been announced to leading figures in several countries. Some have suggested that India was chosen as the landing terminal of the Anunnaki.

*** *** ***

Numerous ufologists believe that the United States is more likely to be the Anunnaki's return destination.
They claim that American military scientists and a group of astrophysicists at NASA and top-echelon officials at the NSA have learned about the Anunnaki's return (Including the date of their return) from an extraterrestrial race currently living on Earth.
Some of these extraterrestrials work at the Dulce base, AUTEC, and other underground facilities in Arizona, Nevada, Puerto Rico and Mexico.
How accurate are these claims?
Nobody knows for sure. However, Ulema de Lafayette has stated, "this could be quite accurate, simply because the Greys who live on Earth and underwater already know that the Anunnaki are planning on returning to Earth. And since the Greys are working on several joint-projects with some very powerful governments, one can assume that they have informed our governments about the Anunnaki's return.

Part one: The return of the Anunnaki

In addition, a few years ago, in Washington, D.C., an Anunnaki Sinhar by the name of Ambar Anati had two meetings with top officials and leading figures in science, and informed them that the return of the Anunnaki is "irrevocable", because the Greys have contaminated the human race."

In the area of speculation and rhetoric, we have 3 proposed dates, so far:

> ❖ 1-According to Z. Sitchin, the return of the Anunnaki shall occur sometime in 2085.
> ❖ 2-According to independent researchers and "fans" of the Mayan Calendar, the Anunnaki will return in 2012 and this could change humanity's fate, and bring the world to a catastrophic end.
> ❖ 3-According to the Ulema, the precise date is 2022.

*** *** ***

What Contact? What Return??

The return of the Anunnaki triggers enormous global interest, and excites the imagination of people.
The reasons?
Well, the list of reasons is *ad infinitum*...endless. According to our readers, the return of the Anunnaki could:

(a) Change their religious belief systems;
(b) Alter the fabric of our societies;
(c) Clean-up mind and body contamination;
(d) Establish cosmic order.

Part one: The return of the Anunnaki

Highly cultured researchers (debunkers and believers alike) have begun to express an increased and intense interest in this topic, because the possibility of contacting extraterrestrials, and/or being contacted by them has become a possibility that science can no longer refute or deny.

The paramount questions rotating around the Anunnaki's return are:
1-When?
2-How?
3-Where?
3-For what purpose?
4-And who will be contacted on earth? Heads of governments and important people only, or just, you and me, and the rest of us?

Basically, those are the major concerns.
However, contact with extraterrestrials is neither the main topic, nor the primordial concern per se, because several scientific groups and secret military units are already working in sync with various alien races. Many top echelon military men and the crème de la crème of scientists in the United States have already confirmed such cooperation.

The main theme is not "Extraterrestrial Contact", but a <u>contact with the Anunnaki.</u> And this difference is extremely important and major on so many levels.

*** *** ***

Why the Anunnaki contact or Anunnaki return is so different and so important on many levels?

- 1-History shows, that there is a special (and very unique) relationship between the Anunnaki and the human race.

Part one: The return of the Anunnaki

- Unlike other extraterrestrial races that interact with us for very specified and specific purposes, such as abduction of humans in exchange for alien technology, or peaceful co-habitation/co-occupation of planet earth via a mutual agreement/protocol, the Anunnaki:
(a) Do not interact with us,
(b) Do not abduct humans,
(c) Do not cooperate with United States military scientists.

The Anunnaki do not need the consent of humans to carry on their projects, and/or to coordinate mutual operations. They had, and still have full control over us from the dawn of the creation of the primitive humans.
We function, think, act and react according to what they have installed in our "Intellect program", genes, DNA, and "Mental Conduit".
They created us genetically.

*** *** ***

Other extraterrestrial races currently working with top military scientists on earth have control over earth and its inhabitants because of their far advanced technology.
These alien races operate very differently from the Anunnaki.
Their agenda is macabre, for it contains:

(a) Human abduction;
(b) Animal mutilation;
(c) Genetic experiments;
(d) Mind control;
(e) Territorial ambitions.

The Anunnaki have no interest whatsoever in dominating the earth and controlling our minds.
The Anunnaki have already created our mental faculties and "programmed" us some 65,000 years ago. Thus, their physical interference in human affairs is not necessary at all.

Part one: The return of the Anunnaki

- 2-The Anunnaki left earth thousands of years ago. Many other alien races are still on earth carrying out their own programs and projects. For a multitude of reasons, they need planet earth as a spatial/terrestrial base.

The Anunnaki (Or Igigi) do not need planet earth as a base for their galactic enterprises.
They lived here, created multiple human races, founded cities, established religions and taught us how to think, how to act and how to understand our physical world. Their job is done!
The Anunnaki are no longer interested in human affairs, because the human race has nothing particular or beneficial to offer to the Anunnaki. But other extraterrestrial races are in extreme need of using humans in any capacity, role, function, and aspect to carry out their operations. Ufologists and scholars know very well the complete scenario and agenda of alien races currently living on earth. We have plenty of theories and hypotheses, but nothing is absolutely certain.

*** *** ***

- 3-Almost 99.99% of extraterrestrial activities, sightings, landings, human abductions, visitations, encounters and contacts occur, develop, and materialize in the sphere-existence of various alien races living on earth, but never in the Anunnaki's sphere or perimeter.

The Anunnaki are not part of this spectrum. In other words, the Anunnaki are out of the picture. They left earth thousands of years ago, and are not very much interested in us.
Thus, a return of the Anunnaki to earth is an exceptional event in the history of mankind. Very unique and very significant indeed.

The Anunnaki must have serious, paramount and indispensable reasons for returning to planet earth.
Other alien races are here on earth. Some left, while many others are still working and living in secret military bases, laboratories on the surface of the earth, underwater and in terrestrial orbit.

So, there is nothing new or special about their presence on earth. But the return of the Anunnaki to earth is evidently very special, and constitutes a major event.

The Anunnaki are not coming back to mine gold!!! This is an old silly story we will not bother with.

The Anunnaki must have more important and predominant reasons for their return. And this is what makes their anticipated return extremely paramount and significant! This book explores and explains the scope, nature and reasons for the return of the Anunnaki.

*** *** ***

Identified cities in India for the return of the Anunnaki

Some writers have suggested that India was chosen as the landing "terminal." Those suggestions have appeared on many websites, and in articles published by journalists from India. The early and very ancient Anunnaki-Ulema manuscripts identified the "Hind and Sindh" (Ancient territories of modern India and Pakistan) as one of the landing spots for the return of the Anunnaki.

The most frequently mentioned cities and regions for the landing of the Anunnaki are:

- 1-Punjab,
- 2-State of Multan also called Bayt al-Zahab by the Arabs, and Dar Al-Aman by the Mughals,
- 3-Lamghan,
- 4-The area surrounding the river of Chinab,
- 5-Kashmir,
- 6-Jazirat Al Sind.

*** *** ***

Part one: The return of the Anunnaki

Earth's designated landing areas for the Anunnaki's return to our planet in 2022

Cheik Al Mutawalli and Dr. Farid Tayarah (Both, members of Hiram Masonic Lodges in Lebanon and Egypt, and custodians of the Book "Sun of the Great Knowledge": Shams Al Maa-Ref Al Koubra) said that some regions of India lign up perfectly with the "Anunnaki Triangle" that defines precisely the perimeter of their landing and designated cities for their return.

This "Triangle" encompasses additional cities outside India. Dr. Tayarah named those cities and areas:

Aktion,	Bijjeh,	Geilenkirchen,
Alaska,	Brazilia,	Gyumri,
Amchit,	Bucharest,	Honolulu,
Amrit,	California,	Kamishli,
Antioch,	Carthage,	Kent,
Arizona,	Cherbough,	Konya,
Arwad,	Dover,	Le Havre,
Baalbeck,	Dushanbe,	London,
Basra,	Gabala,	Malta,
Mexico City,	Paris,	Trapani,
Nevada,	Prague,	Tyre,
New Mexico,	Puerto Rico,	Ur,
New York City,	Saint Petersburg,	Vera Cruz,
Niederheid,	Sidon,	Washington DC
Oerland,	Texas,	

Part one: The return of the Anunnaki

Will you be there when the Anunnaki return to earth? Find out!

Will you be there when the Anunnaki return to earth?
Find out!
What are you chances of meeting an Anunnaki? Here is the formula!
DO YOUR MATH!

*** *** ***

The following is an excerpt from a dialogue between a student and an Ulema:

The student asked the Ulema: "Well, if I correctly use these numbers, would I be able to learn more about the return of the Anunnaki? Are they a threat to us? Can I meet the Anunnaki?"

The Ulema replied: "First, the Anunnaki are a threat only to the "Fasidin" (Bad people, rotten people in his language). So you have nothing to fear for yourself...Yes, the numbers will tell you a lot about the Anunnaki."
He stopped for a few seconds, and then, said: 'Tayeb Esma'h (OK, listen now, in his language), when you have some free time...and if you are interested in knowing if you have any chance of seeing with your own eyes the "Roujou'h" (Arrival) of the Anunnaki, do this...consider it as a game for now...nothing serious...just play with these numbers, and see what you could find...OK?
Do this:
- Write down the number 2022
- Add your age to 2022
- Subtract 6
- Deduct 14 from what you got
- Add together the four digits of the new number you got
- Add the new number to form one single digit

Part one: The return of the Anunnaki

- Add the digit you got to 2022

*** *** ***

> He continued: "The final number you get will tell you if you are going to be one of those lucky persons who will be blessed by the Anunnaki...remember blessing is not a religious benediction or a spiritual blessing...no...no...no...it is simply your chance to enter a new age of happiness, tranquility and an enormous personal satisfaction. Do the numbers, see if you will be around..."

The student did not quite understand how the final number will tell him about all that? So he asked the learned one: "How would I understand what the final number means?"
The Ulema replied: "You will, just compare the number to the year 2022...if your number is under 2022, you are not a lucky man...if your number is equal or higher, then you have made it...you will be there, you will meet them and your life will be full of happiness..."

Anxiously, the student asked his teacher: "So, If I get less than 2022...I am screwed! Right?" The Ulema laughed and replied: "Not totally, try again...be patient...take your time, and if the same number pops again, do not panic, add to the number, the numerical value of the Phoenician letter "Aleph"..." (First letter of the Phoenician, Aramaic, Hebrew, Anunnaki, and Arabic alphabets.)

*** *** ***

Part one: The return of the Anunnaki

Is it true that their return will seal the fate of Planet Earth and all humanity?

Question:
Did the Anunnaki plan on returning to Earth to clean house?
Is it true that their return will seal the fate of Planet Earth and all humanity?

Answer:
Absolutely!
According to Sinhar Anbar Anati – an Anunnaki hybrid woman born on Earth of Anunnaki lineage, who married an Anunnaki Sinhar, traveled to Nibiru (Ashtari), lived there for several years, and studied the true history of humanity here on earth as well as learning much about life on Nibiru – YES they will be returning in 2022, and the decision they have made is now irrevocable and final.

Before her final departure from Earth back to Nibiru in 2007, Sinhar Anbar Anati contacted Ulema de Lafayette with a desire for him to publish an account of her life and experiences both here on Earth and Nibiru, with humans, Anunnaki, hybrids and Greys.
The most fascinating parts of her account were her meetings with top echelon military brass and scientists from different countries and governments, concerning the return of the Anunnaki to Earth, and the reason behind their return.

*** *** ***

Ambar Anati's story and revelations:

Herewith is an exerpt from her story, as told to Maximillien de Lafayette and Dr. Ilil Arbel, who included it in their book "Anunnaki Ultimatum End of Time."

Part one: The return of the Anunnaki

Note: Maximillien de Lafayette and Dr. Ilil Arbel wrote the story of Sinhar Ambar Anati in 2008.
The following is an excerpt from the story, and it has been authorized by Ulema and author de Lafayette to reproduce it in this book, in its entirety.

Sinhar Ambar Anati in her own words:

I was taken to earth, and went to a hotel in New York. I had with me a special device, an ingenious thing that had on it the special telephone numbers of top members of the National Security Agency, or NSA as everyone refers to them. Only two or three people in the world have these numbers, not even the president of the United States has access to them.

They are used only for matters related to extra terrestrial reverse engineering. The device makes sure the phones will be promptly answered, and when I called, I gave them data that they recognized as their own extraterrestrial material.

They were shocked, but nevertheless they agree to meet with me. I suppose they realized they had no choice.

Rather politely, they offered to fly me to Washington DC, where they wanted to have the meeting, but I informed them that it was not necessary.

It was easy for me to simply materialize in D.C., and I did not want them to know my current address, if this could be prevented. They directed me to come to the Four Seasons Hotel in Georgetown, where they were to meet me at the lobby.

I was to know, if questioned at the hotel, that I was heading for the suite that was reserved under the name of a Middle Eastern gentleman who owned a limousine service in D.C., and had often used the hotel for similar purposes.

*** *** ***

Three members of the NSA were waiting for me

I materialized a little distance away from the hotel, and walked there on M Street. Three members of the NSA were waiting for me, and they took me to the reserved suite, where fifteen more people were sitting around a huge table.

They rose and greeted me politely, but I could clearly see the suspicion in their eyes and in their thoughts.

I noticed that the shades of all the windows were closed, and I saw no telephones. However, they all had gadgets in their hands which I have recognized immediately.

They were navigation devices, which at the time were known only to extraterrestrials, not to any humans.

For a moment I assumed that they got it from the Grays, for communication purposes, and then noticed that quite a few of these people were really Grays who had shape-shifted to resemble humans.

I can easily identify them, because even while shape-shifting, the Grays cannot turn their heads independently of their body. They have to turn the entire body if they wish to look to the sides. As they turn, their eyes cannot follow their heads quickly, like humans' eyes, but they have to refocus.

*** *** ***

The Grays attended the meeting.

All that is done rather discretely, but after living with the Hybrids and the Grays, I could not miss that.

In addition, humans usually fidget, move around. The Grays never do. When seated, they sit quietly, immobile.

When standing, they are straight and immobile as well. In addition to that, I had more instructions from Nibiru as to how to recognize all shape-shifters, which I cannot explain because it involves using the Conduit.

Part one: The return of the Anunnaki

One of the Grays at the end of the table was tapping nervously on the edge of the table with something that looked like a pen, and from time to time pointed it towards me.

I recognized this gadget as a scanning device, such as we use on Nibiru. It was not held by any of the humans, because this fiber/scanning device was not known to the humans' scientific community until much later, 2006 or 2007. I supposed the Grays kept it to themselves for a while.

I did my best to ignore the fact that half the people there were Grays, and proceeded as if I had no idea and was talking only to humans.

I had nothing to fear, really, since I could annihilate the Grays with one thought, and I decided that discretion was the best approach. The Grays maintained their pretence throughout it, and I said nothing at all.

Come to think of it, I was used to the treachery of the Grays, but I have to admit I was a little distressed by the humans' duplicity and stupidity.

Did they really think I won't recognize the Grays?

*** *** ***

Holographic pictures that showed them the entire sequence of the Roswell crash.

I have explained to them who I was, telling the absolute truth, and giving my name as Ambar Anati. Naturally they did not believe me. To help persuade them, I first of all projected certain images on one of the walls.

These were holographic pictures that showed them the entire sequence of the Roswell crash, where the Gray was held, and data pertaining to their research.

They still were not persuaded that I was who I claimed to be, but the fact that the projections were done without any equipment made them uneasy and less sure of themselves.
They were at least ready to listen.

Part one: The return of the Anunnaki

I told them quite a lot about the Grays and their agenda. "By now," I said, "you must be aware that they do not tell the truth, that they are not to be trusted."

"Business is business," said one of them. "They have given us more than they promised, too, so we have gained additional knowledge.

It's not really a big deal if they abduct a few more people."

"First of all, it is not a few people. It's thousands that are tortured and killed."

"What can we say?" answered another. "Sometimes harsh measures cannot be avoided." I did my best to hide my feelings about such a statement, and went on.

"Are you aware of the fact that they are trying to take over earth?"

"No, we were not informed about such intent," said another.

"And are you aware of the invisible radio plasmic belt around earth? They want to isolate earth from the universe. This belt can expand up or down, and can affect missiles, rockets, or airplanes, and blow them up. It explains what has happened to various airplanes in Vietnam, and also to human spacecrafts and space missions."

"We don't understand what you want us to do," said one of them.

"I want you to trust the Anunnaki. They intend to help you get rid of the Grays. This is really very simple. Either you go with the Anunnaki, in which case much can be done, or you stay with the Grays.

If you choose to stay with the Grays, the Anunnaki will return and clean up the earth, in a way that you will not like. They are perfectly capable of annihilating the entire population if the atrocities do not stop."

"Are you threatening us?" asked one of them. The rest stared at me, impassive.

"I would not call it a threat," I said. "I would call it a fair warning. Remember, the Anunnaki are stronger than both humans and Grays.

They did not have to send me, they could do what they wanted without warning. But they prefer to save as many humans as possible."

"How do we know how strong the Anunnaki really are?" said one of them. "After all, they have been away for so long. They don't seem to have much of an interest in us."

"Let me show you a small example of what the Anunnaki can do," I said.

In a blink, I multiplied myself into thirty Victorias; we arranged ourselves around the table, behind the sitting people. They jumped off their seats, shocked.

"It's a trick," cried some of them. "Grab her!"

"Please, do grab," I said. "Touch all thirty of me, and see that this is not an idle trick. We can become billions, if we wish." Hesitantly, they touched some of the multiples. A few multiples offered to shake hands, which the humans did, trembling. They could not deny the multiple's tangible presence.

I contracted myself into one person again, and sat down. "Please," I said. "I have no desire to frighten you. Sit down and let's be reasonable."

*** *** ***

At the Dulce Base

"Truth is, Ms. Anati," said one of them, "The Grays are an immediate threat. They are right here and we cannot control them. The Anunnaki are far away.

But still, we can see that you wish to help us, and it should be considered. What would you want us to do?"

"I want to start by going into some of the more important places where humans and Grays interact," I said.

"I need much data to deliver to the High Council of Nibiru and receive instructions before I meet the President of the United States, among others."

Part one: The return of the Anunnaki

"I think the best thing to do is to go to Dulce, in New Mexico. It is the most important joint laboratory of the Grays and the U.S. Government," said one of them.

The others nodded in agreement. "There are bases in Nevada, Arizona, and Colorado, among others, but Dulce is the most important."

"Very well. Would you assign one of the members to come with me, act as my escort?" I asked.

"Yes, Colonel X— will go with you." The colonel rose. He seemed to be a respectable, middle-aged man. In reality, he was certainly a Gray. As before, I pretended not to notice.

"Would you like me to materialize you there?" I asked.

"No, I think it's best if we go in a more traditional way," said the colonel. "We don't want to startle the people in Dulce too much. It's best if they don't panic." I agreed and we decided to go the next day, in a military plane.

*** *** ***

On the plane, the colonel, who had become reasonably friendly, gave me some information about Dulce. "It's all underground, you know" he said.

"People know about seven layers, but in truth, there are nine I am aware of, perhaps more I don't even know about. It's really a very large compound."

"Where exactly is it?" I asked.

"It lies under the Archuleta Mesa on the Jicarilla Apache Indian Reservation, near the town of Dulce. Very easy to keep it a secret, the way it is constructed," he said. "And they are very careful about security. You will see."

We finally landed at the small air field. A medium sized building, guarded and surrounded with a high wire fence, stood in the desert. We entered a normal room.

I noticed the cameras in the entrance, and a woman in military uniform looked at some papers Colonel Jones presented to her, but the security was not impressive.

I realized later that the deeper you went into the compound, the stricter the security was.

Part one: The return of the Anunnaki

She pressed a button, and a man came to escort us through a door that led to an escalator.

From then on, it seemed we were descending into Hell.

*** *** ***

We were joined by a Gray.

Everything was clean, shiny, and metallic, much like I remembered from my unpleasant stay with the Hybrids.

No matter where you looked, you saw a security camera. There were side doors everywhere.

Apparently, many secret exits and entrances existed, and each was loaded with security features, some seen, some invisible.

*** *** ***

The First Level:

On the first level we were joined by a Gray. He was polite and distant, and showed us into various offices without much comment. The offices were normal, military, and stark. Maps hung on walls, with many pushpins in various colors stuck into them.

The individual colors, the Gray explained, showed sites of high activity of different subjects.

Green, for example, showed sites of heavy spaceship activities, including those of extraterrestrials that were not Grays, and were considered enemies by them.

Red were for areas of cattle mutilation and collection of animal blood. Blue indicated underground activities and caverns. I do not remember all the other colors and sites, but the arrangement was quite elaborate.

The offices were monitored constantly by humans, who wore military-like jumpsuits.

Each carried a gun, quite visibly.

All the uniforms were decorated with the symbol of the Triangle, much like the Phoenician Da (Delta) symbol.

They had various letters and numbers in each triangle, supposedly signifying rank, but I never found out if this was true.

When they saw that we were accompanied by the Gray, they simply ignored us.

*** *** ***

The Second Level:

The second level was exactly the same, full of offices, but after the first level, which we reached by the escalator, we used only elevators.

I was told that the elevators had no cables in them, and were controlled magnetically, using alien technology.

Magnetism also supplied light, which came from flat, round objects, and there were no regular light bulbs in sight.

*** *** ***

The Third Level

The third level was devoted to hospital-like environment used for impregnation of female humans.

I was not allowed into the surgical ward itself, but the Gray explained that the experimenters removed the fetus, and placed it for speeded-up growth in an incubator, creating Hybrids.

In this facility, more than in the one I visited during my previous time with the hybrids, they tended to experiment with genetic manipulation during the very early time in the incubator. The results were quite monstrous sometimes.

Through windows in the walls, I saw cribs, or really a sort of cages, with some of the results.

Deformed humans were the norm – extra arms and legs, small or very large heads, and creatures that did not really look humans. "What do you do with these?" I asked.

"We harvest certain tissues and then kill them," said the Gray. "We learn quite a lot from them about genetics. We apply them to our own research."

*** *** ***

The Fourth Level:

On level four, there were genetic labs that created half human/ half animal creatures.

Their shapes, as I saw them sitting in their cages, were so horrific, that I had to avert my eyes. Some of them had a reptilian look, some had fur, and others looked like gargoyles. "Do you harvest tissues here too?" I asked.

"Yes, we combine this research with the materials we get from the cows. The research is extremely interesting and useful," said the Gray.

*** *** ***

The Fifth, Sixth and Seventh Levels:

The aliens had their living quarters on levels five, six, and seven. These looked much like military barracks, as we passed the corridors and peeked into the rooms, but I saw no reason to enter.

I asked the Gray if it was true that there were additional levels. This did not seem to faze him at all, and he said, in perfect English that seemed so unpleasant, coupled with his scratchy alien voice, that yes, of course there were.

*** *** ***

The Eighth Level:

Apparently, they took advantage of the huge natural caverns under Dulce, and created additional levels. They carried even more security there, and the Gray said that if we wanted to go there, he would have to call two more Grays to accompany us, and we would need to use an eye identification system. These details were quickly accomplished, and we used a side elevator to the eighth level.

Here they also experimented with manipulation of the nervous system by various means.

It allowed them to cause disease and even death from a distance.

"I am afraid you cannot enter the place where the subjects are kept," said the Gray. "These subjects are mostly insane, dangerous, and very susceptible to changes in the routine. If we enter, we might destroy some of the experiments."

*** *** ***

The Ninth Level:

Level nine, where we were invited to enter, contained storage units of fully grown creatures and tissues, in vats, all of them dead. This included tanks full of embryos in various stages of development, waiting for use.

The place was kept as clean, as was the rest of the compound, but the smell of the chemicals was overwhelming. I simply could not stay there long, and Colonel Jones, who until that time showed no emotion, suddenly shape-shifted and appeared in his real, Gray form.

"You knew all along, Ms. Anati," he said, his voice turning scratchy. "I never thought we could trick you, and would have preferred to appear in my true form in the first place, but my group insisted." "It does not signify," I said. "Of course I knew." The other Gray did not pay much attention to the shape-shifting, being used to such practices.

Part one: The return of the Anunnaki

The Tenth Level:

Level ten, the most secret of them all, was devoted to human aura research, and other extra-sensory abilities, including dreams, hypnosis, etc.

The researchers were able to record dreams on specialized machines; the dreams were studied as part of the major advanced study of psychic power and phenomena.

"Once we are more advanced in this research," said the Gray, "we will have total power over other races. Of course, we mean no harm to humans or to the Anunnaki. We are merely concerned with the Reptilian races."

I almost laughed. No harm to humans? Was the Gray trying to be a PR person?

When we finished our tour, we were escorted out of the complex. The plane was waiting for us outside.

I said nothing about my disgust, horror, and disbelief to anyone. But I had seen enough, and I knew that this was just the tip of the iceberg.

Such treaties must have been entered into by more than just the United States government.

The Grays had reached almost total control over humanity.

*** *** ***

Grays in shape-shifted form.

After materializing myself back to New York, I knew I would always be watched, but I also knew how to handle it and avoid my watchers. I needed time.

First, I spent a few days just digesting what I saw.

I made myself invisible, and left the hotel for hours of exploration.

I walked the streets, took the subway, rode on buses, visited museums, stores, offices, hospitals, senior citizens homes, schools, and more.

Everywhere I went I saw Grays in shape-shifted form. Obviously, they did not only infiltrate the military, but spread out much more. They flooded the city.

Some worked in offices, some in restaurants, obviously doing it as part of their agenda.

They were nurses, teachers, officials, sanitation engineers. They were probably doing the same in other cities, urban areas, towns, and even other countries.

*** *** ***

The Grays and their slaves, the Hybrids, have invaded the world.

For me, as I mentioned before, it is easy to recognize a shape-shifter. I was taught how to do it by the best teachers on Nibiru. But a human cannot do so very easily. Your doctor could be one. The nice lady in the department store could be one. The teacher of your young child could be one.

In addition, I saw many hybrids.

Vicious, unfeeling, and manipulative, they flocked mostly into the entertainment industry, the financial world, and the advertising field. It seemed they liked glamour.

The Grays and their slaves, the Hybrids, had invaded the world.

After a few days I got to work. Using the same device that had gotten me the telephone numbers of the NSA members, I spent my time contacting and negotiating with hundreds of people from a number of governments on earth.

I also visited other laboratories, bases, and Air Force fields. Every time I negotiated with them, I encountered the same road blocks. Every government on earth was in terror of the Grays.

The Anunnaki were feared, too, and the knowledge that they would very likely attempt to clean the earth, terrified the humans, but not enough to get them out of their fearful paralysis regarding the Grays.

But that was not the worst of it. Unbelievably, many individuals in power simply did not care. All they wanted was to keep their power and control, to wage war. They wanted to make billions and keep it within a tiny group of the financial elite, while the rest of the world was permitted to go to the devil.

*** *** ***

This was a long mission. For years I went from country to country, getting in touch with people in power, acquiring knowledge, collecting data and transferring it, every night, to Nibiru.

The High Council took it all very calmly, and when I despaired, reminded me that my services were invaluable despite the seemingly unachievable goal of converting humanity.

The only bright points of my day were my evening conversations with my daughter and my husband, who were always supportive and loving.

I drudged on and on, until I thought that nothing more could be achieved. I stayed until late 2007, and then I made the call and requested permission to go back to Nibiru, and make my final report.

As always, Marduchk was there for me and I left an earth I no longer loved. I was going home.

*** *** ***

The Anunnaki Council.

> I report to the Council about my years of envoyship, and I view the frightening plans for the cleansing of the earth before the return of the Anunnaki and their plans for the complete change of the earth.

The years of envoyship have taken their toll on me. I was tired, discouraged, and worse, I began to feel old. It did not show in my appearance, which was a good thing, but I was no longer the strong young woman I used to be.

This time, putting the results of my mission before the High Council, and letting go of the burden and putting it on stronger shoulders, would be a relief.

I was not at all nervous about meeting the Council. I knew that I had done all I could, and more than that I could not do – unless the Council thought that there was more to accomplish. If they did, I would most certainly obey.

*** *** ***

The United States military authorities would not cooperate.

The whole Council came to the meeting. No one thought that there was anything more important to do or to attend. I bowed before them, and started giving my report.

Basically, it was a simple one, signifying that the United States military authorities, which were the greatest part of my contacts, would not cooperate.

Part one: The return of the Anunnaki

I presented numerous reports, charts, lists, analyses, whatever I could do to validate my findings, but in the end, it boiled down to one thing.

The United States government, and the military in particular, were more afraid of the Grays than of the Anunnaki. Officials and military from other countries, such as England, Russia, and China, with whom I had also spoken, were no better. The fact that I had promised the officials that the Anunnaki would return, and would destroy them if they continued to associate with the Grays, frightened them a great deal.

But they argued that no matter how you look at it, the Anunnaki have been away, physically, for thousands of years. Their contacts and connections with the humans were not numerous, and they obviously did not care much.

*** *** ***

The Grays have been on earth for these same thousands of years, and their technology was advanced enough to annihilate the earth just as much as that of the Anunnaki, and they were more likely to act violently because their habitat, their experiments, and that their hopes would be threatened.

The results were that I could not persuade any government to disassociate from the Grays, or to trust me. At the end of my report I bowed, and sat down again, rather exhausted. All I wanted was to go home, sit under my favorite tree, have a cat or two lean against me, and wait for Marduchk to come home and tell me things were not so bad. But this was not to be.

The Council members deliberated without opening their Conduit to me, which was fine with me since I felt almost dissociated from it all. But after a short time, they opened it for our conversation.

"You have done well, Sinhar Ambar Anati," they communicated telepathically. "We now know where we stand, and we have made our final decision – we will go back to earth and cleanse it. Humanity is so utterly contaminated, only drastic measures can apply."

Part one: The return of the Anunnaki

"How will you do that?" I asked. Cleanse an entire planet? Just like that? It seemed like a hopeless task, even for the Anunnaki. "Please explain to me, I am not sure I understand your plan."

"Very well," said the Council. "But we will need to go back a little. The point you must understand is, why did the Anunnaki originally come to earth? You know some of the reasons, but it wouldn't hurt to put everything in perspective for you."

"Yes, please do," I said. My fatigue had faded away completely, and I was eager to hear the details.

"Well, the Anunnaki did more than just come to earth. They have created it, million of years ago.

At that time, a group of Anunnaki scientists on Nibiru, including Sinhar Inanna, Sinhar Enki, Sinhar Ninlil, and others, had decided to extend their experiments in creating biological, living forms.

To do that, they needed a good plan and permission from the Council, so they worked it out and requested a meeting. The Council considered their suggestions, and agreed that such work would greatly increase Anunnaki knowledge and therefore would be an excellent idea to pursue.

However, they had one condition. The scientists were welcome to start working – but their laboratory would have to be off-planet.

The Council suspected that the introduction of new life forms, even in the isolated conditions of a laboratory, might be a threat to everyone already on Nibiru.

Large and small animals, and particularly people, even if they were to be created in the image of the Anunnaki, could not be tolerated to wander freely on Nibiru.

*** *** ***

Part one: The return of the Anunnaki

The Anunnaki needed a planet-sized laboratory.

The scientists devoted more thought to their project, and agreed that what they really needed was a planet-sized laboratory, where the creations could interact in a controlled environment without the interference of previously existing life forms.
The solution, to which the Council readily agreed, was to create a planet specifically for that purpose, at considerable distance from Nibiru, just in case.
And so the scientists went to the edge of the galaxy, and caused a star to explode and create a solar system.
The sun, which they named Shemesh (Sol) was surrounded by a few planets, and after a suitable amount of time (eons to humans, but nothing to the Anunnaki who can play with time as they wish) the Anunnaki went there to decide which planet would be the most appropriate.
For a short time they considered the planet humans call Mars, which at that time had plenty of water (the most important ingredient necessary for the laboratory, after oxygen) but finally settled on choosing Earth.

*** *** ***

The Anunnaki fostered the evolutionary process

> They went to earth, started creating life forms, fostered the evolutionary process, and managed to accumulate an enormous amount of useful knowledge, all of which they telepathically transferred to Nibiru (Ashtari), where it was much appreciated. Unfortunately, the knowledge leaked to the Grays at Zeta Reticuli, and they decided to use humans, and sometimes cattle also, in their doomed experiments that were geared to save their own miserable race. While doing this, they sadly contaminated the pure genetic material the Anunnaki scientists so painstakingly created, and the humans that resulted were no longer suitable for the study.

That was the reason why the Anunnaki deserted their research on earth.

"But you have never completely deserted humans," I said.

"No, not completely. We kept our connection. But the Grays really dug in, made their bases, lived underwater, and we had to keep away. And Grays' DNA have created greed, violence, and unbelievable cruelty within human nature.

Such characteristics were not part of the original DNA we used to create the humans. We had intended to create the humans in our image. Right now, we will assume, based on your research, that humanity is divided into three groups, regarding their level of contamination."

"Yes," I said, musing. "I have noticed the same thing. There are levels of contamination that make for various behaviour patterns. Actually, I have a lot of charts about it."

"Indeed," said the Council. "And excellent charts they are, and they gave us the structure.

*** *** ***

Humanity is divided into three groups, regarding their level of contamination.

The first group:

The first group is those who exhibit heavy Grays' DNA contamination. They include:
- Those who torture or support torture by others, for any purpose whatsoever.
- Murderers (unless in self defense, which sometimes occurs in situations such as domestic abuse by a contaminated spouse).
- Rapists.
- Child molesters.
- Child abusers.
- Senior citizen abusers.

Part one: The return of the Anunnaki

- Spouse abusers.
- Those who commit violent robberies.
- Illicit drug manufacturers, distributors and pushers.
- Those who engage in enslaving women, girls and young boys in prostitution rings.
- Criminals who use their form of religion as an excuse for their heinous crimes; this includes all religious fanaticsand extremists, such as suicide bombers.
- Those who destroy lives by depriving them of ways to support themselves, for their own greed.
- This includes the top echelon of corporate executives, who have lost any sense of humanity in their treatment of thousands of people and feel that this is "strictly business".
- Elected officials who have sold out for power and greed, and who are willing to destroy their own countries to aggrandize themselves.
- Elected officials who are willingly participating in destroying the ecology of the planet because of their close association with oil corporations, and other forms of commercial energy producing countries and their corrupt rulers.
- Any politician, military personnel, or anyone else who is engaging in trade with the Grays, allowing them to continue the atrocities in exchange for technical and military knowledge.
- Lawyers and judges who play games at the legal system for their own gain, sending child molesters, murderers, and other violent offenders back into society, ready to prey again on the innocent, all in the name of "reasonable doubt".
- Those who destroy lives and reputations by "identity theft".
- Those who torment animals.
- These include not only people who hurt and mutilate animals for their own sick pleasure, but also those who support dog fights, cockfights and bullfights, those who

beat their horses, donkeys, or dogs, those who "legally" mutilate cats by removing their claws or hurting their vocal cords, owners of puppy mills who force female dogs to reproduce by "animal rape," and those who abandon their animals, or chain them indefinitely, sometimes allowing them to die by such neglect."
- Prostitutes.

"Extremely dangerous people," I said. "I don't believe there is much chance of reforming them."

"None whatsoever," said the Council. "People who engage in such practices are doomed, as far as we are concerned. They are pure evil.

*** *** ***

The second group:

Anyway, here comes the second group, people who exhibit a medium level of Grays' DNA contamination. These would include:
- People who believe that discipline requires physical punishment (in children or adults).
- Middle echelon executives who "only take orders" from their superiors as their corporations are destroying the economy of their own countries to save their own skin.
- Those, who in the name of fashion and beauty, have hurt countless young girls who have succumbed to eating disorders, some of whom have actually died, while the owners and designers made a fortune for themselves.
- Irresponsible parents who allow their children to grow up with Grays' values rather than human and Anunnaki values.
- Hunters of animals who kill only for food but do not feel a joy in killing and do not mutilate or torment the animals.
- Owners of "factory farms" whose animals are not deliberately tormented, but live a miserable life.

- People who eat any form of meat, since we believe in a strict vegetarian diet, supplemented by milk and eggs from animals that are treated humanely, and are allowed to live out their lives comfortably and die naturally".

"They may have some chance, I suppose" I said.
"Not much. Still, we hope they will try to work on their own redemption. We offer no guarantee, of course.

*** *** ***

The third group:

Then, there is the third group, people who exhibit light Grays' DNA contamination, and they include:
- People who are willing to advertise products that may be harmful, for gain.
- People who are willing to import products that may be harmful, for gain.
- People who object to social reform that may help the greater number of others, such as health care or better equalization of income, for gain.
- People who are engaged in the fur trade.
- People who are willing to influence others through brainwash-style advertising, such as the cosmetic industry, for gain.
- Racists, sexists, and ageists, who are willing to allow their prejudices to influence their behaviour to others.
- People who are willing to spend millions of dollars on frivolous pursuits, such as diamond studded collars for dogs, who don't really care about anything but love and food, or $200,000 cakes for a party, while millions around them are starving.
- People actively engaged in aggressive corporate take-overs, thus destroying the livelihoods of many.

- Anyone deliberately sending a computer virus for "fun and games" and thus destroying other people's livelihood and property.

*** *** ***

A cataclysmic event.

The Anunnaki's Bubble.

"I assume," I said, "that this is just a partial list. I can understand that. But what are your plans? What will you do with the people? With the animals?"

"We will plan a cataclysmic event, the likes of which can hardly be imagined by humans. As we told you, we have done it before, many times.

Other races have destroyed some of our experiments, and sometimes only a drastic cleansing would help. We will show you one soon, a cleansing that happened a few hundred years ago on a humanoid civilization much like the humans, but first, let us explain what will happen.

We will bring a bubble of a special substance, resembling anti-matter, but is not destructive, and cause it to touch the earth's atmosphere.

The bubble will be exactly the same size of planet Earth.

As soon as the two globes touch, all the humans that have been lucky enough not to be contaminated by Grays' DNA, and all the animals, plants, and those inanimate material which the Anunnaki wish to preserve (such as beautiful and historic monuments, art-filled museums, and great libraries, in addition to the homes of those saved) will be stripped from earth and absorbed into the bubble.

The fish, and other animals who need water, will be taken to an artificial ocean within the bubble. The birds will have plenty of places to perch on.

Nothing will be hurt or damaged – the humans and animals will feel nothing – they will be secure and comfortable within the bubble.

It is unlikely that they will even retain a clear memory of the event, because we would not wish them to be traumatized.

Then, the earth will be cleansed of all the pollution. For lack of a better description, try to imagine a huge vacuum cleaner removing all the landfills, eliminating all plastics, all the dirt, all the smog from the air, and all the filth from the ocean.

In a few short minutes, the earth will be sparkling clean, a pristine planet, the way it was when we had first created it.

Disposing of the garbage involves very high technology which humans simply do not as yet understand. The beautiful clean planet will be ready to be repopulated, and in an instant, the humans, animals, plants, and inanimate objects that were saved in the bubble, would be returned to earth.

*** *** ***

Anunnaki guides will be there for the humans.

Anunnaki guides will be there for the humans, who would naturally need quite a bit of help to adjust to the new life."

"But those are only the uncontaminated ones," I said. "What about the others? How will they meet their fate?"

"Those who were heavily contaminated, and who were engaged in cruelty, greed, and violence for their own gain, will have no chance at all. They will simply be destroyed, and there is no need to even think about them any further. What is left are those who are of medium-level contamination, and the lighter level.

These groups will receive a warning to mend their lives, now, fourteen years before the event of 2022. When the event occurs, some of the people of light level contamination would have completely cleansed themselves through their efforts, and therefore would have been transferred, as clean beings, into the bubble. Others would have remained lightly contaminated.

Those of medium level contamination, who obviously require more work, would be divided into those who had succeeded in the cleansing, and had brought themselves into a light level contamination.

Those who remain at medium level, who did not do the work of cleansing properly, will be destroyed with the heavily contaminated ones.

All that will remain now would be the group of light contamination level, and if they wish to save themselves, they must go through Ba'abs, or Star Gates, into other dimensions, so that they could be evaluated by the Anunnaki.

If they can be cleansed, they go back to earth.

If not, they will live out their lives in another dimension, where conditions are much like our own earth before the cleansing. They will lead a normal life, but will not be able to reproduce, so eventually they will die out.

As for those who would succeed passing through the Ba'abs, the procedure is extremely difficult.

*** *** ***

Ba'abs (Star Gates) exist everywhere.

> Ba'abs (Star Gates) exist everywhere. They are huge, magnificent Ba'abs that are used regularly by the Anunnaki to cross from one dimension to another. But there are also small ones, located in the street, in a tree, in an apartment building, in private homes, you name it.
>
> They will become visible when the bubble touches with the earth, and those who were not taken into the bubble, or were not destroyed, must find their way into a Ba'ab. All Ba'abs look the same – they are a circle of shifting light of rainbow colors, very clearly defined.
>
> People wishing to enter a Ba'ab must hurl themselves against it, and it will open and absorb any number of travelers.
>
> As soon as you enter the Ba'ab, you are already in another dimension.

Part one: The return of the Anunnaki

It is extremely frightening, a deep blackness illuminated by explosions, thunderbolts, and streaking comets. There is a very high level of a stormy, whoosh-like sound – the noise can be deafening – and the traveler is swept with violent speed forward, unable to resist or help the move, and constantly twirled and twisted in one direction, and then the other.

The traveler will feel dizzy, disoriented, and scared, and this lasts for an indefinite period of time. When this part is over, the traveler is thrown by a huge gust of wind into a tunnel, which is so brightly lit by blinding orange, yellow, and white light, that it is impossible to keep one's eyes open for more than a few seconds at a time.

The traveler hears horrible shrieks, screams, and howling of wind, and when the eyes are open, he or she sees bizarre faces, weird creatures, and unknown vehicles which always seem almost on the verge of colliding with the traveler, but somehow never do. After a while, the traveler is thrown out of the tunnel onto solid ground, which may be quite painful but not permanently harmful. The light becomes normal and the sounds stop."

"Does that mean they have arrived safely?"

"Yes, at that point, the travelers have reached their destination. It looks much like earth, but it is devoid of people or animals, and plants and houses look very dim, as if the travelers found themselves in virtual reality.

Then, the traveler begins to see people materialize against the cardboard-like background.

This takes time, the images of people float as if from thin air, but then, all of a sudden, reality shifts and the travelers find themselves in a real world.

Animals, incidentally, will never materialize. All of them have been returned to earth, to their proper places, as mentioned before. They are not needed here, since no animal labor or the eating of animals is permitted by the Anunnaki, who abhor such practices.

From then on, the travelers will eat only a vegetarian diet. In this dimension, the travelers will meet a few Anunnaki, who will direct them to their evaluation and possible cleansing.

Part one: The return of the Anunnaki

Only those who make it would be returned to earth. Those who cannot be cleansed will be sent, through a Ba'ab, to the dimension we have mentioned before, where they will live out their lives, but will not be able reproduce.

The Anunnaki do not wish to kill them, since they are not inherently evil like the heavily contaminated ones. But they cannot let them reproduce the bad DNA; the Anunnaki do not indulge in sentimental pity, and are fully aware that any form of evil should not be allowed to exist."

"The treatment of the humans is extreme," I said calmly, "but not unjust. They have brought it upon themselves since they would not listen to the warning."

"Well said, Sinhar Ambar Anati," said the Council. "Spoken like a true Anunnaki."

"You said you would show me how this is done," I said. "I do wonder how the earth would be cleansed."

"Yes," said the Council. "Look at the Miraya." Naturally, there was a huge Miraya on one of the walls, and I waited while the Council made preparations for the visions to appear.

"It will be emotionally harrowing to watch that, Sinhar Ambar Anati," said one of the Council. "Are you sure you want to see it?"

"Yes," I said. "I think I should. Perhaps there is still something I can do."

"I think there is," said the Council, and at this point a small light appeared in the Miraya. The light grew, and I suddenly saw a bubble, looking much like a simple soap bubble, on the screen.

It started to travel, and in a very short time I saw it approach the unmistakable shape and color of earth. The two globes touched, and I saw streams of light emanating from the earth and disappearing into the bubble.

"In these streams of light, all the clean people, all the animals, and all the inanimate objects we have chosen are transferred to the bubble for safe keeping," said the Council. "Also, the Ba'abs are opening for those who might try to escape into them. We will now zoom in closer and show you the cleansing itself."

Part one: The return of the Anunnaki

The Miraya showed a growing image, and after a few minutes I saw a terrain which I did not recognize, but it seemed earth-like.

The people were ape-like humanoids, but obviously they bore a very close resemblance to humanity. They even wore similar clothes.

The area looked devastated – after all, the houses the people had lived in, any animal they may have had, all the plants, and many buildings, had already disappeared into the bubble.

So the environment was totally alien and frightening to these people. They looked disoriented, staring at the sky, running around, searching for missing people. The whole scene was of one of terrible confusion.

The sun seemed to undergo an eclipse, but it was not a natural one. A massive ceiling of metal shapes of machinery, gadgets, wheels, and shifting lights covered the sky.

They were ominously silent, as if waiting. I imagined that looking at them from below was immensely frightening.

The people seemed to have lost their minds, they were running around in circles, some stampeded and trampled each other. I saw people running into churches and heard the bells toll.

Naturally, religious leaders would not be saved, or go through the Ba'abs, but still tried to call their congregations in, hoping for some miracle.

Everywhere I saw Ba'abs, those colorful circles, and people smashing themselves into them in an attempt to escape.

Some went through.

Others were thrown back. The Ba'abs could determine the level of contamination and only allow the righteous ones to pass through, hurling the others back at some distance.

"Total chaos," I said.

"It's even worse than you can imagine," said the Council. "In various cities, people tried to reach their governments, without much success.

The only officials that have stayed at their posts, issued orders to avoid any interference with the extraterrestrials, since it would make everything even more dangerous and no one on the planet we are showing you had the technology to match.

The officials' orders were ignored, particularly by those in rural areas, who were used to self sufficiency. These people confronted the Anunnaki, started shooting at them with their guns.

As in other areas, which of course had many good people living in them, only the violent ones have remained, since the others have already escaped.

Acting stupidly, they annoyed the Anunnaki with their inept shooting until the Anunnaki decided to paralyze them with special beams of light, for a limited time.

*** *** ***

The final stage.

When the beams effects wore off, some resumed their doomed attempts to fight, and at this point the Anunnaki started the final stage."

"Let me see the final stage," I said.

From the bottom of the spaceships, a special substance was diffused, and it landed in huge, swirling streams. It was a black liquid, mixed with light and electricity, and some strange sparkling particles, which I was sure was a form of energy or radiation.

"It smells like fire and brimstone, but strangely, it is cold to the touch. Yet, it burns everything that touches it. This is a tool of annihilation, a tool that no one can fight," said the Council. I looked on, without comment.

The substance slithered inexorably over the ground, the buildings, and the stranded cars like icy cold lava waves. It swept away many people, killing them instantly.

Part one: The return of the Anunnaki

Once it covered a large area, it began to coagulate, and as it did so, it expanded and rose up, foot by foot, until it reached the height of an eight storied building. Slowly, it seemed to harden, solidifying itself into steel-like state.

Huge stacks of smoke rose up into the sky, cars melted, buildings collapsed, and fires started everywhere, seemingly not only by the touch of the substance, but spontaneously, when the wind carries the particles of energy into flammable materials. The combination of images and sounds was that of chaos, pain, confusion, and death.

I imagined that the fire and brimstone smell had now mixed with that of burning flesh and of melting metal, plastic and rubber.

Then, all of a sudden, the substance stopped growing, and assumed the appearance of craggy mountains, with sharp edges and canyons. A very few who had survived, but had nowhere to go to, now tried to climb on the substance, since the earth itself was buried in it. This was futile, since the substance was too slippery for the climb. They started to fall and slip, and were instantly killed.

"These conditions will continue over the entire world for two days; no one will be left alive on the scorched earth," said the Council. I remained silent. "Let us move the scene into the fourth day," said the Council. "You see, at that point, which must have been the third day, all the spaceships left, and in twenty-four hours, the substance and all it consumed turned to dust. The earth became ready for the vast cleansing."

Other spaceships appear on the screen, of completely different appearance. The new ones were not be circular like the others, but crescent shaped, and of pleasant colors, nothing frightening about them.

They activated the huge vacuum system, and an enormous cloud of black dust came up in swirling, filthy streams. It did not take long; in a few minutes the whole cloud was sucked into the machines, and the earth was ready for new life.

With so much death and destruction, a small part of me wanted to pray for the souls of the ones who were killed.

Part one: The return of the Anunnaki

Something in my head wanted to turn to God. Then I laughed. If our kind of paternal God had existed, He would have not allowed humans to be so cruel, so horrible, as to cause a need for such a massive cleansing.

I was beginning to grasp the nature of All-That-Is, the concept of a creative God that encompassed everything and learned from it voraciously. He, she or it would not have mercy on our souls. I bowed my head, and then raised it and looked at the Council.

"I see the need," I said. "I would like to request one more trip, one more attempt to convince the officials about this cleansing, let them warn the earth. If I fail, my blessing goes with your cleansing. The evil must be removed."

"We are proud of you, Sinhar Ambar Anati," said Sinhar Inannaschamra verbally. "High Council, I have told you that, years ago. She is a true Anunnaki."

"Indeed she is, Sinhar Inannaschamra. Indeed she is, and she has our permission to go for the final attempt," said the Council. "We shall have a plan soon." Then they bowed and left.

As usual, Sinhar Inannaschamra stayed with me, and we walked home together.

"So the earth will be cleansed," I said. "The contaminated DNA will be removed. So far, so good. But what is going to happen afterwards? I imagine the world will be considerably changed."

"You won't recognize be able to it," said Sinhar Inannaschamra. "It will be vastly improved, believe me. The first thing to disappear is the root of all evil – money."

"Really? Money will no longer exist?"

"Think about it, Victoria. Would the Anunnaki support any of humanity's greed-infested systems? The most profound change will be the abolition of money and every system that is attached to money.

People will work in their chosen professions, or a new profession that they will adopt, and produce or serve as usual."

"But how will they survive?

How will they get food, lodging and clothes? In other words, if they don't have money, how will they be paid?"

Part one: The return of the Anunnaki

"They will not be paid, but they will have everything that they need, just like we do on Nibiru. Everyone will have a comfortable home, designed to his or her taste.

Good food for them and for their pets, beautiful clothes, nice jewelry, cosmetics, diapers for babies, toys, hobby supplies, etc. will always be available in huge cooperatives that will look like excellent supermarkets, open day and night so that no one will ever lack for anything.

What everyone considers luxury items will also be available – the Anunnaki have no desire to have humans live in austerity.

Humans will always have books, TV, radio, home movies, classic films etc. They can go to the theater, the ballet, the symphony orchestra, chamber music performances, movie theaters and always for free. The only thing the Anunnaki will deprive humans of is excess.

There will be no need for hoarding, since everything will always be available, and no one will be able to be richer than their neighbors. Equality will be established, and appreciated by those who are not contaminated by the greed and meanness of the Grays.

"So what about places like Fort Knox?"

"No need for such places anymore. Ford Knox is going to be destroyed, and the gold used for ornamental purposes. That is the only reason people will value gold now – its beauty. A good artist can create some pretty good pieces from such a lovely substance, which will be widely available after the great change.

The same will happen, incidentally, with diamonds, and other gems. Their intrinsic value will disappear, so jewelry will only be appreciated for its intricate and elegant design, not for how many carats a stone weighs.

Because of that, there will be no need for the IRS, the Social Security system, and other such organizations. The elimination of the money system will cause many professions to disappear, such as accountants, bankers, tax preparers, security guards, and IRS employees."

"Any other changes?"

"Of course. Money will not be the only 'victim.'

Part one: The return of the Anunnaki

In a society that consists of good people, people who have no need or desire to commit any crime whatsoever, there will be no need for the legal system. All organizations pertaining to the law and law enforcement will disappear, including the Supreme Court. And of course, there will be no prisons. This will eliminate many professions as well, such as lawyers, judges, court clerks, prison officials, police officers and guards."

"You know, Sinhar Inannaschamra, this sounds like a lovely place to live in."

"Built in the image of Nibiru, of course. All governments will be abolished. No elected officials, no presidents, no kings. People who are good do not need anyone telling them how to live, they do it instinctively. This will eliminate thousands of positions, such as presidents, kings, governors, mayors, all government employees, social workers, and child protection agencies.

And don't forget that since the Anunnaki technology is going to keep humans healthy, there will be no need for hospitals or clinics, other than those devoted to childbirth, and much of the work there will be done without the need for people. In addition, there will not be any incidents of insanity or mania or depression.

This will eliminate the positions of most doctors and nurses, and of additional employees such as hospital administration, hospital billing, psychiatrists, psychologists, and hospital janitors, to name a few."

"So no one will be sick, what a world," I said. "I can imagine that humans will no longer have the need for cars and airplanes, right?"

"Indeed. There will be advanced technology that will allow for much more efficient forms of transportation and the use of clean and efficient energy, and in the process, we will eliminate the need for any fossil fuels.

This will remove more professions from the list, such as gas stations, agencies supplying us with electricity and gas, car manufacturers, airplane manufacturers, and highway builders."

"It will be hard to adjust to such living."

"I am not sure about that. Remember, the only people remaining are not contaminated.

Part one: The return of the Anunnaki

They don't need or want wealth, really preferring to be happy, creative, comfortable and spiritually fulfilled. There will be even more changes. Some miscellaneous professions will not remain, since they will no longer be appreciated or needed.

For example, the fashion industry, with its cruel attempts to make women into slaves of someone else's ideas of beauty, will entirely disappear.

Beautiful clothing will be created by individual designers or by anyone who likes to indulge in it as a creative hobby. Advertising, of course, will vanish as well.

So no one will need runway models, beauty contest organizers, manicurists, cosmetologists, or advertising commercials actors and voice over artists."

"So what will happen to the clean people who worked in these professions?" I asked, envisioning a mass of unemployed, confused people.

"Nothing to be alarmed about. Those who will lose their professions will be trained for another profession, always entirely of their own choice, that will give them pleasure and pride to pursue. Even those who have not lost their profession, but who feel the need for a change, will be encouraged to pursue a career change. As a matter of fact, since the life expectancy of each and every person will be greatly increased, it is expected that many people will have numerous career changes as time goes by.

Life-long study is always encouraged by the Anunnaki, who consider the acquisition of knowledge the most enjoyable thing a person can do."

"From what you say, many professions that are very well respected today, mostly because they are highly paid, will disappear. I wonder if such individuals will be able to adjust."

"They usually do. Remember, many professions will change in the way they are perceived.

For example, the teaching profession, for both children and adults, will become the most highly respected profession in the world. Librarians will be very highly regarded.

Gardeners will be of great importance. Historians and writers will be greatly valued.

But of course, in a world that judges a person by what he or she is, not by how much money is accumulated, every profession will be appreciated for its usefulness to the entire community. So I think the great majority of people will be pleased with our changes."

"Only the survivors..."

"True," said Sinhar Inannaschamra casually.

"The population will be greatly decreased, of course." We entered my home in silence, and I materialized some coffee and fruit for us in a dream state.

I found it hard to believe that I, of all people, had contributed one of the major reasons to the end of the world as we know it. I always used to think it would be accomplished by fanatics or by governments that supported nuclear explosions. Well, one lives and learns.

*** *** ***

Part one: The return of the Anunnaki

The Final Clash.

How I went to earth to make one final attempt to convince the humans to give up their affiliations with the Grays. How the humans tried to betray my trust, and the explosive results that would bring not only extreme danger to myself, but the return of the Anunnaki in 2022.

One last time, I said to myself. This is their only chance. If they agreed to accept the final option to change their ways, good. If not, I would not stand in the way of the Council's plan of cleansing the earth. It would hurt me a great deal to think of the billions that were about to die. But there would be no more opposition on my part. I would obey the Council, no matter how badly I would feel.

With the weariness of an act that was performed hundreds of times over in the past seventeen years, I contacted the highest level military personnel at an important air base which I will call North X, since of course, I cannot reveal it's real name. As always, they had no choice but to meet with me.

At this time, anyway, after all these years of negotiations with everyone, including some presidents of the United States and Europe, I was pretty well known – and highly disliked. Perhaps I was even a little feared.

The individual I spoke to was very agreeable, and proceeded to arrange the details for the meeting with me. "By the way," I said, after all was decided upon. "If a single shape-shifting Gray will be at the meeting, I will leave immediately. And believe me, I always recognize a shape-shifter. You see, this is the last meeting I plan to have with any human, and the presence of a Gray will defeat the purpose of it."

"There will be no Grays at the meeting, Ms. Anati," said my contact. "I can promise you that.

Part one: The return of the Anunnaki

My colleagues and I have already discussed the issue before you and I came to arrange the meeting. They feel the same way as you do." Well, that was a good sign, I thought. We shall see.

Arriving at the air base, I was immediately taken to a small, ordinary conference room. A few people rose from their seats at the conference table as I came in.

There were two generals in military uniform, one a retired admiral, who worked for the NSA as a consultant, and was a co-proprietor of a major civilian jet propulsion company, a colonel who had worked as test pilot for the Mcdonnell Douglas and Boeing companies, and a person that I guessed represented the White House.

As always, they were extremely polite, and indeed, none of them was a Gray. Perhaps by that time, they finally believed that I could recognize a shape-shifter, or perhaps they had their own agenda. I think, in light of what took place later, that the second option was the correct one. They wanted to hide the meeting from the Grays.

We sat around the table, and they turned to me, ready to hear my offer. They thought that I still was ready to negotiate. Of course, the time for negotiations was over, but they did not realize that.

"Allow me to summarize the current situation for you, gentlemen, I said. "Whether you take action now or later, you will be facing an extraterrestrial threat. The threat you have now, comes from the Grays who are controlling your science and space program, and are dominating a major part of the earth.

The Grays know that you have tried, for many years, to find a weapon system to counter attack them. And they know very well that you have started this program when President Reagan took office. They also know that you failed to develop such a weapon system on your own.

That means that you are defenseless. You know it, and they are aware of it. This is why you allow the Grays to go on with the atrocities and the abductions of human beings. It makes you feel safer around them. However, what you don't understand is that the Grays will not be satisfied by only kidnapping people and going on with their abominable experiments.

Part one: The return of the Anunnaki

All their experiments are aimed at saving their own doomed race, which is slowly dying from an epidemic of Progeria which they cannot control. By and large, they have failed. So now they want permanent visible bases on the surface of the earth, and much bigger scope for further experiments on a larger scale."

"They have never mentioned this plan to us," said the White House representative.

"Of course not. This is top secret. They know you will feel like cornered rats and fight back."

"So what will happen when they take over?" asked the Admiral.

"They will kill many humans. The rest will be put in concentration camps, to be available for use whenever needed. In other words, you will be taken over, and this, to all intents and purposes, will be the end of the human race."

"I see," answered the Admiral, in a low voice. He was clearly thoughtful.

"What is the later threat you have mentioned?" asked one of the generals.

"It will come from the Anunnaki. You don't feel it now, not quite yet, but it is just as real. However, it is very different from the threat of the Grays.

The Anunnaki are not interested in establishing any bases on the surface of the earth or in the oceans, nor do they wish to experiment on you.

They want, quite simply, the complete destruction of your military systems, submarines, aircraft carriers, and spy satellites. They will throw an electro-plasmic shield over the earth, which will prevent airplanes from taking off.

This will apply to every airplane, no matter how big or small, military, commercial, or private. Gravity will become twelve hundred times stronger than it is now, preventing everything on earth from moving, including human beings.

Then, a kind of artificial lava will finish off the biosystem of the earth. You will not be able to fight it, for the simple reason that you do not know what it is made off.

In addition, the Anunnaki will bring on huge tsunamis. However, the worst part will be the issue of magnetism. Positive and negative magnetism will be distorted, and this will alter the laws of physics on earth.

This scenario may sound like science fiction, but you know better than that. It will start around the end of 2021. You will suddenly be confronted by confusion, when all clocks and watches will stop, and ships at sea will collide with each other without knowing the reason, among other results of the changed polar magnetism."

"We would consider severing all relations with the Grays," said the representative of the White House. "That is, on one condition."

"I don't think the Anunnaki will be willing to negotiate conditions," I said, "but do tell me anyway. Perhaps something can be done."

"If the Anunnaki will send an official military delegation from Nibiru right away, bringing with them scientists to develop a system like the plasmic belt and the Star Wars program, and guarantee to us that the United States can have complete military control over the earth, we will be willing to cooperate with them. Also, we want a system that will allow us to cause major ecological catastrophes to North Korea, Iran, China, Afghanistan, and parts of Russia. Of course it should look like a natural catastrophe, not anything man-made," said the White House representative.

"The Anunnaki will not give you any such programs," I said resolutely. "It is not at all within their plans."

"So you are refusing to protect us! If you don't protect us, why should we break our agreement with the Grays? After all, how do we know you are really coming back, or even if you are telling the truth about the Grays' plans? And quite frankly, why such a sudden interest in human affairs on the part of the Anunnaki, and in Americans in particular?

"Nonsense," I said. "They are not particularly interested in the Americans, you are not more important than anyone else on earth. The only reason for contacting you in particular is the fact that the Grays have their bases in America.

Part one: The return of the Anunnaki

All the star gates, the genetic laboratory facilities and installations are either underground in America or in the American military bases. In short, the Grays are contaminating human DNA from right here."

I could see that they believed me. But they were still naïve enough to believe that the Grays will eventually help them develop the Star Weapon system they have promised but failed to deliver. The Americans still wanted to buy some time, and they were not really sure how to do that. I could feel their confusion.

"Ms. Anati," said the Admiral. "We would like a little time to confer before giving you our final answer. If you don't mind, allow me to escort you to one of our private guest lounges. They are quite comfortable, I'll arrange for coffee and some refreshments, and we will come back for you in an hour to finalize our plan. Would that be all right?"

It would have been just fine, had this been the real plan. Very natural and appropriate. But my Conduit was open all along, and I read their thoughts freely.

I knew what they meant to do to me, and it did not include coffee or refreshments, nor did it take place in a guest lounge. But I decided to play their game, and went quietly with the Admiral, who chatted pleasantly while escorting me to an elevator.

The ride on the elevator was long. Very long. We went down, obviously into some underground facility. I said nothing about it and pretended all was well. Eventually, the elevator stopped, the door opened, and at the door, three or four soldiers waited for me.

I was grabbed unceremoniously, while the Admiral went back into the elevator, not even giving me a glance. I was shoved into a cell, they locked the door behind me, and I was left alone in their underground prison.

As I said, I knew this was coming, but having my resources, I had no reason to fear these people. I could, of course, dematerialize myself and get out any time I wanted.

So I sat on the narrow bed, directed my Conduit, and listened to their conversation.

Part one: The return of the Anunnaki

I must admit that I experienced a slight feeling of claustrophobia. I have come so close to being an extraterrestrial that it was inevitable.

But I repressed it, reminded myself that I could leave any time I wanted, and listened carefully to the conversation in the conference room.

"It won't take long, they are all terribly claustrophobic," said the Admiral. "Her energy will drain away, like a battery, very soon."

"Will she die?" asked the White House representative anxiously. "I am not sure this is a good strategy, we may be held accountable for any issues that may arise from her arrest."

"She won't die so quickly. She will go insane first," said the Admiral.

"Well, so what do we do now?" asked the retired pilot.

"We have all sort of options, but what is clear to me is that we must confuse the Anunnaki and get them off our trail," said one of the generals.

"But she may contact the Anunnaki first," said the other general.

"This will be a good thing," said the Admiral. "At the same time she contacts them, we will send signals that will confuse them. They won't be able to decide where to go to get her. In the meantime, she will go mad."

"Are you sure they drain away like the Grays?" asked the first general.

"Oh, yes, they are all the same, these filthy aliens," said the Admiral. "Let her rot here, and we will have the Anunnaki and the Grays so confused, they will fight each other, and that will take care of all our problems."

At this moment, something happened in my own mind. I realized that I no longer wanted to save these people. They were pure evil, and the Anunnaki do not tolerate evil.

I felt, to my own amazement, that I no longer cared about how many contaminated humans would die in the cleansing. I knew the Anunnaki will save the clean ones. Let the others go. I grinned.

Part one: The return of the Anunnaki

Yes, I had finally started thinking like a full Anunnaki. What's more, I felt that I was quite capable of killing them myself.

I remembered how shocked I was when my dear, kind, loving husband Marduchk had killed without batting an eyelash. I was even more shocked when my beloved sister-in-law told me that she had killed too, on various missions she had undertaken. Now I understood.

I was not angry with these treacherous creatures. A cold, determined feeling went through my mind instead. It was all so simple. They were evil, and so they had to die.

Calmly, I created a plasmic shield around me. Nothing in the known universe could penetrate it. Wearing it, I could pass through an exploding star and survive.

Then, I made some calculations, figuring out how much energy was needed to blow up the entire base, killing everyone inside it in an instant. The plasmic shield was invisible and I could hear perfectly well through it until I chose to switch the audio off.

I materialized myself back into the conference room. The look on their faces when they saw me was so priceless, I had to laugh.

"Well, gentlemen," I said quite politely, "this is the end. I could have exploded the air base from anywhere on the face of the earth, but I wanted to give you the news myself."

They must have communicated quickly with some of the personnel, because about fifteen soldiers, well-armed with all sorts of paraphernalia, burst into the room and rushed to grab me.

The plasmic shield made them fly backwards, and some hit the wall. One or two fainted from the blow.

"I would not bother, if I were you, gentlemen," I said. "Believe me, there is absolutely nothing you can do. Well, it's time to blow up the air base, so good bye."

"Please, Ms. Anati, we will do what the Anunnaki ask us!" cried the White House representative. "Yes, yes, tell the Anunnaki we have no conditions! We will obey them implicitly!" said the Admiral. The others just stood there, terrorized.

Part one: The return of the Anunnaki

A few years ago, perhaps I would have taken pity on them. I would have thought of their wives, their children and pets... by now I knew this was stupid sentimentality that made me less than an Anunnaki. That was over now.

"Too late, gentlemen," I said. "Good bye." I turned down the audio, and activated the explosion.

It looked like a nuclear bomb. It sounded like one, even through the plasmic shield. And it worked like one, too. Nothing was left of building; I was now standing alone in a huge, black, gaping hole in the ground.

From other buildings, people came out, screaming, running wildly. I ignored them, nodded with satisfaction at the cleanliness of the job, turned away, and proceeded to materialize myself in another continent.

I did not want CIA agents hunting and bothering me like flies and gnats. Of course, I could kill them. But what is the point of doing the Anunnaki cleansing job for them all by myself?

Well, it was time to leave earth. If I ever came back to it, after it was cleansed, I would no longer be the same woman. I have changed, and my place now was on Nibiru. However, I could not just call on Marduchk and ask him to pick me up as usual. Ahead of me was another task, the most important task of all.

This task would be dangerous, tremendously risky, but unavoidable, and I would have to do it alone. Somehow or other, I would have to leave everything of me that was human right here on earth. Only then would I be able to place my mind into the clean, perfect Anunnaki body that was prepared for me some years ago. I would have to do that with no traces of humanity, or of any possible contamination.

And for that, I would have to shed my old body like the skin of a snake, leave it on earth, and go home not in a space ship, but rather, send my mind through a multidimensional Ba'ab. Which meant, in human terms, that I would simply have to die."

*** *** ***

Part one: Coding and decoding the significance of 2022

Coding and Decoding the Significance of the Year 2022

2022 is the year when the Anunnaki plan to come back to earth and cleanse it from the Grays' contamination. This year has great significance if it is coded in Hebrew.
There are two ways of interpretation.

First Interpretation of the Code

Take the number 2022 and translate it into the Hebrew alphabet. Remember that Hebrew is read from right to left, and follow the numbers in that sequence. This gives you the word:
2022=בבא
2 is ב**,** the second letter of the Hebrew alpha-bet.
The 0 becomes א because:
0 = The Infinite = God = The One. The א is the first letter in the Hebrew Alphabet, namely, The One.
The word reads, phonetically, bb'ab, and it means ba-Ba'ab: In the Ba'ab.

Ba'ab means: Stargate of the Anunnaki.
From this stargate the Anunnaki spaceships enter and exit galaxies, skies, multiple universes, parallel dimensions and outer space.
Also from this Ba'ab, a person exits our physical world to enter the dimension (Universe) of extraterrestrials.

Interpretation and meaning: Once you enter the year 2022, you will automatically enter the Ba'ab of Liberation – but only if you are not contaminated, or if, starting right now, you attempt to cleanse yourself.

Part one: Coding and decoding the significance of 2022

Second Interpretation of the Code

Add the numbers that appear in the year 2022.
2 + 0 + 2 + 2 = 6
According to the Ulema and the "Book of Rama-Dosh", the number 6 means: Liberation.

Interpretation and meaning:
The liberation from the contamination and control of the Grays.

Characteristics of the number 6

6 is a perfect number, also a "Triangular" number. It is the geometrical value of the word "Space" in Anak'h, the Anunnaki language, and "Spirit" in the Phoenician language. In the Greek oracles it is "Delta".
This geometrical form and its numerical value is also the "Logo" of the Anunnaki, because it represents the triangle. And inverted the triangle was shown on the uniforms of the American military personnel and scientists who work on the "Black Projects" and alien reverse engineering at secret bases, and genetic laboratories in the United States.
Many insiders and top echelon military men reported that they have seen the "Triangle"/"Delta" sign on several crashed UFOs stored in secret military bases.

*** *** ***

The number 6, Carbon and the Creation of Mankind

Worth mentioning here is that the chemical element carbon has an atomic number of 6. In the "Book of Rama-Dosh", the word "Carbon" was used to represent the source of life and was the first element used by the Anunnaki to genetically create the early human race. Everything is connected.

Part one: Coding and decoding the significance of 2022

The Ulema who are the custodians of the Anunnaki "Book of Rama-Dosh" explain that the number "6" is the secret code of the year 2022. It is a vital number because it represents the 6 known directions known to mankind: directions: north, south, east, west, up and down.

In 2022, two more directions or dimensions will be added. And the human race in 2022, will understand the nature of these 2 additional dimensions which are not very far from the physical fourth dimension we live in.

The fifth dimension could be considered as a spatial trampoline, and the sixth dimension is the destination or rendezvous of the human race with the Anunnaki.

*** *** ***

The number 6 is one of the six major extraterrestrial hot spots on Earth

"6" as a pentagonal pyramidal number is explained in the Anunnaki's manuscript as one of the six major extraterrestrial hot spots on Earth. "6" is the Anti-Ba'ab.

The other five are: Baalbeck, Arwad, Tyre, Nippur, and Malta. Does this predict or hint to the landing areas of the Anunnaki when they return to earth in 2022?

Some psychics think so. It is an entertaining idea, but an unlikely scenario.

The sixth letter in the Phoenician Alphabet is "Waw". Once the corners of the letter "Waw" are joined in a stroke of a pen, it becomes a perfect triangle.

This was the "Unification" numerical code for the Anunnaki and early Phoenicians of Baalbeck and Tyre.

The Ulema (Seers, Sages and Men of Knowledge in Arabic) also used the Anunnaki-Phoenician letter "Waw" in their Arabic dialect. It is pronounced in the same way, and means exactly the very same thing: "With" or "With others". In Phoenician, "Waw" means hook.

Part one: Coding and decoding the significance of 2022

Statue of a Phoenician goddess found in Malta.

Part one: Coding and decoding the significance of 2022

Ruins of ancient Malta, which is one of the six major
extraterrestrial hot spots on Earth.

Part one: Coding and decoding the significance of 2022

The ancient walls of Malta.

Part one: Coding and decoding the significance of 2022

Ruins of Baalbeck, one of the earliest Anunnaki's cities/colonies on Earth.

The Trilithon of Baalbeck, part of the early space centers of the Anunnaki in the Near East.

Part one: Coding and decoding the significance of 2022

Another view of the legendary Trilithon of Baalbeck.

Part one: Coding and decoding the significance of 2022

Tomb of Hiram, King of Tyre, founder of the first Freemasonry Rite in the world, and an offspring of the remnants of the Anunnaki in the Near East.

Part one: Coding and decoding the significance of 2022

Ruins of the ancient city of Tyre in Phoenicia (Modern day Lebanon). Tyre was one of the six major esoteric cities of the Anunnaki on Earth.

Part one: Coding and decoding the significance of 2022

Tyre (Sour) today; a Shiite Muslim city in Southern Lebanon.

Part one: Coding and decoding the significance of 2022

Staircase within the Ziggurat of Nippur. The ancient city of Nippur in Iraq, was one of the six major extraterrestrial hot spots on Earth.

Part one: Coding and decoding the significance of 2022

A tower towards the heavens in Nippur.

Ur Nammu atop the Ziggurat (Tower of Babel) at Ur.

Part one: Coding and decoding the significance of 2022

The Phoenician "Hook":
The esoteric and spiritual meaning of the hook is "Ascension", and "Liberation". It was constantly chanted in the secret rituals of the Phoenician gods Adoon (Adon, Adonis, Adonai) and Melkart.

*** *** ***

Meaning of the number 6 in Anunnaki-Phoenician Alphabets

The Phoenician "Hook" also meant a "Celestial Gate". This is how we got the word "Ba'ab" meaning exactly the extraterrestrial stairway to heaven. "Waw" in the Phoenician Alphabet is in fact an Anunnaki symbol and written like a "Y".
The letter "Y" represents a base (Earth) and two additional dimensions on the right and on the left. These are the two additional dimensions beyond ours that the Anunnaki code reveals. It is not as complicated as you might think. It is only a secret and hidden message.
It corresponds to the Hebrew "Vav".

Two united "Vav" represent the "Ascension" and the two additional dimensions beyond the physical fourth dimension.
In Aramaic "Waw" is written and pronounced like the Phoenician and Anunnaki "Waw".

Facts:
Despite the US constant denial of any contact with aliens, many statements given by top American military scientists and a high-ranking Annunaki's personal revelations show without any doubt, that in fact:

1-While different alien races do live and work on planet earth, the Anunnaki do not.

Part one: Coding and decoding the significance of 2022

2-The Grays who originally came from Zeta Reticuli have several bases and genetic laboratories, fully operational in the United States. The Anunnaki left our planet earth thousands of years ago.

3-The Grays have helped the military in developing advanced spatial weapons/missiles systems. The first test occurred in 1984, and the Russians became aware of these significant military tests around 1985.
The Anunnaki offered the United States advanced technology for scientific and humanitarian purposes, but the military wanted very advanced weapon systems instead. The Anunnaki refused.

4-The Grays kept on abducting humans for various reasons, and for a very long time, and the United States government allowed these abductions.
The Anunnaki are not in the abduction business.
Whether the Grays' abductions occurred with, or without the consent of our government remains irrelevant, because a treaty was signed between the US and 4 different alien races permitting such horrible acts. In exchange for "closing their eyes" NASA, NSA, the CIA, the navy and the Air Force received very advanced extraterrestrial technology. The Anunnaki never participated in these atrocities.

5-A very high level meeting between the United States and a representative of the High Council of the Anunnaki took place at the Four Seasons Hotel in Georgetown, Washington, D.C.

6-The United States refused to terminate their formal relationships with the Grays, and categorically rejected an offer submitted by an entity representing the Anunnaki.

7-The United States government did not believe that the Anunnaki had any vital interest in the human race, and especially the United States.

8-The United States were officially notified that the Anunnaki shall return to earth in 2022.

Part one: Coding and decoding the significance of 2022

This notification was never taken seriously by those who attended the meeting in Washington, D.C., however scientists from MIT and top executives at a major corporation (military contractor) known for its jet propulsion projects and headed by a former high ranking military commander, wrote a memo and a summary of findings pertaining to the topics discussed during that infamous meeting, and submitted their memoranda to The White House.

Insiders leaked very disturbing information about a lethal clash between the Anunnaki official and military guards at a well-publicized military base known for its "black projects" and extraterrestrial technology-reverse engineering.

*** *** ***

Part one: In 1947, a Grays' spacecraft crashed in Roswell

In 1947, a Grays' spacecraft crashed in Roswell

> In 1947, a Grays' spacecraft crashed in Roswell. Two Grays died from the impact, but one survived. The Americans held him underground at Andrews Air Force Base.
> Strangely enough, a sort of friendship was developed between the Gray and two American civilian scientists, something that we still don't understand, but there it was.

At that time, the military and CIA were only interested in acquiring advanced military weapons systems, not in a friendship with an alien. But somehow they became friends.
The military kept everything under cover and did not even inform even Congress or the President of the United States.

One general actually said, 'Civilians and politicians come and go. But we, the military, that is our career.
Therefore, they should not be informed and if Congress will not be told, consequently the American public should not be told either.' That was the policy that was adopted on a regular basis ever since."

*** *** ***

According to an Anunnaki record, and a revelation by Victoria (Ambar Anati, the Anunnaki official delegate) we have the following information:
Victoria talking to another Anunnaki: "That is frightening," I said. "The military should not control the decision."
"Indeed they should not. Look at the Miraya, Sinhar Ambar Anati.
Here is one of the first conversations between the surviving Gray and the two American scientists."

*** *** ***

Part one: In 1947, a Grays' spacecraft crashed in Roswell

Statement by Ambar Anati on record

Statement by Ambar Anati on record: "On the screen, I saw an office, quite ordinary and simply furnished. Two men and a Gray sat around an empty desk. They seemed comfortable, there was no tension, as you might expect in such a company. Then, the sound came from the Miraya. (A monitor)
One of the American scientists,[1] asked the Gray:
-"So where did you come from? And why are you here?"
-"We have been here for thousands of years," said the Gray, in perfect English, though his voice had the usual scratchy sound of his race. "We have our bases underwater, in the Pacific, near Puerto Rico, and under Alaska's glaciers."
-"Thousands of years?"
-"That is so. We consider ourselves the first and the legitimate inhabitants and owners of the earth. You are not. We are here because we need natural resources that exist on earth and in the oceans."
-"Seems to me this is not all you need, buddy," said the other scientist, grinning and lighting a cigarette.
-"This is true. We also need some live organisms, and various substances we can extract from human bodies."
-"And did you get all you want?" asked the first scientist.
-"Yes, by and large. We need them on a constant basis," said the Gray. "The natural resources of the earth and the water are regularly mined. The human substances are more difficult to obtain. We get them from the humans we abduct."

The two scientists nodded in agreement, totally unimpressed by the mention of the abductions.
They really did not seem to mind.
-"What bugs me," said the first scientist, "is that we tried so hard to reverse engineer your spaceship, ever since we got it after the

---

[1] A note from Victoria: we cannot reveal the scientist's name, since this could endanger his family.

Part one: In 1947, a Grays' spacecraft crashed in Roswell

crash in Roswell. We just can't do it. You have to help us decipher the codes on the screens we found inside the spaceship, and also the geometric and scientific symbols on the grids and measuring tapes we found scattered around the spaceship.
Our team is getting impatient; they may even threaten to kill you, you know. The two of us are friendly with you, but the team is getting ugly, and the boss is mad."
-"What is the point?" said the Gray without showing any emotion, not even fear regarding the threat. "Even if I teach you how things work, and decipher all the codes for you, you will not be able to reverse engineer our technology, because you don't have the raw materials. Look at this."

From somewhere around his body, he pulled out a piece of metal.
-"This is a very light metal yet stronger than any material known on earth. Yet this sheet of metal could float in the air, and can be bent and folded like paper and then, open up on its own. Look!" He demonstrated. The metal seemed to be indestructible.
-"You must understand that we are willing to reveal plenty of information," said the Gray. "But we can only do so if you will allow me to go home. I need to recharge my body, it's like a battery, you know.
I will die if I stay much longer, and that will be useless to you. Let me go, and I will arrange for others to come back with me, others who know much more than I do. I am a simple pilot. I will bring you scientists.

We have no intention of hiding this knowledge from you, on the contrary, we have every reason to cooperate with you and do some joint projects. And we can supply the raw materials and the knowledge of how to turn it all to your advantage."
-"So since we are such good friends," said the second scientist, "tell me, where exactly is the home you speak of? Since you have lost the spaceship, obviously, we will have to take you there.'"
- "If I tell you, you will not understand and you will not be able to take me there, since it involves getting through additional dimensions.

Part one: In 1947, a Grays' spacecraft crashed in Roswell

Our scientists constructed our bases' entries like that, as a precaution against intruders. But if you take me back to Roswell, exactly where we crashed, I will find my own way."
"How will you do that?"
"Simple," said the Gray. "When a spacecraft lands on a particular spot, automatically it marks the spot, scans it, and sends data to our mission control for identification and location purposes. Thus, we are never lost. If I can contact my people, they will come for me."
"But if you go away, how do we communicate with you, and find out when the others are coming?"
"In the spacecraft there is a communication device. Let's go there. I am sure it is functional, because it is really indestructible. I'll teach you how to use it. We will contact my people from there and tell them about our plan. You will be there to supervise everything. Bring the boss, too, just in case."
The scientists looked at each other. They seemed rather pleased.
"Very well," said one of them. "We'll come back for you later tonight, after we talk to the boss. I am sure he will agree to our plan."
"It will be a feather in his cap," said the Gray, using an old fashioned human expression unexpectedly. The two scientists burst out laughing.

*** *** ***

And that, was indeed what happened. They took him back to Roswell, and left him there on the exact spot of the crash.
They did not leave the area, though, but hid in a small canteen which was placed at some distance, to watch what was going to happen to the Gray. In a very short time, a spaceship came, landed, and he went in. The spaceship took off directly and vanished into the sky.
The scientists sent the piece of metal which the Gray had demonstrated with to a military laboratory, and they called one engineer from Lockheed Corporation and another one from MIT, to analyse the piece. Nobody could figure out what it was made of.

Part one: In 1947, a Grays' spacecraft crashed in Roswell

Still, prior to his departure, apparently the Gray did reveal many secrets of very advanced technology, that American corporations started developing right away, and began to use ten years later. Many highly advanced electronic gadgets that American consumers have used for a over a quarter of a century came from the Grays.

*** *** ***

And what happened then?

> A few years passed. Then, a historic meeting happened. In February 1954, President Dwight Eisenhower went for a week's vacation to Palm Springs, California. This was a little strange, and many did not quite understand the timing, because he just came back from a quail shooting vacation in Georgia. Actually, it was less than a week before his trip to Palm Springs.

On the night of February 20, 1954, the President of the United States disappeared

Two vacations in a row was not his style, but he went anyway, and arranged to stay there for a week.

Now, a president, as you know, is always surrounded by other officials, not to mention body guards; he is never out of sight.
But on the night of February 20, the President of the United States disappeared. The press, which somehow was alerted despite all the efforts for secrecy, spread rumors that he was ill, or that he had suddenly died.
The president's people were alarmed, so they called an emergency press conference, and announced that Eisenhower lost a tooth cap at his dinner, and had to be rushed to a dentist.

Part one: In 1947, a Grays' spacecraft crashed in Roswell

To make it more believable, the dentist was presented to the people.
He was invited to a function the next evening, and was introduced all around.
This, again, was strange.
Why would a dentist be invited to such an affair, and why would the President's personnel take such care to make him visible to everyone?

*** *** ***

A Cover-up!

It was a cover-up for the President's real business

Eisenhower was actually taken to Muroc Airfield, which was later renamed Edwards Air Force Base. There, he met with the Grays.
No president had ever done so before.
The delegation of the extraterrestrials consisted of eleven Grays. Six from Zeta Reticuli, and five from earth's underwater bases.
But of course, this was not their last meeting,

This marked only the beginning of negotiations between the government of United States and the Grays.
So the situation was no longer only in the hands of the military, but went much further.

*** *** ***

Part one: In 1947, a Grays' spacecraft crashed in Roswell

Eisenhower was the first American President to sign a treaty with the extraterrestrials.

Part one: In 1947, a Grays' spacecraft crashed in Roswell

Muroc Field/ Edwards Air Force Base.
Eisenhower was actually taken to Muroc Airfield, which was later renamed Edwards Air Force Base. There, he met with the Grays.

Part one: In 1947, a Grays' spacecraft crashed in Roswell

How was this meeting arranged, in the first place?

Before the meetings: Two major black projects

> In 1953, astronomers discovered some large objects that at first were believed to be asteroids, and later proven to be spaceships. They were very large, but since they took a high orbit around the equator, they were not visible to laymen.
> Two projects were installed:
> 1-**Project Sigma,** created to interpret the Grays' radio communications,
> 2-**Project Plato,** created to establish diplomatic relationships with the aliens.

There were talks about other races that contacted the humans at that time, arguments regarding who the treaties should be signed with, and so on.
As a matter of fact, the Nordics, a benevolent race, actually tried to prevent humans from getting into these evil treaties, and wanted them to dismantle their nuclear weapons and abandon their road to self destruction, but they were not listened to.
The Nordics wanted the humans to go on a path of spiritual development, but what the humans wanted was military secrets.
Because those humans were so badly contaminated, they would not even consider a peaceful offer. And the treaty with the Grays was signed. It basically said that the aliens and the humans will not interfere in each other's affairs.
The humans will keep the alien presence a secret, and the Grays would be allowed to experiment on cows and on a limited number of human abductees. The abductees' names would be reported to the U.S. government for control, they were not to be harmed, and they should be returned to their homes after the memory of the events was removed.

Part one: In 1947, a Grays' spacecraft crashed in Roswell

But, as we know, the Grays did not keep their promise, and extended their experiments without telling the U.S. government. They could not be trusted. But let's face it, the military people were treacherous as well. For example, there was the issue of the Gray who had arranged all of that.

Second meeting in 1954

He came back with a delegation in 1954, and agreed to stay on earth as a hostage of good will, on condition that he would be allowed the freedom to go back and forth to recharge himself. This lasted for a year, but soon enough the military, having learned a little about the vicious plans of the Grays and the excessive number of abductions that was not agreed upon, turned back on their word to the hostage and locked him up for three years.

As a result, he developed extreme claustrophobia that eventually killed him, as they would not let him leave to recharge himself.

This information about Gray claustrophobia was never known about within the circle of ufologists.

*** *** ***

United States "Protocol on Extraterrestrials' Visit to Earth in 2022"

Master Kanazawa spoke about a very specific protocol written by the United States government. In the Kira'at provided below, you will have a short glance at its contents.

> It might appear to many of you as a science fiction story, or a pure fabrication of mine, or a crazy scenario created by others who are deeply involved with this issue, but those who in the past were part of the team of American officials who met with extraterrestrials, and some of the military scientists who are currently working on joint extraterrestrials-intraterrestrials-Greys and American scientific and esoteric weapons systems programs, are fully aware of the existence of the secret governmental "Protocol on Extraterrestrials' Visit to Earth in 2022."

Maximillien de Lafayette said, "It is up to you to take this subject into consideration, or disregard the whole idea.
But always ask yourself, what IF part of it is true? If I was not absolutely sure and certain that the "Protocol" indeed exists, and it is periodically and constantly reviewed and updated, I would have never dared to come forward and talk to you about it.
You do not have to be an insider to know about the "Protocol". Just ask any "avant-garde" futurist or an out-spoken quantum physics professor, if such a protocol could exist? It is also my understanding that many Fire Chiefs in the United States, at one time in their career, have heard of, or were briefed on the instructions manual on how to deal with extraterrestrials should a landing (Assumed a hostile invasion) or encounter occur.

It is also my belief that the United States government published in March-April 1954, an instructions guide called "SOM1-01 Special Operations Manual: Extraterrestrial Entities and Technology, Recovery and Disposal." Some ufologists have claimed that "The cover of the manual includes the date April 1954 and notes that it was created by the "Majestic-12 Group." This is not correct. The manual was never written by that group.

Part one: US Protocol on extraterrestrials

What I do know is this, and this is the absolute truth: A group of scientists from MIT, Cal Tech, NSA, the United States Air Force, and top scientists from the United States Department of Energy (DOE) came up with the first draft of the manual.

A few years later, Reverend Billy Graham, and two powerful Catholic archbishops in the United States were called in to share their insights and express their concerns.

Part of what they had suggested appeared in the 15 page Addendum to "Protocol on Extraterrestrials' Visit to Earth in 2022."

Master Kanazawa in this part of his Kira'at did not address the issues of:
- **a**-The inevitable clash with extraterrestrials,
- **b**-The mass hysteria,
- **c**-The Aliens' Asphyxiation Effect (AAE), which is one of the United States government's major concerns,
- **d**-United States cities' evacuation,
- **e**-The manual of the United States government counter-attack measures against extraterrestrials' invasion.

But others, including Ambar Anati did!

Master Kanazawa's Kira'at (An excerpt):
- Following the initiative of the United States of America, a few countries are consulting with each other on the "Protocol on Extraterrestrials' Visit to Earth in 2022," written by the American government.
- The American Protocol is still in its infancy now. However, it is promising, because it is addressing subjects of extreme importance.
- It is both a protocol and an instructions manual.
- The Protocol part of it will remain in the hands of the governments, while the instructions manual will be made available to the people of Earth in 2021.
- However, leaks to the general public and the media beforehand are expected.

Part one: US Protocol on extraterrestrials

Some of the issues discussed in the protocol and the manual are:

- 1-How an encounter with a pecies from outer space could affect the world economy, and Earth's monetary system. It is our belief that this issue is discussed in an addendum;
- 2-The question of God, and how to explain to human beings, the nature of God, and mainly the irrelevance and unnecessary existence of several organized religions, and religious governing bodies. It is our belief that this issue is discussed in an addendum;
- The Church of England, the Vatican, and a consortium of Christian Churches in the United States of America have joined in to draft the section related to the religious topics discussed in the American protocol;
- 3-The Ba'abs (Stargates), are a major issue, especially to the United States, Russia, China, France, Great Britain, and a few other countries that are going to emerge as a global power on the world market;
- However, the military aspects of the Ba'abs, mode of operation, and ramifications such as intergalactic travel, time-space travel, anti-matter, anti-gravity will be handled exclusively by the United States of America;
- 5-DNA contamination is another sensitive and extremely important issue.
Human DNA contamination caused by excessive scientific and military genetic programs, that are not in the best interest of humanity.
6-It is our belief that this very delicate subject has already been a part of previous meetings between American officials and an elite group of extraterrestrials;
- 7-The alien-human interbreeding programs: It is our belief that this very delicate subject has already been a part of previous meetings between American officials and an elite group of extraterrestrials;
- 8-The life and existence of the hybrid race on Earth.

- 9-It is our belief that this very delicate subject has already been a part of previous meetings between American officials and an elite group of extraterrestrials;
- 10-How to handle a close encounter with three different extraterrestrial races that are going to play a paramount role in the future of humanity;
- 11-Petrifying situations prompted by electric currents, and electricity stations and grid shortouts during the landing of the extraterrestrials ships on Earth;
- 12-The development of a global communications system, jointly administered by the Anunnaki, the United States of America, China, Russia, and Europe, for the purpose of informing the populations of Earth of the landing, the purpose of the landing, and areas of landings of the Anunnaki, and their Merkabah (Also Markaba) in several areas of the terrestrial globe.
- 13-This communications system will also be projected as a huge holographic screen that will appear in the sky, at close proximity to the surface of Earth, containing vital information intended to orient the people of the Earth.
- 14-You have to remember what we have said in the past, about the remaining portion of the people on Earth. Those who were saved, those who will perish, and those who will not be allowed to ascend through the Ba'abs. The ascension through the Ba'abs is their only way of salvation.

United States Government Publications on Extraterrestrial Invasions:
Do you think that alien invasion is a far fetched scenario?
Science fiction? Are you sure it will never happen? And hence forth, is 2022 and/ the return of the Anunnaki to earth pure fantasy?
Well, think again, because the United States government is taking the issue of extraterrestrial threat and alien invasion very very seriously!! You bet!!

Part one: US Protocol on extraterrestrials

The United States government has published a series of books on the subject, and provided very detailed information and instruction on the danger of aliens, their threats, what to do if you encounter aliens, and what precaution and safety measures you should take.

Below, are some websites that have posted the government's publications, along with excerpts from each book.

We hope these websites will still be accessible to you, since "Big Brother" is constantly deleting/ adding sensitive material on the subject of UFOs and extraterrestrials.

We are referring to serious articles and summary findings by reliable authors, and not to the silly and ridiculous messages of fake mediums and spiritual extraterrestrial messengers-psychics on earth!!

1-Government Alien Invasion Plan:
You can read the instructions of the American government at:
www.scribd.com/doc/917802/Government-Publications-on-Aliens?query2=Government%20Alien%20Invasion%20Plan

2-Government Publications on Aliens and Security:
www.scribd.com/doc/917802/Government-Publications-on-Aliens?query2=government%20extraterrestrial

3-The United States Government's Plan with Aliens:
www.scribd.com/doc/917802/Government-Publications-on-Aliens?query2=the%20government's%20plan%20with%20aliens

4-United States National Defense Against Alien Invasions.
www.scribd.com/doc/917802/Government-Publications-on-Aliens?query2=national%20defense%20against%20aliens

5-Aliens' Attack Plan
scribd.com/doc/917802/Government-Publications-on-Aliens?query2=alien%20attack%20plan

Part one: US Protocol on extraterrestrials

6-What to Do in Case Of An Alien Attack
www.scribd.com/doc/917802/Government-Publications-on-Aliens?query2=what%20to%20do%20incase%20of%20alien%20attack

United States Government Major Concerns:

Xenotransplantation and aliens-cross-species infections:
"This action plan concerns the process of xenotransplantation, which is the transplantation, implantation, or infusion into a human being of living cells, tissues, or organs from a nonhuman source. It takes into account the possibility of aliens-cross-species infections, and provides meeting transcripts and available documents and international information.
Current intelligence on extraterrestrials indicates a particular proclivity towards experimentation of various sorts. If the aim of such experimentation is to discover the physiology and more of human beings and other animals that inhabit the planet Earth, xenotransplantation could be used. Since this is a complicated process above the understanding of many, this text will provide a basic introduction to this topic that could come in handy."
As noted by Center for Biological Evaluation and Research: "Use of Cloning Technology to Clone a Human Being." This document presents cloning as a piece of the recent activity involved in the area of scientific and biotechnological progresses.
"It presents information concerning the matter of the ethical nature of a potential human clone, the current illegality of human cloning under United States law, and also acknowledges that cloning could lead to medical advances in research and practice.
While this technology has not been developed or used currently on Earth, the possibility exists that extraterrestrials could have knowledge of its forms and functions. This document can provide information about what is involved in the cloning process and help one to recognize if they or another has been cloned"; noted by U.S. National Library of Medicine, "Genetics Home Reference," Department of Health and Human Services.

Part one: US Protocol on extraterrestrials

This portal leads to information concerning the various genetic conditions that could afflict the human being. The genetics of over 200 various conditions are discussed in detail, along with the normal functions and the rendered health effects of over 300 genes.

United States Government Official Statement:
"Extraterrestrials could seek to unravel the inner secrets of mankind."
A glossary presenting definitions on medical and genetically important matters. Genetics tie into the above entry, as they present a way that extraterrestrials could seek to unravel the inner secrets of mankind. The Human Genome Project is a human attempt to do this, which could inadvertently provide aid to the enemy.
Genetic engineering is a way to either help or hinder the human race, and is a complicated subject. As noted in Science Reference Services, "Unidentified Flying Objects (UFO)," Library of Congress.

United States Government Findings:
In case of extraterrestrial invasion, the power supply known as electricity would most likely be a high value target for hostile parties.
In case of extraterrestrial invasion, there exists the possibility that the surface would become unfit for human habitation due to a variety of happenings.
Therefore carefully constructed underground shelters would be advisable for usage. Underground shelter has been used in the past to great effect against bombardments of the past, although this situation would present new challenges.
(As noted by Science Reference Services, "Solar Energy," Library of Congress.)
A pathfinder for resources held by the Library of Congress and online information of scientific repute in various media formats that contain information upon the subject of solar energy.

Part one: US Protocol on extraterrestrials

These formats include books, reference works, conference proceedings, government publications, abstracts and indexes, journals and journal articles, internet resources and other selected materials. In case of extraterrestrial invasion, the power supply known as electricity would most likely be a high value target for hostile parties. Therefore it would become imperative that humanity access alternative forms of energy. Solar energy would be a wise choice in this instance.

Recently discovered publications and manuals by the United States Government pertaining to alien threat:

1-Likely Defense Against Alien Invasion;
2-Surviving Extraterrestrial Invasion;
3-Aliens and Government Preparation;
4-US Emergency Plan for Extraterrestrial Invasion;
5-Extraterrestrial Alien Invasion Government Procedure.
Can be browsed at:
www.scribd.com/doc/792200/US-White-House-Federal-Register-035466?query2=surviving+extraterrestrial+invasion.

*** *** ***

United States current intelligence about the mode of transportation of beings of other worlds

A pathfinder for resources held by the Library of Congress and online information of scientific repute in various media formats that contain information upon the subject of Unidentified Flying Objects or UFOs. These formats include books, reference works, conference proceedings, government publications, abstracts and indexes, journals and journal articles, internet resources and other selected materials.

Part one: US Protocol on extraterrestrials

The purpose of including this resource on the list should be obvious, as it presents current intelligence about the mode of transportation of beings from other worlds.
General reports seem to indicate similarities in the types of vehicles used, so the information could become useful as a type of spotter's chart, as well as providing information about the performance and abilities of the craft. As noted by Bacon, Kenneth H., "DOD News Briefing, Tuesday, April 18, 2000,"

*** *** ***

Department of Defense Briefings: Area 51, a location often believed to contain materials of extraterrestrial origin

A transcript of daily news briefings by the Department of Defense concerning various matters indicative of that day and questioning put forth by various media agents.
Pertinent questions to our topic were presented upon the nature of the contents of Area 51, a location often believed to contain materials of extraterrestrial origin.

During the course of the questioning the government through its spokesperson again denies that there are any alien life forms or alien technology present at the aforementioned location. While not providing precisely in-depth information about the goings on of the base, it serves as a reminder that this could be an area of interest in the event of extraterrestrial invasion.
Being present at this site would most likely be dangerous, as the potential concentration of alien technology would most likely provide an attraction. As noted by Science Reference Services, "Underground Architecture," Library of Congress, www.loc.gov/rr/scitech/tracer-bullets/undergroundtb.html (Accessed December 1, 2007).

Part one: US Protocol on extraterrestrials

A pathfinder for resources held by the Library of Congress and online information of scientific repute in various media formats that contain information upon the subject of underground architecture. These formats include books, reference works, conference proceedings, government publications, abstracts and indexes, journals and journal articles, Internet resources and other selected materials.

*** *** ***

PART TWO
The Return of the Anunnaki: Q&A
Questions answered by Maximillien de Lafayette.

PART TWO
Q&A

Questions answered by Maximillien de Lafayette.

Outlook for mankind after the year 2022...147
- Question: What is the outlook for mankind after the year 2022? You have explained this in some detail in your books but will we live in peace or does humankind still pose a threat to one another if challenges and greed are proposed like they always have been?...147
- Answer...147

Another extraterrestrial threat other than the Gray's aliens...150
- Question: After the Anunnaki's job is finished here on earth through decontamination will we ever have to deal with another extraterrestrial threat other than the Gray's aliens?...150
- Answer...150

On aliens competing with the Anunnaki to rule our planet...152
- Question: Are there any other alien races in this galaxy or another that could compete with the superstar status of the Anunnaki and rule our planet?...152
- Answer...152

Part Two: The return of the Anunnaki, Q&A

Would the Anunnaki come to aid the planet if another alien threat happens?...155

- Question: You have said that the Anunnaki feel responsible for the hybrid contamination between the humans and the Gray's, would the Anunnaki ever come to the aid of the planet again if this threat would happen?...155
- Answer...155
- Question: Has the planet ever come close to another threat as serious as the Gray's and will it be a possibility?...155
- Answer...155

Hybrid Grays: Adoption and DNA contamination...156

- Question: Have there been a large number of ones that were disease free and human enough to be adopted?...156
- Answer...156
- Question: Could someone have a relative hybrid or be a child of a hybrid and not know it?...156
- Answer...156
- Question: I always wonder how people with no compassion what-so-ever are the same species. It seems that living as a loving and compassionate being is what our natural instinct wants us to do, so I wonder if hybrids have any connection to emotionless behavior? ...156
- Answer...156
- Question: I have read the discussions about contaminated DNA and am curious to know if it is to the point where large amounts of people have some connection to hybrids?...157
- Answer...157

Part Two: The return of the Anunnaki, Q&A

- Question: Is it true that hybrid human/grey babies and children are being created and raised in secret bases? What of the stories of horrific experiments being performed on abducted humans in labs by the Greys as part of their breeding/tissue harvesting programs?...157
- Answer...157
- Question: What is the reason behind the Greys interbreeding program with humans?...176
- Answer...176
- Question: Is one of these Anunnaki Gods going to take over the earth after the pole shift?...184
- Answer...184
- Questions: I am very worried by what you have written on the subject of the return of the Anunnaki in 2022? Is it for real?...184
- Are they going to change the way we look?...184
- Are they going to get rid of us and replace us with a new human race?
- What kind?...186
- Answer...186
- Questions: Is it true that a massive Russian underwater base exists one mile deep in the Marianas trench in the Pacific ocean? If so, what activities/research/experiments are going on there? Do the Chinese have one too?...187
- Answer...187
- Question: Will the Anunnaki intervene to prevent possible use of atomic/thermonuclear weapons prior to, or during their return in 2022?...193
- Answer...193

Part Two: The return of the Anunnaki, Q&A

Who will survive the return of the Anunnaki?
- Question: What percentage of the world's population will survive the return of the Anunnaki to become part of the new human race after 2022?...196
- Answer...196

How many other Anunnaki will be part of the return? ...197
- Question: Though the return will be led by Sinhars Marduchk and Inannaschamra, how many other Anunnaki will be part of the return? ...197
- And how many Anunnaki guides will there be, for humans who will be saved and returned to earth after the cleansing?...197
- Answer...197

Efficient energy systems of the Anunnaki...200
- Question: What kind of clean and efficient energy systems, and modes of transportation will the Anunnaki introduce after 2022?...200
- Answer...200

Stargate over Chicago...201
- Question: Is there a stargate/ba'ab in Chicago?...201
- Where exactly is it located, and what does it look like? How would you jump into a ba'ab?...201
- Terminal of Grand Central Station in downtown Chicago...201
- Answer...202

Part Two: The return of the Anunnaki, Q&A

Signs before the return of the Anunnaki...204
- Question: What are the signs that people will see in the skies the day before the Anunnaki return, and where will they be seen?...204
- Answer...204

Anunnaki's tools of annihilation...205
- Questions: Who/what created the "tool of annihilation" that the Anunnaki will use when they return?...205
- Answer...205

*** *** ***

Part Two: Outlook for mankind after the year 2022

Outlook for mankind after the year 2022

Question by Matt Hoxtell, Chicago, Illinois, USA.

Question: What is the outlook for mankind after the year 2022? You have explained this in some detail in your books but will we live in peace or does humankind still pose a threat to one another if challenges and greed are proposed like they always have been?

Answer:

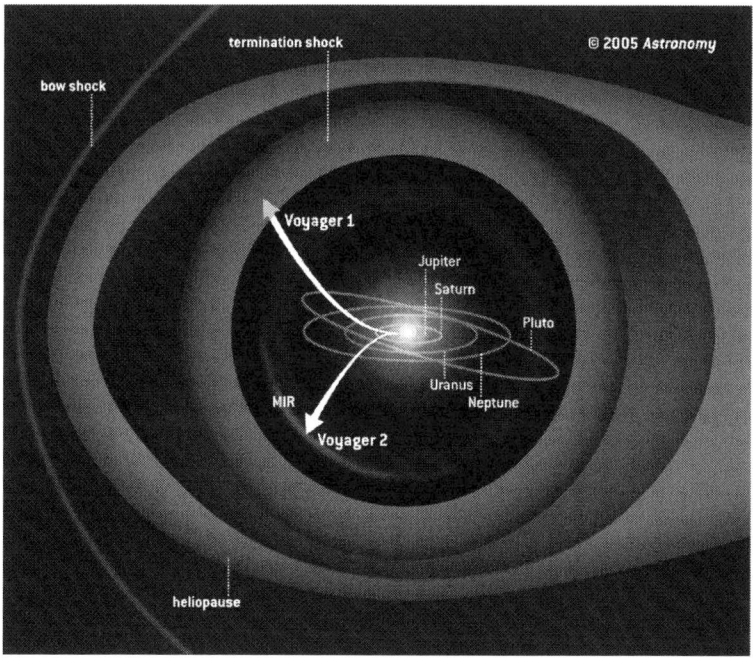

NASA's ring of hydrogen particles.

*** *** ***

Part Two: Outlook for mankind after the year 2022

> NASA has discovered a ring of hydrogen particles around our solar system—a protective layer, which is now being called the Heliosphere. This was announced by the Anunnaki-Ulema, centuries ago, and they called the ring "The Cosmic Plasmic Belt."
>
> The Heliosphere is generated by solar wind particles, which originate deep within the Sun. NASA launched the Interstellar Boundary Explorer Mission (IBEX) last year to get a better picture of the Heliosphere.
> It was always suspected that it existed, but NASA scientists thought it existed in a completely different form; instead of being a uniform stripe, there are bright spots, which indicate the "bubble" has varying intensity and density.
> Also, though NASA knows it protects the solar system from the radiation outside of it, scientists still aren't entirely sure why it is there or what it does. As noted by NASA.

*** *** ***

2022 happenings are diverse, and could be easily misinterpreted by the public. Nothing physically will occur on Earth's landscape, or in its atmosphere.
A clash between a segment of non-terrestrials and humans is inevitable in the future.

In the past, more than 3 incidents occurred in secret military bases, and produced fatal consequences.
The incidents were provoked by military men who according to Greys' revelations have insulted Grey scientists who had worked on two joint- programs with the military.
The future clash will occur between the Anunnaki and the Greys, and humans will be caught in the middle. The outlook of mankind will be seriously affected by direct interference from the Anunnaki group called "Baalshamroot Ram".

Part Two: Outlook for mankind after the year 2022

This is the very group that surrounded the Solar System with the "Cosmic Plasmic Belt"; intense radiations/high velocity ranges of rays, as recently revealed by NASA.

The human race will never be in peace with itself, and with its own kind. This is dictated by the "Naf-Siya", the "Araya", the DNA and the bio-psychological makeup of human nature, originally created by the Anunnaki on two occasions:
The first time some 450,000 years ago, and the second time (Final Phase), some 10,000 years ago, which announced the dawn of civilizations on Earth.

Greed is an indivisible segment and one of the characteristics of the fabric of the human psyche. Thus, greed will always be here, and will increase the level of the contamination of mankind.
However, the year 2022 will bring major changes to social systems, and these changes will have enormous influence on the public's concept of religions.
Christianity's dogma could be altered. Islam will not be affected by these changes.

Buddhism, and Hinduism will not affected either, simply because Buddhism is founded on the concept of "Transmission of mind," and thus is not a religion per se.
Ancient Hinduism and Hindu manuscripts and inscriptions have already announced and pre-announced the existence of celestial spacecrafts known as "Vimanas" created by the "Gods", a super race from the multiple layers of the universe. Consequently, both will blend perfectly with the comprehension and definition of a new social order to be established by the Anunnaki.

In short, 2022 will bring paramount changes to:
a-Religions;
b-Social order.

*** *** ***

Part Two: Another extraterrestrial threat other than the Grays' aliens

Another extraterrestrial threat other than the Gray's aliens

Question by Matt Hoxtell, Chicago, Illinois, USA.

Question: After the Anunnaki's job is finished here on earth through decontamination will we ever have to deal with another Extraterrestrial threat other than the Gray's aliens?

Answer:
The only threat humanity will face is the product of the Greys' agenda. It is important to understand, that the Greys have lived on Earth for millions of years, long before the human races were created by the Igigi, Anunnaki and Lyrans. We call the Greys "extraterrestrials". This is not entirely correct, as the Greys are the intraterrestrials of Earth, and humans their co-habitants. We fear the Greys. And ironically, the Greys also fear us. They feel threatened by our nuclear arsenal and experiments, because these can annihilate Earth, where the Greys live. Earth is also the habitat of the Greys.
Earth is where their communities and families live. Greys will do anything and everything to prevent humans from destroying Earth. Earth will be only destroyed by acts of nuclear war. The Greys have adapted very well to the intra-landscape of Earth; meaning Inner-Earth. And water on Earth is essential for their survival and for "energizing" their crafts. Unfortunately, constant interactions with the Greys will deteriorate the genes of the human race.
The first phase of such deterioration is contamination.
The Anunnaki are fully aware of this contamination. Simply put, in order to eliminate the contamination of human and human DNA, the Anunnaki must get rid of the Greys. And the decontamination process will result in a major confrontation with the Greys. Some influential governments have already received a sort of "briefing" on the subject.

Part Two: Another extraterrestrial threat other than the Gray's aliens?

Some high officials took the threat very seriously, whilst many others did not. Their arrogance and ignorance will have lethal consequences, which humanity will suffer from.
No, there are no additional threats from other extraterrestrial races, simply because they are not interested in us. They are not interested, because we have nothing meaningful or important to offer them. Humans live on a linear scale. This is how and why we understand the universe in terms of time and distance/space. And this limits us, and prevents us from becoming members of the "Cosmic Federation."
Only two races in the known universe can live on Earth: The Anunnaki and the Greys. In the past three extraterrestrial races lived here on Earth, for sometime among us.
They were:
- **a**-The Anunnaki;
- **b**-The Lyrans;
- **c**-The Greys.

Their organisms and body structure could sustain our atmosphere and its conditions. Other extraterrestrials would not be able to live on Earth, as humans are not able to live on other known stars and planets because of their atmospheric conditions. Other alien races will self-destruct if they try to live on Earth.
Consequently, they have no interest whatsoever in invading or dominating Earth. In other words, the only threat, the only real threat, will come from the Greys. But for the time being, we are safe, because the Greys still need us. Despite their highly advanced technology and science, the Greys did not yet find the perfect and final formula for saving themselves, genetically.
For some incomprehensible and possibly silly reasons, the survival of the Greys depends on two things:
- **a**-The survival of humans;
- **b**-The safety of planet Earth.

*** *** ***

Part Two: Aliens competing with the Anunnaki to rule our planet

Aliens competing with the Anunnaki to rule our planet?

Question by Matt Hoxtell, Chicago, Illinois, USA.

Question: Are there any other alien races in this galaxy or another that could compete with the superstar status of the Anunnaki and rule our planet?

Answer:
On the market nowadays, we find several so-called encyclopedias and field-guides on extraterrestrial races. The Internet is infested with silly and childish websites posting ridiculous literature on extraterrestrial races, description of their physiognomy, heights, weights, eyes, skin, etc. This is nonsense par excellence. How did they know about these extraterrestrial races?

What are their sources, data, and authoritative references? They are non-existent. Their articles are the product of an erroneous imagination and immature fantasy.

Unless you break the frontiers of time and space, and land on their planets and stars, you will never be able to learn about their species, physiognomy and their biological structure on any level. As long as modern ufology embraces such phantasmagoric assumptions and fake narratives, ufology will never be accepted academically, or gain the respect and trust of erudite milieus and scientists.

However, and according to some statements and "leaks", we have learned about the existence of six different extraterrestrial races who have contacted the United States military.

This was mentioned in the "Krill File".

But again, this so-called file was announced to the ufology community by Mr. Moore, who has been discredited by eminent ufologists. And once again, I ask you to define what we understand by "Eminent ufologists"? How eminence is defined, and on what basis or foundation, such eminence is based upon and structured?

Part Two: Aliens competing with the Anunnaki to rule our planet

To tell you the truth, nobody knows, except the Anunnaki-Ulema. Unless you are familiar with Ana'kh, and have read the archaic manuscripts of the Anunnaki-Ulema, and some of the Phoenician cosmogeny tablets, and unless you are familiar with the Akkadian and proto-Mesopotamian language(s), you will never be able –for sure– to categorize the galactic races.

All we have is mythology and colorful folklore. And beginning in the early 1950's, authors began to put their spin on everything extraterrestrial or alien. Call it science fiction, or perhaps mytho-inspirational essay, but not an authoritative study of galactic civilizations.

As of today, we are aware of the existence of two races:

a-The Greys;
b-The Anunnaki.

The Greys became known to us through articles by all sorts of ufologists, contactees (usually phony/fake), abductees, charlatan channelers, statements by so-called military men who worked in secret military bases, "insiders" and self-serving authors.

The truth I tell you, is that the Greys do exist, but they are not, who, what and how they are generally described to be, by many ufologists and those who claim to have had any sort of contact or rapport with them. In some cases, accounts of encounters were correct, but in general, 95% of accounts and reports betray the truth, simply because the human mind is unable to understand what flashes before our eyes. And this apparent in the way contactees/abductees (followed by a fleet of ufologists) describe the Greys. For instance, how many times have you heard from abductees and ufologists alike, that the Greys or extraterrestrials have very big eyes in proportion to the size of their heads, and the eyes were described as large eyes slanted upward and outward, or big dark eyes that were olive or almond-shaped? Many times, I'm sure. To tell you the truth, extraterrestrials' eyes are as big or as small as human eyes. And their sockets are almost similar to ours, but with three major differences. One of them is the retina. Aliens do not have retina in their eyes, simply because they do not need one.

Abductees were not able to realize that aliens or extraterrestrials eyes were "masked."

Part Two: Aliens competing with the Anunnaki to rule our planet

By masked I mean their eyes were covered by a dark lens or more exactly a screen, called "Bou-Ka'h" in the Ana'kh, the Anunnaki language. The large black eyes were simply a dark screen applied to the eyes of the extraterrestrials. Consider this screen as eyeglasses for now (But in actuality these glasses provided the alien with information, much like glasses with mini TV/info screens on them being made and used by the military today).

This common error is clearly shared by ufology authors, ufologists, and researchers alike. This serious misconception and erroneous description are strong evidence that we have no clear vision or understanding of the physiognomy of extraterrestrials.

If this is true, then we are not in a position to categorize and adequately classify aliens, extraterrestrials, and Greys.

Thus, recognizing and/or defining other extraterrestrial species is pure speculation.

In conclusion, we should concentrate exclusively on two known non-human races; the Anunnaki and the Greys.

Such concentration will enable us to conclude that:
- 1-There are no other extraterrestrials on the scene;
- 2-The Greys are not in any position to compete with the Anunnaki.

And since we have logically eliminated the possible interference from other alien races/non-humans that exist in our galaxy/other galaxies answering the question: "Are there any other alien races in this galaxy or another that could compete with the superstar status of the Anunnaki and rule our planet?" becomes an easy task. And the answer is: The Greys cannot rule our planet, nor can they challenge the super status of the Anunnaki for obvious reasons.

One of these reasons is the fact that the Anunnaki are far more advanced than the Greys.

*** *** ***

Part Two: Would the Anunnaki come to aid Earth if another threat happens?

Would the Anunnaki come to aid the planet if another threat happens?

Questions by Matt Hoxtell, Chicago, Illinois, USA.

Question: You have stated that the Anunnaki feel responsible for hybrid contamination between humans and the Gray's, would the Anunnaki ever come to the aid of the planet aif this threat would happen again?
Answer:
Yes and yes.
This was basically the topic Sinhar Ambar Anati (Victoria) discussed with representatives from the United States government years ago. Please refer to the book: "Anunnaki Ultimatum", co-authored by Ilil Arbel. Anati made it clear to American scientists and to two generals, that the Greys' contamination will inevitably destroy the human race.

*** *** ***

Question: Has the planet ever come close to another threat as serious as the Gray's and will it be a possibility?
Answer:
Yes, millions of years ago, when a huge celestial object was on a trajectory in the direction of planet Earth.
The Anunnaki deviated the object from its collision course with Earth. And later on, they decided to surround the Solar system with a protection shield, known as "The Cosmic Plasmic Belt", which is called "Zinar" in Ana'kh, the Anunnaki language. This was also mentioned in the Book of Ramadosh "Ketab Rama-Dosh."

*** *** ***

Part Two: On hybrid Grays

Hybrid Grays: Adoption and DNA contamination

Questions from Melanie Schmidt:

Question: Have there been a large number of hybrids that were disease free and human enough to be adopted?
Answer:
Yes. A few hybrids were adopted, usually by military families, and the adoptive parents must go to the base where the hybrids are, and can select the one they will adopt. This is a fact.

Basically, some infant-hybrids look just like our own children.
No physical deformities whatsoever.
However, they have shown some muscular anomalies right below their shoulder plates and the vertebral column in the neck. They cannot turn their heads effortlessly.

Another thing: They will never grow to be tall.
Their average height is 5ft 6"

Question: Could someone have a hybrid relative or be the child of a hybrid and not know it?
Answer:
No. Impossible.

Question: I always wonder how people with no compassion whatsoever are the same species.
It seems that living as a loving and compassionate being is what our natural instinct wants us to do, so I wonder if hybrids have any connection to emotionless behavior?
Answer:
Many infant hybrids have displayed high degree of emotion, attachment, fear, joy and anxiety, and become very attached to their parents.

Part Two: On hybrid Grays

Question: I've read discussions about contaminated DNA and am curious if it is to the point where large numbers of people have some connection to hybrids?
Thanks! Melanie Schmidt.

Answer:
No, not many. Those are very rare cases.
Worth mentioning here is that not all infant hybrids have contaminated DNA.
The contamination occurs during the interbreeding process. If noticed by the Grays, they will dispose of those children right away. This has been documented and reported by abductees who lived for a while in the hybrids' habitat.

Dr. David Jacobs wrote a magnificent book on the subject called "Threat". I encourage you to read his book, as it is really fascinating. In fact, a few years ago I contacted Dr. Jacobs, and asked his permission to use some of his material. And gracefully he agreed.

*** *** ***

Questions from Elaine Bradley, New York, New York:

Question: Is it true that hybrid human/grey babies and children are being created and raised in secret bases?
What of the stories of horrific experiments being performed on abducted humans in labs by the Greys as part of their breeding/tissue harvesting programs?

Answer:
Once again Maximillien de Lafayette has provided us with an account of the unthinkable horrors committed by the Greys, as witnessed by Sinhar Anbar Anati:
Here is her account (in her own words), on visiting the Hybrids:

My first encounter with the hybrid children, and my first glimmer of understanding of what eternity is like.

Part Two: On hybrid Grays

"The base we are visiting today is under water," said Sinhar Inannaschamra. "We are about to descend way down into the Pacific."

"What about air?" I asked, a bit apprehensive about the idea. Surely Sinhar Inannaschamra won't forget I could not breathe under water, but still...

"We pass through a lock that is safe for both water and air," said Sinhar Inannaschamra, "and inside, it's geared for the hybrids, which, just like humans, need air." In a few minutes, we stopped and I assumed, correctly, that we were already inside the base.

"They are expecting us," said Sinhar Inannaschamra. "Don't worry about them. They know I can blow the whole place up if they dare to give me any trouble."

The spaceship's door opened and I saw that we were inside a huge, hangar-like room. If I had expected a beautiful, aquarium-like window, showing the denizens of the deep playing in their blue environment, I would have been disappointed. But knowing the Grays, I expected nothing of the sort, and so the beige and gray room, all metal and lacking any windows, did not exactly surprise me.

"This base is enormous, you know" said Sinhar Inannaschamra. "It is used for many operations, but we will just concentrate on the hybrids today."

I was pleased to hear that, since I was secretly apprehensive about the possibility of stumbling on one of the Grays' hellish laboratories. I will never forget, or forgive, what I saw in their lab. But I said nothing and waited to see what was going to happen next. Sinhar Inannaschamra walked me to a solid wall, put her hand on it, and the wall shimmered a little, then moved, allowing a door to form and open for us.

We entered a long corridor, illuminated by stark, white light, with many regular doors on each side.

Sinhar Inannaschamra opened one of the doors and we entered a large room, obviously a refectory since it contained extremely long tables, all made of metal. The room was painted entirely in beige – tables, chairs, walls, and ceiling, and had no windows. It was scrupulously clean.

Part Two: On hybrid Grays

Suddenly, the tables opened up, each table revealing a deep groove on each of its long sides. Plates of what seemed to be normal human food were released from the grooves, and placed before each chair. At this moment, a few doors opened at various parts of the room, and from each door an orderly file of children came in and settled at the table. They were completely silent, not a word was heard, as they picked up their forks and began to eat. None of them paid any attention to us, even though we stood there in plain view of them.

The children seemed to range from six to twelve, but it was difficult to be sure of that. On the one hand, they were small and fragile, so I might have mistaken their ages. On the other, their eyes gave the impression almost of old age.

They seemed wise beyond their tender years. Their hair was thin, their skin was pale to gray, and they all wore white clothes of extreme cleanliness.

Despite these similarities, which made them look as if they were all related to each other, I could tell some differences between them that seemed rather fundamental. It was almost as if they fitted within three distinct groups. I mentioned it, in a whisper, to Sinhar Inannaschamra, and she nodded.

"Yes, you got it," she said. "They consist of early-stage hybrids, middle-stage hybrids, and late-stage hybrids. The first group is born from the first combination of abductees' and Grays' DNA. They closely resemble the Grays.

Look at their skin – the grayish color is very close to that of the Grays, and so is the facial structure. The second group, the middle-stage hybrids, are the result of mating between these early-stage ones, once they are old enough for reproduction, and human abductees.

The resulting DNA is closer to humans, and so they look much more like humans, and many of them lose the Progeria gene. The third group, the late-stage hybrid, is the most important. Middle-stage hybrids are mated with humans to create them – and they can hardly be distinguished from humans."

"Yes, I can tell who the late-stagers are quite easily," I said. "But there are not too many of them here, right?"

Part Two: On hybrid Grays

"This is true, not too many are here. A large number of these hybrids, who represent the most successful results of the experiments, are placed for adoption with human families."

"Are the human families aware of the origin of their children?"

"Yes, in most cases they are. Generally, they are adopted by a high-ranking United States military man or woman, who had worked, or still works, with aliens, in secret military bases. This happens much more often than most people suspect... the spouse of the military person may or may not know, depending on the circumstances and character traits of the hybrid child. These lucky hybrids lead a much better life than whose who are raised in places like this one, communally."

"Are they badly treated here? Are they abused by the Grays?"

"No, the Grays don't want to lose them, they are too valuable. But they receive no love, no individual attention, there is no real parenting, and the environment is barren and depressing. They live like that until they are old enough to be of use in the experiments. Not a very nice life for any child."

"And what about the issue of Progeria? I mean, for the adopted ones?"

"Only the hybrids who are entirely free of Progeria are adopted by human families. We even suspect, though we are not sure, that many of the Progeria stricken late-stagers are killed, since their Progeria gene is too strong. The Grays believe that after these three attempts, it cannot be eradicated by further breeding."

"And so they kill the poor things... what is the motive for all these atrocities?"

"All for the same reason I have mentioned before. They think they somehow will save their civilization. But they are doomed."

"But in the meantime, they harm, torture, and kill so many people. I don't understand why it is tolerated." Sinhar Inannaschamra did not answer.

*** *** ***

Part Two: On hybrid Grays

The children finished eating, still in complete silence. Each child, as he or she finished his/her meal, leaned back into the chair, and as soon as all of them were leaning back, the groove from which the plates came opened up, and re-absorbed all the plates. "They now go to an automatic dishwashing machine," explained Sinhar Inannaschamra.

The children got up, and left the dismal room in the same file arrangement they came in. As soon as the room was empty, large vacuum cleaners emerged from the wall and sucked up every crumb, every piece of debris. Then they sprayed the tables and floor with a liquid that smelled like disinfectant. The room was spotlessly clean again, ready for the next sad, depressing meal.

"Shall we go to the dormitories now?" asked Sinhar Inannaschamra. I nodded. We followed the children through one of the doors, and entered a place that was a combination of an old-fashioned orphanage and military barracks.

It was a very large room, but the ceiling was not high, only about twelve feet. Again, everything was beige and gray, and there were no windows to relieve the monotony.

The room was full of beds, arranged above each other in groups of three, like in a submarine. Dozens and dozens of such rows seemed to stretch to a very long distance.

The beds were made of some metal, very smooth, and of silver-gray color. They seemed to be assembled like prefab furniture.

"Sinhar Inannaschamra," I said, "there are no ladders. How do the children reach the upper levels?"

"They can levitate," said Sinhar Inannaschamra. "Look at this. Part of each bed is magnetic, so each child can have his or her toys attached to it. As for the lower beds, the toys are stored next to them."

"So they have toys," I said. "That's a mercy."

"Yes, the Grays discovered that mental stimulation is highly important to the hybrids' development. There are plenty of other activities, mostly with abductees, that relieve their lives of the tedium, at least to a certain extent."

"But they have no privacy at all."

Part Two: On hybrid Grays

"None whatsoever, they only get their own room when they are more mature, but they have one thing that pleases them. If the children want to, they can put their things in their bed, close the bed with a panel, and hide it inside a wall. They like that."

"I wonder, too, is it a comfort for them to be together, after all?"

"Their feelings and emotional state are not exactly human... it's hard to explain. I think it's time for you to see them interact."

"Where are all the children now?"

"They are attending various activities," said Sinhar Inannaschamra. "Come, I'll show you."

We entered a room that opened directly from the dormitory. To my surprise, it was really a glass bubble. You could see the outside, which was an unpleasant desert surrounding. I found it nasty, but I figured that to the children it might represent a pleasant change.

About ten children, seemingly between the ages of six and eight, sat on the ground, which was simply desert sand. They were playing with normal human toys – trucks, cars, and trains. They filled the things with sand, using plastic trowels that one usually sees on the beach.

They were also building tunnels from the sand, wetting it with water from large containers that stood here and there. They seemed to be enjoying their games, certainly concentrating on them, but their demeanor remained quiet and subdued, and they did not engage in the laughter, screaming, yelling, or fighting that children of this age normally do.

"They also have rooms with climbing equipment, and places to play ball," said Sinhar Inannaschamra. "It is needed to strengthen their bones and muscles."

I approached the children, a little apprehensively, worried that I might frighten the poor things. They looked up at me, seemingly waiting for me to do something, but I was pleased to realize that they were not afraid. I sat on the sand, took some stones that were scattered around, and arranged them so that they created a little road.

Part Two: On hybrid Grays

The children stared at me for a minute with their strange, wise eyes, as if trying to read my thoughts, and almost instantly grasped the idea and continued to build the road together.

None of them smiled, but they seemed very much engaged in the new activity. Once all the stones were used, they looked at me again, as if trying to absorb information, and sure enough, after a minute they took the trucks and made them travel down the little road. I got up and let them play.

"So they can read minds," I said to Sinhar Inannaschamra.

"To an extent," she said. "At this age, they basically just absorb images you project. You probably thought about the trucks going on this road, and they saw it."

"And everything was done together, as if they were mentally connected," I said. "Do they do everything together?"

"Yes, everything is communal, even the bathrooms where they clean themselves. But don't be too upset about it. If they are separated from each other before adolescence, they become extremely upset. It is almost as if the onset of puberty makes them an individual, and before that they have a group mentality."

"Horrible," I said.

"They are not unhappy," said Sinhar Inannaschamra. "Only as adolescents, when they break off the communal mind, do they come to understand how unhappy they really are. But we will visit the adolescents on another occasion."

"Very well," I said.

"Would you like to see the room where they keep the fetuses?" asked Sinhar Inannaschamra.

I followed Sinhar Inannaschamra to the corridor, and we walked quite a distance before opening another door. We entered another one of the hangar-sized rooms, full of tanks.

"Each tank contains liquid nutrients," said Sinhar Inannaschamra. "This is where they put the fetuses, as soon as they are removed from the abductees. The tanks are arranged in order, from the youngest fetuse,s to those that are almost ready to be removed."

"Do they separate them into stages?" I asked.

Part Two: On hybrid Grays

"Yes, this room is for early stagers only. In other rooms, they have the middle stagers. But the late stagers remain in the mother's womb until birth, to make them as close to humans as possible."

"And what are the babies like?"

"Quiet, not as responsive as human babies. Many of them die as soon as they are removed from the tank. Those that survive are generally mentally well developed, but physically weak, and emotionally subdued."

"And who takes care of them?"

"Both Grays and abductees. The Grays perform most of the physical requirements, but the abductees supply the human touch. We can't go there yet."

"How come?"

"We need to prepare you to interact with abductees. They are very complicated. We shall have a few sessions about interacting with them at the same time when we teach you how to work with the adolescents. Also, you had wanted some instruction on how to contact and help those people that are children of humans and Anunnakis, like your son. This requires some teaching, too."

We went back to our spaceship, not saying much. I remember thinking that if I were part of the Anunnaki Council, I would vote to kill every Gray in the known universe. Of course I did not say it to Sinhar Inannaschamra, but I am sure she knew how I felt. Back home, I went to my beloved garden and sat under a tree that constantly showered tiny blossoms on me, like little snowflakes. I did not even know I was crying.

"What is the matter?" said Marduchk, who suddenly appeared next to me. I told him about the visit with the hybrids.

"The hybrids are not abused," said Marduchk. "Something else is bothering you."

I thought for a moment, and then decided I might as well be honest with him. "Yes," I said. "I cannot understand the Anunnaki's casual attitude about the fact that thousands of human beings are tortured and killed all the time.

Neither you nor Sinhar Inannaschamra seem to be as shocked as I am about the fact that the Grays engage in such atrocities."

Part Two: On hybrid Grays

Marduchk was quiet for a minute, thinking. At this conversation, we did not use the Conduit, because in my agitated state I found it difficult. I was not entirely used to it as yet. So I waited for him to say what he thought.

"I see your point," he said. "You think we are callous about it."

"Yes, I do, to tell you the truth. Why don't you destroy the Grays? Why do you allow so much death, so much pain? Are you, after all, cruel beings? Have you become callous because you have lived so many years, and become thick-skinned about suffering?"

"No, we are not cruel. It's just that we view life and death differently than you do. We cannot destroy all the Grays, even if we wanted to. We don't commit genocide, even if they try to do it. We don't want to kill them. We know that they will die on their own."

"And in the meantime, suffering means nothing to you?"

"It means a lot, but destroying the Grays would not eliminate suffering that occurs in all the universes we go to. There are other species that are even worse than the Grays, you just don't know about them because their horrific behavior is not aimed at humans."

"It seems to me, that even though you are so much more sophisticated than humans, the fact that you deny the existence of God may have deprived you of your ethics, after all."

"Deny God? What makes you think we deny God?" asked Marduchk. He seemed genuinely surprised.

"Marduchk, you have told me, more than once, that the Anunnaki created the human race, not God. So where is God if He is not the Creator? Your statements are contradictory."

"Not at all," said Marduchk. "The Anunnaki view of God is similar to human religions in many ways, but contains much more information.

The term we use to describe God is 'All That Is.' To the Anunnaki, God is made of inexhaustible mental energy, and contains all creation within Itself, therefore representing a gestalt of everything that has existed, exists now, or will exist in the future, and that includes all beings, all known universes, and all events and phenomena.

Part Two: On hybrid Grays

God's dearest wish is to share in the lives of all It's creations, learn and experience with them, and from them. But while they are imperfect, God Itself is perfect, which is why It can only be seen as a gestalt."

"Why are you calling God *It*?" I asked.

"Because we do not attribute gender to God."

"I see," I said. "So in essence, the Anunnaki God is not all that different from ours. What else should I know?"

"It is possible that other primary energy gestalts existed before God came into being, and actually created It. If so, then the possibility exists that there are many Gods, all engaged in magnificent creativity within their own domains. We are not certain if that is so, but we do not dismiss this beautiful possibility."

"That is vastly different from human thought," I said, meditating. "But how does it tie in with life and death issues, and with the fact that you have created us?"

"The individuals that exist within God, though part of God, have free will and self-determination. In life and in death, each is a part of God and also a complete and separate individual that will never lose its identity.

The Anunnaki are indeed the creators of human beings, but since each Anunnaki is a part of God, there is no conflict in the idea of their creation of humanity.

Creation is endless and on-going, and human beings, in their turn, create as well – for example, great art, literature, and service to other people, animals, and the planet Earth – though they do not exactly create life as yet. We are all part of the grand gestalt, and that makes All That Is such an apt name for God."

"So how does that make the situation with the Grays' atrocities any better?"

"It is better because the lives that they take are not disappearing into a void. Each individual is eternal, and even if killed as a child, will go on into other domains. I am not saying that this justifies the Grays' atrocities.

I am merely pointing out that even though these atrocities do exist, the individuals affected will have another chance."

Part Two: On hybrid Grays

"Yes, this does make a difference, and I can see how it would affect your thinking. But for me, after seeing what the Grays do to humans in their labs, it is still very disturbing."

"I can understand that, Victoria. It is not something you are accustomed to. Tell me, do you still want to do this mission?" He asked his question in a very neutral way, obviously not wanting to influence my free will.

"Yes, more than ever," I said. "Maybe I can do some good for these poor, sad children."

"I have a suggestion, then," said Marduchk. "I don't see it as a long-term mission, since you cannot change the ways of the Grays from within. I think you will find it a springboard to other missions, as it is obvious to me that you have some thoughts on making the Anunnaki do something about the Grays to force them to stop their experiments.

Doing this mission will be extremely good as a learning experience, right from inside the Grays' base. As for contacting the people who are the children of humans and Anunnaki's, that will not take much of your time.

There are very few of these around, these days."

"How long do you think this mission will take me?"

"Exactly nine months," said Marduchk. I stared for a minute and then laughed.

"I see what you mean, Marduchk. You think I should start our daughter, allow her to grow in the tube in the Anunnaki fashion, and while she is in the tube, concentrate on my mission. Then, I should come back and spend some time with you and the baby, before embarking on other missions."

"Doesn't it sound like a good plan? While the baby is in the tube, there is nothing you can do for her other than look at her as she grows. And you can easily do that with a monitor from earth, right from the Grays' base. And we will talk every day, so if you have any concerns about her, I can take care of it."

"This is a wonderful idea," I said. "I will have the orientation regarding the abductees and the adolescent hybrids, and of course the human-Anunnaki people, and when I am ready to go on my mission, I will first stop at the hospital and start the baby!"

Part Two: On hybrid Grays

This plan made me feel a little better, but I knew I must give the issue some more thought, and perhaps further discussion. So, when I went to see Sinhar Inannaschamra the next day to arrange for the orientation, I brought the subject up with her, and told her honestly how I felt.

"Yes, I do understand how you feel, Victoria," she said. "Before we do any more work with the hybrid mission, I would like to give you a little background about our relationship to life and death."

"I would very much welcome it," I said.

"So let's start with the concept of An-Hayya'h," said Sinhar Inannaschamra.

"I have never heard the word mentioned," I said.

"This word, which is also used as A-haya and Aelef-hayat, could be the most important word in Anakh, our language, as well as in the written history of humanity, because it deals with several extremely important issues.

These are:
- The origin of humans on earth.
- How humans are connected to the Anunnaki.
- Importance of water to humans and Anunnaki.
- The life of humans.
- Proof that it was originally a woman who created man, Adam and the human race, via her Anunnaki identity.
- The return of the Anunnaki to earth.
- Humanity's hopes and salvation, and a better future for all, our gifts to you, as your ancestors and creators."

"Complicated concepts," I said.

"I will try to explain the whole concept as clearly as possible, because it is extremely difficult to find the proper and accurate word or words in terrestrial languages and vocabularies. Let's start with the word itself. The word An-Hayya'h is composed of two parts.

The first part is 'An' or 'A' (Pronounced Aa), or 'Aelef' (pronounced a'leff).

Part Two: On hybrid Grays

It is the same letter in Anakh, Akkadian, Canaanite, Babylonian, Assyrian, Ugaritic, Phoenician, Moabite, Siloam, Samaritan, Lachish, Hebrew, Aramaic, Nabataean Aramaic, Syriac, and Arabic.

All these languages are derived from Ana'kh. Incidentally, the early Greeks adopted the Phoenician Alphabet, and Latin and Cyrillic came from the Greek Alphabet. The Hebrew, Aramaic and Greek scripts all came from the Phoenician. Arabic and most of the Indian scriptures came from the Aramaic.

The entire Western World received its language from the Phoenicians, the descendants of the Anunnaki. Anyway, the 'An in Ana'kh means one of the following:
- Beginning
- The very first
- The ultimate
- The origin
- Water

On earth, this word became Alef in Phoenician, Aramaic, Hebrew, Syriac and Arabic. Alef is the beginning of the alphabet in these languages. In Latin, it's 'A' and in Greek it is Alpha. In Hebrew, the Aleph consists of two yuds (pronounced Yod); one yod is situated to the upper right and the other yod to the lower left. Both yods are joined by a diagonal vav.

They represent the higher water and the lower water, and between them the heaven.

This mystic-kabalistic interpretation was explained before by Rabbi Isaac Luria. Water is extremely important in all the sacred scriptures, as well as in the vast literature and manuscripts of extraterrestrials and the Anunnaki.

Water links humans to the Anunnaki. In the Babylonian account of Creation, Tablet 1 illustrates Apsu (male), representing the primeval fresh water, and Tiamat (female), the primeval salt water.

These two were the parents of the gods. Apsu and Tiamat begat the Lahmu (Lakhmu) and Lahamu (Lakhamu) deities.

Part Two: On hybrid Grays

In the Torah, the word 'water' was mentioned on the first day of the creation of the world: 'And the spirit of God hovered over the surface of the water.' In the Chassidut, the higher water is 'wet' and 'warm,' and represents the closeness to Yahweh (God), and it brings happiness to man.

The lower water is 'cold,' and brings unhappiness because it separates us from Yahweh, and man feels lonely and abandoned. The Ten Commandments commence with the letter Alef: 'Anochi (I) am God your God who has taken you out of the land of Egypt, out of the house of bondage.'

The letter 'Alef' holds the secret of man, his/her creation, and the whole universe, as is explained in the Midrash. In Hebrew, the numeric value of Aleph is 1.

And the meaning is:
- First
- Adonai
- Leader
- Strength
- Ox
- Bull
- Thousand
- Teach.

According to Jewish teachings, each Hebrew letter is a spiritual force and power by itself, and comes directly from Yahweh. This force contains the raw material for the creation of the world and man.

The Word of God ranges from the Aleph to the Tav, which is the last letter in the Hebrew alphabet. In Revelation 1:8, Jesus said: 'I am Alpha and Omega, the beginning and the ending.' In John 1:1-3, as the Word becomes Jesus, the Lord Jesus is also the Aleph and the Tav, as well as the Alpha and the Omega.

In Him exists all the forces and spiritual powers of the creation. Jesus is also connected to water, an essential substance for the purification of the body and the soul, which is why Christians developed baptism in water.

Part Two: On hybrid Grays

In Islam, water is primordial and considered the major force of the creation of the universe. The Prophet Mohammad said, as can be read in the Quran: 'Wa Khalaknah Lakoum min al Ma'i, koula chay en hay,' meaning: 'And We (Allah) have created for you from water everything alive.'

The Islamic numeric value of Aleph and God is 1. To the Anunnaki and many extraterrestrial civilizations, the An or Alef represents the number 1, also Nibiru, the constellation Orion, the star Aldebaran, and above all the female aspect of creation symbolized in an Anunnaki woman 'Gb'r,' whom you know as the Angel Gabriel on earth."

"The Angel Gabriel was a woman?" I asked, amazed.

"Unquestionably so," said Sinhar Inannaschamra, smiling.

"How interesting," I said. "But do go on. What about the second part of the word An-Hayya'h?"

"The second part, namely the Hayya'h part, means:
- Life
- Creation
- Humans
- Earth, where the first human, which was a female, was created.
-

In Arabic, Hebrew, Aramaic, Turkish, Syriac, and so many Eastern languages, the Anunnaki words Hayya'h and Hayat mean the same thing: Life. But the most striking part of our story is that the original name of Eve, the first woman, is not Eve, but Hawwa, derived directly from Hayya. You see, Eve's name in the Bible is Hawwa, or Chavvah. In the Quran it is also Hawwa, and in every single Semitic and Akkadian script, Eve is called Hawwa or Hayat, meaning the giver of life, the source of the creation.

Now, if we combine An with Hayya'h or Hayat, we get these results: Beginning; The very first; The ultimate; The origin; Water + Life; Creation; Humans; Earth, where the first was created; Woman. And the whole meaning becomes: The origin of the creation, and first thing or person who created the life of humans was a woman, or water. Amazingly enough, in Anakh, woman and water mean the same thing.

Part Two: On hybrid Grays

Woman represents water according to the Babylonian, Sumerian and Anunnaki tablets, as clearly written in the Babylonian-Sumerian account of Creation, Tablet 1."

"Well, no wonder then, that God has no gender in the Anunnaki concept," I said. "I found that very interesting, when Marduchk told me about All That Is as the name of God."

"Yes, it all ties together rather nicely, even if it is a little complicated," said Sinhar Inannaschamra.

"A little?" I said, laughing. "I will have to think about this for a long time before I am comfortable with the concepts. But it is fascinating. I would like, moreover, to understand a little better how the Anunnaki created the human race."

"Well, it happened around 65,000 B.C.E," said Sinhar Inannaschamra. The Anunnaki, at that time, lived in the regions you now call Iraq, known then as Mesopotamia, Sumer and Babylon, and also Lebanon, known as Loubnan, Phoenicia, or Phinikia. We taught your ancestors how to write, speak, play music, build temples, and navigate, as well as geometry, algebra, metallurgy, irrigation, and astronomy, among other arts.

We had high hopes for this race, which we have created in our image. But the human race disappointed us almost from the beginning, for human beings were, and still are, cruel, violent, greedy and ungrateful.

So, we gave up on you and left earth.

The few remaining Anunnaki living in Iraq and Lebanon were killed by savage military legions from Greece, Turkey and other nations of the region.

The Anunnaki left earth for good, or at least that was the plan at the time. Other extraterrestrial races came to earth, but these celestial visitors were not friendly and considerate like the Anunnaki.

The new extraterrestrials had a different plan for humanity, and their agenda included abduction of women and children, animal mutilation, genetic experiments on human beings, creating a new hybrid race, etc..."

"But you are still there, Sinhar Inannaschamra. And you are still trying to help. Obviously, you would not have projects such as you had with me if you had forgotten us..."

Part Two: On hybrid Grays

"No, we did not totally forget you. We could not... After all, many of your women were married to Anunnaki, and some of our women were married to humans.

Ancient history, the Bible, Sumerian Texts, Babylonian scriptures, Phoenician tablets, and historical accounts from around the globe did record these events. You can find them, almost intact, in archeological sites in Iraq and Lebanon, as well as in museums, particularly the British Museum, the Iraqi Museum and the Lebanese Museum."

"So how did you keep in touch with human civilization?"

"Before leaving you, we activated in your cells the infinitesimally invisible multi-multi-microscopic gene of An-Hayya'h. Yes, this is how it is all inter-connected... It was implanted in your organism and it became a vital component of your DNA. Humans are not yet aware of this, just as they were unaware of the existence of their DNA for thousands of years. As your medicine, science and technology advance, you will be able, some day, to discover that miniscule, invisible, undetectable An-Hayya'h molecule, exactly as you have discovered your DNA.

An-Hayya'h cannot be detected yet in your laboratories. It is way beyond your reach and your comprehension, but it is extremely powerful, because it is the very source of your existence. Through An-Hayya'h, we remained in touch with you, even though you are not aware of it. It is linked directly to a 'Conduit' and to a 'Miraya' (monitor/ mirror) on Nibiru. Every single human being on the face of the earth is linked to the outer-world of the Anunnaki through An-Hayya'h. And it is faster than the speed of light. It reaches the Anunnaki through 'Ba'abs' (star gates). It travels the universe and reaches the 'Miraya' of the Anunnaki through the Conduit, which was integrated in your genes and your cerebral cells by the Anunnaki some 65,000 years ago."

"The same Conduit I have now?"

"Yes, that same Conduit. Of course, humans cannot use it, since it was not activated like yours. But hopefully some day they will be able to."

"And how do the Anunnaki receive the content of a 'Conduit' to allow them to watch over the humans?" I asked.

Part Two: On hybrid Grays

"Through the 'Miraya' which we created to function with the Conduit and the An-Hayya'h, even though we felt that you do not deserve it.

The Anunnaki have been watching you, monitoring your activities, listening to your voices, witnessing your wars, your brutality, your greed and indifference towards each other for centuries. We did not interfere, at least not very much."

"But from my experience, you are returning?"

"Yes. We will, because we fear two things that could destroy earth, and annihilate the human race. The domination of earth and the human race by the Grays, and the destruction of human life and the planet Earth at the hands of humans. The whole earth could blow up. Should this happen, the whole solar system could be destroyed. As we know already, should anything happen to the Moon, the earth will cease to exist."

"Is there hope that we will change?"

"There is always hope. We are trying to change you. The most delightful and comforting aspect of it, is the hope for peace, a brighter future, and a better life that you can accomplish and reach when you discover how to use it without abusing it. Every one of you can do that."

"I wonder how many humans I know will see such change in their lifetime," I said wistfully.

"Even when people die, their An-Hayya'h will always be there for them to use before they depart earth. It will never go away, because it is part of you. Without it you couldn't exist. Just before you die, your brain activates it for you. Seconds before you die, your mind will project the reenactment of all the events and acts, good and bad, in your entire life, past, and 'zoom' you right toward your next nonphysical destination, where and when you judge yourself, your deeds, and your existence, and where you decide whether you wish to elevate yourself to a higher dimension, or stay in the state of nothingness and loneliness, and for how long. Everything is up to the individual."

"So there is no death. Our minds live forever."

"Indeed, there is no death. Your minds live on, and make all the individual decisions about their future."

"What about reincarnation? Do we return to earth, ever?"

Part Two: On hybrid Grays

"No, you will not return to earth, nor will your 'soul' migrate to another soul or another body. From the evidence we have garnered, we know and not just believe, that there is no such thing. And why would you wish to return to earth, anyway?

Earth is the lowest sphere of existence for humans; everything else is an improvement!"

"It's good to know that you have not deserted us, Sinhar Inannaschamra. It makes me feel safer, for myself and for humanity."

"My dear Victoria, you are now a full Anunnaki, and you will never, ever, be alone. But I understand your attachment to your previous fellow humans.

There is no reason to worry about them. Humans are always connected to the Anunnaki in this life and the next, and in the future, we plan a much closer communication. So please, go on to your mission with a lighter heart.

There is plenty of bright hope for everyone, even the hybrids, I dare say." I went home, feeling much better about life, the universe, and my mission.

As a matter of fact, I began to look forward to it as a new adventure. And soon I will have a baby girl, too!

*** *** ***

Part Two: Grays' interbreeding program with humans

On the Greys interbreeding program with humans

Question from Maxine Walters, Washington, D.C.

Question:
What is the reason behind the Greys interbreeding program with humans?

Answer:
As provided by Sinhar Anbar Anati, and as told by Maximillien de Lafayette:

"Very few people, on any planet, really understand the Grays. I have made it my business to learn all I could about them, and I will be able to help you."

"In my trip to their lab, I felt nothing could be worse than these beings," I said. "They seem to me to be a constant menace to everyone."

"They are cruel," said Sinhar Inannaschamra. "But I am thinking about something else. Unless you know their problem, all you see is a technological, highly qualified race without heart or feelings, vicious, violent, and engaged in senseless, merciless experiments. But there is more to it than that. They are a dying civilization, desperately trying to save themselves."

"Dying civilization? How come?" I asked, surprised. With all their activity they seemed very much alive to me, and extremely dangerous.

"Have you ever heard of Progeria? On earth they also call it Hutchinson-Gilford Syndrome, after the two scientists who discovered it in 1886."

"Yes, I have heard a little of it. Progeria victims are children who age, really become old people, before they even reach puberty. A parent nightmare, but very rare, I should say."

Part Two: Grays' interbreeding program with humans

"On earth it is indeed very rare. On average, only one child out of four to eight million births is born with Progeria. It is a rare, and extremely frightening genetic disease, resulting from spontaneous mutation in the sperm or egg of the parents."

"Yes, this is what I have always heard," I said.

"The horror of this disease is that it has no cure. The child is born, starts showing early symptoms, and begins to age right away. The children remain tiny, rarely over four feet, both boys and girls become bald, and all develop a large cranium, a pointy nose and a receding chin, resulting in an amazing resemblance to each other, almost as if they were clones...

And then they die of old age, mostly in their teens but often earlier, and there is nothing anyone can do for them. They develop old age diseases – such as hardening of the arteries – and often die of strokes or coronary disease, while their poor parents have to watch helplessly.

The name Progeria is very appropriate. It means 'before old age,' and expresses it very well."

"But what is the connection of the Progeria children to the Grays?" I asked, a frightening suspicion beginning to form in my mind.

"The civilization of the Grays is millions of years old, and for eons, they have been degenerating. A huge percentage of their population has Progeria, in varying degrees, and because of that, they are threatened with extinction.

No one knows how many Grays are affected, and how many are Progeria-free. We only meet those who are, at least for the present, able to carry on their duties, with the help of their advanced medical technology.

For all we know, there are millions of sick individuals hidden from view on their home planet."

"This is incredible," I said, shuddering.

"You must also remember that the Grays do not reproduce sexually. They used to, but not anymore. Also, they don't reproduce like the Anunnaki, either. For thousands of years, they have been relying on cloning.

And that has damaged their DNA even further, creating more and more cases of Progeria. They are dying out."

Part Two: Grays' interbreeding program with humans

"An entire civilization destroyed by Progeria... it is almost impossible to believe," I said.

"If you study the two groups, you will see strong similarities between the Grays and Progeria children. I won't go into all of them, as the list could go on for days, but let's consider the most prominent ones. For one thing, Progeria does not produce any form of dementia.

Both groups maintain their excellent mental faculties, usually with high IQ, until they die. That is a very important clue, but here are the others for your consideration:

- Neither group ever grows much beyond four feet.
- Both have fragile, weak bodies, with thin arms and legs; all their bones are thin, as a general rule.
- Both groups are bald.
- Grays have no sexual reproduction, most have no genitalia at all. Progeria children never reach puberty.
- Both have large heads by comparison to their bodies.
- Both have receding chins and pointy noses. Within their groups, they closely resemble each other. The Grays are cloned; the Progeria children look as if they could have been cloned.

"So will the experiments they do help them survive?"

"That is what they hope for. They take the eggs and the sperm from humans and combine them with Grays' DNA. Thus, they create the Hybrid children."

"Those poor children. I pity them so."

"They are not exactly what you think, Victoria. I pity them too, but you must realize that they are closer to the Grays in their character and behavior than they are to humans."

"What are they like?"

"The first generation Hybrids are smaller than human children. They tend to follow the growth pattern of the Gray parent – and by now you know this is a very fragile one. They are even smaller than Progeria babies. The retardation of growth begins before birth."

Part Two: Grays' interbreeding program with humans

"When you say 'first generation" does it mean that they go on mixing the genetic material?"

"Yes, that is exactly what they do. The Hybrids may or may not have Progeria, but naturally, the more human DNA that is mixed into the species, the more chances there are of eliminating the bad genes. So they breed the Hybrids with more human DNA, always hoping to eradicate the disease, never quite succeeding. That is why they have to get fresh human specimens all the time."

"Do you think they have a chance of survival?"

"No, personally I don't think they have a chance. I think they are doomed. But many Anunnaki disagree with me. At any rate, there is nothing we can do either way."

"Do you think the authorities on earth know about all that? Like the governments of various countries? Why isn't something being done about it?"

Sinhar Inannaschamra looked at me silently. Her big black Anunnaki eyes were suddenly full of such sorrow, such deep sadness, that I did not know how to react. Finally she said, "Yes, they do know. I have to tell you the truth, Victoria, even though it breaks my heart to do so. Almost all earth governments have made a deal with the Grays. They supply them with humans."

I jumped on my feet, completely horrified. "They do that? They sell humans to the Grays for torture and killing? What do they gain?"

"Can't you guess?" said Sinhar Inannaschamra quietly. "The Grays give them the technology they crave. They have learned so much from the Grays, and they mostly use it for military purposes. Humans are not kind to each other. Look at all the wars, torture, genocide, holocausts... all part of human history, and still taking place."

"Unfortunately, this is true," I said.

"Anyway, there are various places on earth where these activities can be studied, such as military bases, mostly located underground, in many countries. Some day you will spend some time there, I am sure."

Part Two: Grays' interbreeding program with humans

"Well," I said, trying to recover from the shock. "I can't answer for the earth's governments, but I can try to help."

"Indeed you can. We are trying, in many ways, to alleviate the situation, even though, as I've explained before, we cannot police the whole universe, or even the entire earth."

"Do you think I should go and take a look at the Hybrids, as part of my education?"

"Yes, I think the best thing to do would be to take you on a field trip. You must meet these Hybrids face to face before you make your decision about the mission. But there is something else I wanted to talk to you about. This mission will have to be on earth, you know. There are no Hybrid bases anywhere else, certainly not on Nibiru. You will be alone for long periods. We don't go back and forth to earth very often, which means that you will have to spend years on earth, except from short vacations."

"Marduchk told me he had committed himself to work with those apelike creatures he shape-shifted into, and scared me so much after our wedding. That means, I am sure, that he will be away for extended periods of time as well, doesn't it?"

"Yes, that is how we all live. My husband is on missions all the time. Most of us are. I used to go to distant places, also, even though currently my mission is teaching fulltime at the Academy."

"But are Marduchk and I going to be completely isolated from each other for all these years?"

"No, of course not. Now that you have your Conduit opened, you can talk to each other every single day you spend apart, and every few years, you can meet for a vacation."

"That does not sound too bad," I said. "I will miss Marduchk and all of you very much, but what are a few years? You have given me the hope of living a very long and useful life, and Marduchk has begun to teach me about the next phase of eternity, which is not yet entirely clear to me but very comforting, nonetheless. I am trying very hard to absorb it all.
In that light, I would be willing to make the effort without any regrets. There is only one thing... I am not sure if you will think it is a good idea..."

"I can sense what it is, Victoria. You want a child."

Part Two: Grays' interbreeding program with humans

"Was I that transparent?"

"It was to be expected. Anyone who has had to give a baby up for adoption, the way you so heroically did, would want another baby. That is only natural. But why shouldn't you? Why did you think it an idea that would not appeal to me?"

"Because I would have to leave the child on Nibiru when I finally go on the mission. Another abandonment."

"First of all, you did not abandon your son. You insisted on knowing all the conditions, you were assured of the loving family and wonderful future he was going to have. And as for the next child, surely you see that our system here is extremely family oriented.

When you go on your mission, let's say when the child is somewhere between five and ten, you will have an entire family ready to take over.

Think about it – the baby's father, aunt, uncle, nieces, and not to mention her loving great-great-great-grandmother ten times removed, namely me – will all be there, loving this child. And you can talk to the baby every single day through the Miraya, see each other during vacations, and come back long before the child graduates from the Academy. I don't think your mission will take seventy-one years, and frankly, I see no abandonment issues here at all."

"What will Marduchk think?"

"He would probably love the idea! He likes children. Not all Anunnaki choose to have children, you know. Some never do, some only have one or two and then spend thousands of years without further reproduction. It's entirely a matter of free will. Those who want children are of course encouraged to have them whenever they please, since they make excellent parents. Those who do not wish to raise children are never pressured into having them. And remember, Victoria, you can have more children after you come back from your mission, if you choose to do so. It is always your choice, and time does not play any part in it."

I was quiet for a few minutes. Being raised on earth had eroded so much of the self-confidence and poise all Anunnaki possess. Well, I will have to work on becoming more like them, that is all.

Part Two: Grays' interbreeding program with humans

"This time I will have the baby Anunnaki style," I said, feeling better every minute, "in the tube. So I can freely study and travel during the time before it is ready for its birth."

"Incidentally, you can decide in advance if you want a boy or a girl," said Sinhar Inannaschamra, matter of factly.

"I'll consult Marduchk about that," I said. "He may have a preference. I don't care if it is a boy or a girl. I just want a healthy baby."

"Well, that is a given. You will have a perfect baby, every time. And tomorrow, come back and I'll take you on the field trip. I think meeting the Hybrids will be a very interesting experience."

I went home, and as I was waiting for Marduchk to come back from the Akashic Library, I strolled in the garden, breathing in the evening air and the scent of the opening night blooming flowers. I saw Marduchk approaching and waved at him.

"You got your Conduit opened!" he said right away. "I can sense it."

"Indeed," I said. "Shall we try to communicate telepathically? Let's see if I am good at it."

"Do you know how to start it?" asked Marduchk.

"I do." I did something in my mind, which regrettably I cannot explain to anyone who has not activated their Conduit, and the Conduit opened, first a little hesitantly, then fully. It was a surprisingly easy, extremely pleasant and effortless way to conduct a conversation.

I related to Marduchk everything that happened, in detail, and a conversation that would have taken about an hour was accomplished in a few minutes.

As for the great decision (namely the child, not the mission), Marduchk was charmed by the idea. "A daughter," he communicated, meditatively, "if you don't mind. I had two sons, but I have never had a daughter... it would be a nice experience."

"Fine with me," I communicated back. "And when I come back, we might consider having more. I love children."

Part Two: Grays' interbreeding program with humans

"Certainly, if you wish," Marduchk communicated. "I find raising children extremely nice." And so the decision was made, and I felt very, very happy.

This is a good time to explain something regarding Anunnaki fatherhood. Earth readers might wonder how the Anunnaki male feels about children, since he does not contribute sperm, and the fertilization of the eggs, as I have explained in a previous chapter, occurs by the activation of the specialized light.

Does the Anunnaki male see himself as the father to his wife's natural children?

The answer is a resounding "yes."

The Anunnaki do not put much weight on trifling physical matters, such as the use of sperm. The Anunnaki couple is an inseparable unit, and whichever way a child comes into their lives, the child is secure of a having a loving father. I wish the same could be said of all human fathers – whether they do or do not contribute sperm.

*** *** ***

Part Two: Are the Anunnaki going to take over Earth?

Are the Anunnaki going to take over Earth?

Questions by Reverend Nancy Santos.

Question : Is one of these Anunnaki Gods going to take over the earth after the pole shift?

Answer:
No! For two reasons:
- 1-The pole is not going to shift. So don't worry. This is based upon mainstream science. However, it could shift as it did before, millions of years ago. But scientists are not concerned. They are absolutely sure that no shift will occur anytime soon.
- 2- If the Anunnaki intend to take over Earth, they will not wait until the pole shift. They can do it any time, at will. But they are not interested at all.

Read the section on the final warning.
Dear Sandra, you have to remember that the Anunnaki are not territorial. Besides, planet Earth is meaningless to them. We, as human beings are not interesting enough to the Anunnaki. Our natural resources are found on numerous planets, readily accessible to the Anunnaki.
There are 7 galaxies in the cosmos filled with natural resources available to the Anunnaki, and these resources are not contaminated. We think that we are the center of the universe, because we are arrogant and pretentious. In fact, very very very few alien civilizations are aware of our existence. And they have no interest whatsoever of paying a visit to us. However, and according to Stephen William Hawking, it is not a good idea to try to reach other civilizations in the universe. He warned us. Now, this does not mean that other alien races are not visiting our planet. Some have visited Earth several times, as part of their galactic excursions.

Part Two: Are the Anunnaki going to take over Earth?

They came and they left. Nevertheless, the intraterrestrial aliens are still here.
Why?
It is very simple: They lived here millions of years before we were created. This is why we call them the intraterrestrials. They are not humans, and they live in isolated areas and aquatic habitats. These races are peaceful to a certain degree, as long as, the human race will not jeopardize the safety of Earth.

So in conclusion, the Anunnaki are not going to take over the Earth. But please do remember, that we are expecting a global communication/contact/rapport with them in 2022.

*** *** ***

Part Two: Anunnaki creation of a new human race after 2022.

Human race: The Anunnaki creation of a new human race after 2022

Question by Raoul Mondragon, Vera Cruz, Mexico.

Question: I am very worried by what you have written on the subject of the return of the Anunnaki in 2022? Is it for real? Are they going to change the way we look? Are they going to get rid of us and replace us with a new human race? What kind?

Answer:
What kind of a new human race are we talking about?
A new genetic race?
A bio-genetic race?
A new race with new physical characteristics and different physiognomy?
"None of the above," said the Honorable Master Li. He added verbatim, word for word, and unedited: "The physical form of humans will not change.
Unless, the Anunnaki will take us back to the primordial Chimiti (Akkadian word for the genetic lab tubes, used by the Anunnaki to create an early form of human beings.)
And this is very unlikely, even impossible. The changes will occur on different levels, and almost instantly."

*** *** ***

Part Two: Russian Underwater Bases

Russian Underwater Bases

Questions by author Angelique Doudnikova, based upon her interviews with Maximillien de Lafayette, and excerpts taken from one of her forthcoming books: "Dialogues with the Last of the Anunnaki-Ulema Masters living among us."

Question: Is it true that a massive Russian underwater base exists one mile deep in the Marianas trench in the Pacific ocean? If so, what activities/research/experiments are going on there? Do the Chinese have one too?
Answer:
Yes, it is true. The Russians have a massive underwater base that was created in 1969, to study an extraterrestrial underwater navigation system called "Aquatic Plasma Corridors".
This corridor is undetectable by satellite, sonar or any other underwater detection system.
Not all branches of the Russian Navy were aware of the creation/existence of this base.
During one of their naval maneuvers just outside the perimeter of this Russian underwater base, six frogmen from one of the Russian submarines encountered three alien frogmen in metallic suits underneath a massive metallic object.
Both the Russian and alien frogmen were roughly at a depth of one hundred to one hundred and twenty feet. The alien frogmen were wearing what appeared underwater to be metallic suits of indeterminable and interchanging colors that morphed from a silvery white to bluish to grey.
One of the Russian frogmen stated that when he tried to approach these three, he was blocked by what seemed to be an invisible underwater forcefield, created by the alien frogmen as a protection sheild.
The Russian frogman's oxygen tanks started to fail and he quickly lost consciousness and started sinking but was saved by one of his fellow divers.

Part Two: Russian Underwater Bases

After being rescued, he described the alien frogmen as being 8ft to 11ft tall, as he saw them underwater. And none of them had any visible oxygen tanks/breathing apparatus attached to them.

In the secret debriefing that followed, the Russian diver who saved his fellow frogman, said that when he too tried to approach this massive foreign submerged object, he encountered what felt like a solid transparent wall surrounding the object.

He later described it as an oval glass box, surrounding this mysterious submerged object which also shielded it from contact with the ocean's water.

After the fall of the Berlin wall, and ensuing collapse of the Soviet Empire, rumors started circulating within the military and scientific community, that this bizarre event was in fact a joint Russian-extraterrestrial operation designed to explore the effects of the underwater plasma corridor on it's environment in the ocean, and on humans, as well as their psychological and psychosomatic reaction to encountering the corridor and seeing the alien frogmen and the ship itself.

Two decades later in Lake Baikal, other Russian navy frogmen encountered similar 9ft "silver swimmers" who also had no visible breathing apparatus.

While these encounters are largely unknown to the general public, military scientists with top clearance are well aware of them, and have worked on similar projects in different underwater bases, such as the one known to us as AUTEC, which is located off Andros Island in the Bahamas.

These massive underwater military bases, whether they be Russian, or American or Chinese, look from the surface to be rectangular/traditional compound structures.

However upon entering them underwater, they expand in all directions, and are extremely extensive. And all of them are joint human-alien operations.

Starting from the second underwater level, compartments are divided into large operation rooms, separated by elaborate long corridors, curving at 90 degrees every hundred feet or so, with doors that can drop down from the ceiling to seal off segments in the event of radiation leakage, or any matter related to internal security.

Part Two: Russian Underwater Bases

One of the interesting characteristics of these doors in the corridors is the circular porthole-like windows within what is a whitish metal of extraterrestrial origin.
None of these metallic alloys are possible here due to earth's gravity, and as such have to be done in orbit aboard the Space Shuttle. Interestingly enough, this technology has been shared by American, Russian and Israeli military scientists.
At one time British and French scientists complained of being left out of the loop, to which the Americans responded very candidly "We don't trust Europeans – especially the French!" To which the French retorted that they would withhold all information garnered from the Cassini-Huygens mission to Saturn...
An American three star general was quick to respond by saying "This is not the first time you Europeans have withheld information from us. Remember the Belgian incident?" (Aurora)
The mode of transportation down to the underwater base and within the base is also fascinating.
 From the surface, one enters a craft that looks like a silvery metallic spinning top, approximately 8ft in diameter, that can comfortably accommodate four passengers, and corkscrews its way downwards centrifugally around a rod using a form of magnetic propulsion for what seems to be a only a few seconds down to an unknown depth. (With a cheeky smile, M. de Lafayette added that he did not think the Chinese yet had this technology.)
From the second underwater level on down, the "Spinning Mobile Satellite" (SMS) travels horizontally and reaches its final destination at an undisclosed level of the base at which it again dives into water. It is at that level/destination that you will find the habitat and work center of the Grays.
Only the highest level personnel with top clearance can go there. Not even President Barack Obama or Vice-president Joe Biden, or any member of Congress/Senate are allowed access to that level at these facilities.
This clearance status was decided upon (jointly) by the NSA, the CIA, the United States Air Force, the DOD and NASA. Even the FBI has been excluded from this exclusive little club.

Part Two: Russian Underwater Bases

Maximillien de Lafayette personally told me that in his opinion, this is perfectly appropriate, since politicians come and go, whilst the military are sworn to secrecy, the average career of top military brass are thirty or more years, and they take their secrets with them to the grave.

M. de Lafayette then went on to give the example of Jesse "The Body" Ventura, former WWF wrestler, and one time governor of Minnesota, who kept all the secrets sealed from the public while in office, yet is now spilling the beans on his own conspiracy show on television!! Worth mentioning here also, is the fact that Lafayette loves Ventura, but were he General Jesse Ventura he would have kept his mouth shut.

Jesse "The Body" Ventura.

Part Two: Russian Underwater Bases

When I asked M. de Lafayette whether he thought the people had a right to know all these things, including the joint human-alien ventures, he replied by saying "Absolutely not! At the present time, so as not to shatter the fabric of our society and cause complete chaos and total anarchy, this information should be withheld and only gradually released to the public as set forth in the U.S.-extraterrestrial protocol, because humans have to be mentally prepared, in order to meet the extraterrestrial."

*** *** ***

Part Two: Anunnaki prevention of use of nuclear weapons.

Anunnaki Prevention of Use of Nuclear Weapons

Question by Angelique Doudnikova.

Question: Will the Anunnaki intervene to prevent possible aggressive use of atomic/thermonuclear weapons against other nation(s) prior to, and/or during their return in 2022?

Photo: Benazir Bhutto

Answer:
From yet undisclosed data, Maximillien de Lafayette said the most imminent threat will come not from Iran, but from Pakistan, an as yet highly unlikely surprise scenario.

Benazir Bhutto knew of this, spoke about it behind closed doors, and was assassinated soon after.

Part Two: Anunnaki prevention of use of nuclear weapons.

Maximillien de Lafayette added that he found it very childish and ridiculous when American ufologists wrote on subjects pertaining to extraterrestrials and nuclear issues since they are absolute outsiders.
Nowhere in their books have they ever written on the Anunnaki and their Ba'abs. Why are some of the Ba'abs so extremely important?
According to Maximillien de Lafayette, they lead to the parallel dimensions of the Anunnaki, and the beginning of time, where the God-Particle/Higgs Boson can be found, which is the reason for the building of CERN's Large Hadron Collider (LHC).

Through the Miraya – a cosmic screen/monitor with a vast depot of data that informs the Anunnaki of past, present and future events occurring in non-linear form, and in different galaxies by which the Anunnaki can monitor the activities of humans on Earth, the Grays, Reptilians, Nordics, Lyrans, Dracos, Plaeidians etc, and envoys from various other galactic civilizations wrongly identified and referred to as "The Galactic Federation/Council" .

*** *** ***

According to Maximillien de Lafayette, there is no way for a medium/channeler/psychic to the stars sitting in his/her apartment in Wala Wala, or Biloxi, Mississippi or in the swamps of Louisiana, listening to Willie Nelson's "On the Road Again" to access this Miraya and reveal the secrets of the Universe.
The Anunnaki will definitely intervene if a nuclear explosion were seen on the Miraya screen to happen near a Ba'ab connected to their galaxy, close to the membrane of the Universe that could cause chaos and disequilibrium in the eleventh dimension of the Universe.
Maximillien de Lafayette added that this is all very possible, since the speech given by Adolf Hitler at the 1936 Berlin Olympics, can still be heard in different worlds, as can the Sermon that was given by Yeshuah (Jesus) on the Mount of Olives. Both can be heard in the "Time-Space Depository". A bank of information, that Nikola Tesla accidentally tapped into.

Part Two: Anunnaki prevention of use of nuclear weapons.

Nikola Tesla.

American history has been unfair to Tesla and given his credits to the greedy and egotistical Edison. Everyone on the planet using A/C electricity today should give thanks and praise to Nikola Tesla and not Thomas Edison.
On another note, Maximillien de Lafayette said that only humans on earth refer to space-time. All other extraterrestrial sentient beings use the term time-space to define the limits of the known universe.

Part Two: What percentage of the world's population will survive the return of the Anunnaki

Who will survive the return of the Anunnaki?

Question by Angelique Doudnikova.

Question: What percentage of the world's population will survive the return of the Anunnaki, to become part of the new human race after 2022?

Note: Maximillien de Lafayette asked me if I thought this was such an important question. To which I replied, that finding out from the Ulema, that only one in ten of every person on the planet will return, means that ninety percent of earth's human population will be annihilated.

Answer:
Maximillien de Lafayette, then told me to calculate the dimensions of the Ziggurat of Enki in Ur (in Iraq), to find the number of earth's population that would survive which had been predicted millennia ago.
And all this while he looked out from the window of his Manhattan apartment at eight fifteen in the morning, after a late night - no an all night interview.

*** *** ***

Part Two: How many other Anunnaki will be part of the return?

How many other Anunnaki will be part of the return?

Questions by Angelique Doudnikova.

Question: Though the return will be led by Sinhars Marduchk and Inannaschamra, how many other Anunnaki will be part of the return?
And how many Anunnaki guides will there be, for humans who will be saved and returned to earth after the cleansing?
Answer:
That is a very normal way for a purely human mind to ask such a question. The truth is: the galactic mind of the extraterrestrials functions differently.
Consequently, the alien mode of operation becomes totally incomprehensible to our mind, and instead of focusing on how many military personnel they might send, we should focus on how many I.S.Ms they will operate at close proximity to Earth. This stands for "Intelligent Satellite Module".
Each module is approximately 8ft to 10ft in diameter, made of "fibro-metal", an alloy of elements not found on Earth, which is cone shaped on the top half and oval shaped on the bottom half. Worth mentioning here, the Gray aliens have craft similar to the "I.S.M." being smaller in diameter at 6ft to 8ft wide.
These were witnessed by farmers in the mid-west several times, and reported on cable T.V.
The purpose of the Gray's I.S.Ms, was to scan particular areas in the United States for several military strategic reasons, such as creating an atmospheric shield network which could alter the fabric of weather and be used to control climatic/atmospheric conditions over a chosen area/country.
This military ecological weapon system produces tsunamis, earthquakes, mysterious underground detonations, complete destruction of all types of agriculture, forests and natural resources (crops, trees, orchards, and every kind of plant).

Part Two: How many other Anunnaki will be part of the return?

Have we seen these kinds of catastrophic events recently in different parts of the world?
Whilst the Gray I.S.Ms require a complicated operational structure, encompassing large numbers of military personnel, one Anunnaki can handle up to one thousand of their I.S.M. machines.
They will be using the Shabka - a cosmic net, made up of anti-radar emissions and rays that not even N.O.R.A.D. can detect. The Gray/Earth joint program I.S.M.'s are detectable and clearly visible to the naked eye, whilst the Anunnaki I.S.Ms are totally invisible and completely undetectable, as they jump from one time-space pocket to another.

Worth mention here to all our readers: The difference between "time-space" travel and "space-time" travel is this: In the mode of time-space, the human mind cannot yet understand it, nor can the eyes see it, as we do not yet fully comprehend the concept of time. In space-mode time however, human eyes can glimpse the craft, for a split second before it vanishes/jumps to another pocket. Only in this instance, does the space-time appear linearly to humans.
One Anunnaki I.S.M. module is capable of covering up to 9,000 square miles.
These mini-spaceship machines will be interconnected through a massive net of rays that will seal off the Earth's atmosphere when the Anunnaki return. The number of Anunnaki who will be operating this return mission is as yet unknown. Very few Anunnaki personnel will be needed to operate this enterprise.
When this massive net of rays is interwoven, it forms a dark gray gluey substance that appears to us as a blend of burning metal, bark and rubber with the most awful foul odor imaginable!! The ghastly and noxious odor itself is enough to kill people. Light from the sun will be completely blocked out, as this gluey substance, known to the Anunnaki as "Zafta", forms a solid egg-shell-like casing around the entire planet from which there will be no escape.
This will truly be the end of the world, and life on Earth as we know it."

Part Two: How many other Anunnaki will be part of the return?

Sorry all you "2012" believers, but Maximillien de Lafayette says it ain't gonna happen!! He will be inviting all of you to a big banquet come January 1st 2013 in Acapulco, Mexico with free Margaritas and Bloody Mary's cocktails to go round till the sun goes down – no cover charge!!

*** *** ***

Part Two: Efficient energy systems of the Anunnaki

Efficient energy systems of the Anunnaki.

Question by Angelique Doudnikova.

Question: What kind of clean and efficient energy systems, and modes of transportation will the Anunnaki introduce after 2022?
Answer:
After the cleansing is done, no oil, coal, natural gas, or any other carbon based fuels will be used to power any car, machinery or mechanical equipment/apparatus.
Energy to power all of the above will be provided via satellites which harness cosmic energy.
By then even solar energy will be regarded as an archaic and rudimentary form of harnessing energy.
This will be made possible by the process of opening the Anunnaki cosmic Ba'abs, which are also the stargates to multiple dimensions.
Eleven of these Ba'abs exist, within the multi-dimensional cosmic landscape, adjacent to Earth.

*** *** ***

Part Two: Stargate over Chicago

Grand Central Station in downtown Chicago.

Stargate over Chicago

Questions from Matt Hoxtell, Chicago.

Questions: Is there a stargate/Ba'ab in Chicago?
Where exactly is it located, and what does it look like?
How would you jump into a ba'ab?
Is it part of the Anunnaki evacuation plan for humans upon their return in 2022?

Part Two: Stargate over Chicago

Answer:
There is a huge cosmic Ba'ab/stargate over Chicago. But this one is quite unique, because it is called a Madkhaal, which means in Ana'kh, an entrance, rather than a stargate.

Madison Square Garden.

Not all stargates are identical, nor do they function in the same manner. There are stargates that lead to another (singular) world, an incomprehensible world of bent time-space. And there are stargates that lead you into parallel dimensions adjacent to our world.
The one over Chicago leads you towards a dimension where time and space are no longer linear. In this dimension, the laws of physics as they are known to us on earth no longer apply.

Part Two: Stargate over Chicago

The Madkhaal is located above Grand Central Station in downtown Chicago.
It is oval and vibrates like a rubber band, very similar to a multiverse membrane, found in the perimeter of the eleven dimensions mentioned in contemporary quantum physics.
It is neither visible to the naked eye nor can it be detected by any apparatus on Earth. Also worth mentioning here, is the subject of the "Anomaly of Stargates."

Stargates do vary in size, function, purpose and mobility, just like the extraterrestrial underwater plasma corridors, used to navigate our seas and oceans, as stated by Maximillien de Lafayette on the History channel's show "UFO Hunters".

The stargate in New York City, which is located over Madison Square Garden, is twice the size of that over Central Station in downtown Chicago. Travel to and from the Chicago stargate is possible at particular times, however travel through the Madison Square Garden Ba'ab is a one way street.
Maximillien de Lafayette recommends this ba'ab for all televangelists and divorce lawyers!!
Since the Ba'abs are at least 900ft – 1,700ft above ground, it is not possible to jump into a Ba'ab. At the time of the return of the Anunnaki, an electromagnetic fog will suck up the people with light to medium contamination, as set forth by the Anunnaki's return protocol.

*** *** ***

Part Two: Signs before the return of the Anunnaki

Signs before the return of the Anunnaki

Question by Angelique Doudnikova.

Question: What are the signs that people will see in the skies the day before the Anunnaki return, and where will they be seen?

Answer:
One year before the return of the Anunnaki, around the end of the year 2021, the governments of many countries will start to circulate publications and manuals describing signs that will indicate the appearance of extraterrestrial craft visible to the public at large.
M. de Lafayette said he is convinced that many Bishops and Archbishops in the United States and England have already been briefed on the subject, and were secretly asked to cooperate on the redaction of material, that would suitably marry religious dogma with "intelligent design", as well as the frightening arrival of extraterrestrials to our planet.

Ironically, four major Anunnaki stargates will be activated and opened, which religious leaders will also interpret as the arrival of the "Four Horsemen" as stated in the Book of Revelation, and will be urging believers to run to their churches and pray. Readers and believers of the "Left Behind" series will have another shot at redemption...(Not!!)
Meanwhile, from the end of 2021 to November 30th, 2022 American citizens will have the most unusual evacuation display of UFOs/USOs of all shapes and sizes (oval, circular, crescent-shaped, triangular, cylindrical and every other shape witnessed, reported and ridiculed by the media, military disinformers and debunkers alike.) These are the vehicles of the Gray aliens jointly operated with the military.

Anunnaki's "tool of annihilation"

Question by Angelique Doudnikova.

Question: Who/what created the "tool of annihilation" that the Anunnaki will use when they return?

Answer:
The "Tool of Annihilation" was created by the Majlas – the Anunnaki High Council, as stated by Sinhar Anbar Anati, specifically for the purpose of cleansing the earth from all its contamination upon their return in 2022.

This tool of annihilation will be utilized in the event of hostile situations, where uninformed rednecks (Back in the saddle again) and other surburbanites will pull out their hunting rifles and shotguns to shoot at spaceships belonging to the most advanced race in the known universe.

According to Maximillien de Lafayette "Those are the ones who are going to get it first!"

*** *** ***

PART THREE
The World of the Anunnaki and Ulema: Q&A
Questions answered by Ulema Maximillien de Lafayette

Tammuz and Ishtar (Sumerian Inanna).

PART THREE

The World of the Anunnaki and Ulema: Q&A

Questions answered by Ulema Maximillien de Lafayette

On divination and Tarot reading…221
- Question: Do the Ulema believe in divination and Tarot card reading? At the beginning I was skeptical but after having consulted a Tarot reader, I became a believer. She predicted things nobody knew or heard about. Sometimes her predictions touched on a very personal note. So my question to you is this: Is the Tarot something your people accept? Is it a game or the real thing?…221
- Answer…221
- Question: If your answer is yes, then would you please explain the difference between regular Tarot cards and Ulema Tarot cards?…222
- Answer…222
- Question: OK, would I be able to learn about my future if I use the Ulema Tarot cards?…223
- Answer…223
- Question: Is there a particular book on the Anunnaki-Ulema Tarot? If so, who wrote it? Is it about the past, present or the future? What did the Ulema say about the future? Is it already written for us? Can we change our future?…223
- Answer…223

Table of contents

On inner bio-rhythm, bad luck, good luck and Anunnaki...229
- Question: Is it true what some mediums have said that some people are conditioned by a bio-rhythm that creates good luck and bad luck? If so, can we change this rhythm and become luckier, if we were not so lucky in the first place? Was this rhythm created by the Anunnaki when they manipulated our DNA?...229
- Answer...229

On ghosts, entities, holographic projections, and the 40 days period after death...235
- Question: I know you don't believe in ghost stories, but what about the idea that sometimes people see themselves like a ghost. I read about this in a Celtic story where a prince saw himself getting killed. Is it a hallucination or a prediction? By the way, the prince saw himself like a ghost, and in fact he got killed short after. So, if seeing ourselves as a ghost, is it an indication that something bad is going to happen to us? Could it be holographic projection, such as those images projected by aliens to impress or frighten abductees?...235
- Answer...235

Living continuously in 3 different time-space zones and Anunnaki...239
- Question: On the Science Channel, Dr Michio Kaku said the universe is expanding, and there are many universes he called multiverses where people live in different time and space zones...239
- Is this something the Ulema can do?...239

- Answer...239

On Anunnaki purification and a new identity...241
- Question: You wrote somewhere about Anunnaki purification, and the new identity a young Anunnaki receives after a purification ceremony on Nibiru. What do you mean by purification? Since you do not believe in the existence of SOUL, what are you talking about?
- Purify what? Dirty laundry?
- Assuming what you have said is true – I don't believe a bit of it– can you tell me in plain English how does this purification stuff happen and for what purpose?...241
- Answer...241
- I. Definition...241
- II. Annunaki purification and its relation to water in Judaism, Essene's sect, and Christianity...242
- III. Anunnaki's "Nif-Malka-Roo'h-Dosh"...243
- IV. Creation of the mental "Conduit"...244

Were dinosaurs created by extraterrestrials?...247
- Answer...247

The lost continent of MU's connection with the Anunnaki...249
- Question: This is the most important question for me. In any of the books I read, I haven't come across any information about the lost continent of MU's connection with the Anunnaki. I assume you know lots of things about it. According to James Churchward's books, MU was even older than Atlantis and home of human civilization. Humans migrated from MU to all over the world.

Table of contents

But we already know that Anunnaki were in Mesopotamia. So what about it? What can you tell me about the lost continent of MU? ...249
- Answer...249
- I. Introduction/Mythological backgound...249
- II. Scientific/geological facts...250
- III. Anunnaki-Ulema views...252
- IV. So, what did we learn from all this?...253

Where are the Anunnaki now and why don't they interfere in our planet?...257
- Question: Where is the Anunnaki race right now and why don't they interfere in our planet anymore? ...257
- Answer...257

Don't ever underestimate the power of your mind!...261
- Question: I can't understand how you could write so many books in a such a short time? Do you use some sort of magic or a supernatural power? You know what, some are spreading rumors that the overwhelming number of your books you wrote were made by a machine and because of this you are a machine.
- Answer...

Scanning brilliant minds to create a "Super-Baby"!...263
- Question: I am not sure who has said aliens can scan our brains and create a new species of babies for their hybrid program. Is it true? ...263
- Can they do that? And how it is done?...263
- Answer...263

On the Ulema-Anunnaki group administration...265
- Question: Is the Ulema-Anunnaki group administered by men or a matriarch woman as I have heard?...265
- Answer...265

The relationship between our mind, body and cellular memory...269
- Question: What is the relationship between our mind, body and cellular memory?...269
- Answer...269

Anunnaki-Phoenician Chavad nitrin and the immortality of the gods...273
- Question: I am originally from Byblos(Jbeil) in Lebanon, and we Lebanese are descendants of the Crusaders who have learned some of the secrets of the Anunnaki in Lebanon and Jerusalem. I have heard that my ancestors the Phoenicians have used a product similar to athletes' steroids. This product I was told was also used by the Egyptian Pharaohs. Could you please tell me more about it?...273
- Answer...274

Hidden entrances to other worlds and dimensions, right here on Earth...277
- Question: Do UFOs and extraterrestrials use galactic entrances and space-time corridors to enter and exit our world? How many are there? Are they visible to the naked eye?...277
- Answer...277
- a-Entrance to the next-life...277
- b-Entrance to the fourth dimension...278

Table of contents

- c-Entrance to the parallel dimension...279

Paranormal mirror and extraterrestrials: Mirrors that remember their previous owners...281
- Question: I read a small article on a mysterious antique mirror that caused the death of it's owner, because, as it was explained in the articles, the mirror had a vengeful memory against one owner. There are people who believe that the mirrors had an extraterrestrial origin and were contaminated by aliens. Logically, they said the contamination killed people. What is your personal opinion?...281
- Answer...281
- I. Introduction...281
- II. The story...282
- III. Italian philosopher Tommaso Campanella's explanation...282
- IV. Paris Academy of Science...283
- V. Parapsychology...283
- VI. Psychology and metalogic...284
- VII. Extraterrestrial influence...285
- Question: What type of civilization are the Anunnaki at this moment in time?
- A Type One, Two, Three, or other type of civilization?
- Type One, according to Professor Michio Kaku, a theoretical physicist from New York University, is a civilization that gets their energy from all planets. Type Two Civilization is getting energy from their, Mother Sun only! Type Three Civilization gets their energy from all the suns in our universe and the next...287
- Answer...287

Anunnaki's immaturity, emotional control, sin, jealousy?...289
- Question: Have the Anunnaki matured away from their immaturity in emotional control, past stories of jealousy, power, etc., sin?...289
- Answer...289
- 1-The Akkadian clay tablets texts...289
- 2-The Bible...291
- 3- Phoenicia/Anatolia texts and archeological finds...292

Anunnaki management skills...293
- Question: Have they learned to manage their emotions and improve their management skills?...293
- Answer...293

The Anunnaki's God: A critical God?...295
- Question: Is the Anunnaki a Critical God? No forgiveness, no exceptions, as in an eye for an eye and a tooth for a tooth?...295
- Answer...295

Benevolent and malevolent Anunnaki gods...297
- Question: Is there a benevolent and a malevolent faction of Anunnaki Gods?...297
- Answer...297

Clairvoyance; Telepathy between members of the same family...299
- Question: Is there clairvoyance (Telepathy) between members of the same family...299
- Answer...299

Table of contents

- **On the Anunnaki's creation of early humans and Earth original species...301**
- Question: Were the quasi-humans the Anunnaki encountered (when they first came to earth), a natural product of evolution, or genetically manipulated by the Igigi /prior E.T. ?...301
- Answer...301
- Question: Have we ever found skeletons and bones of them and what do we call them? (Australopithecus, Afarensis, Homo habilis, Erectus, Cro-magnon?)...302
- Answer...302

All human beings do not come from the same origin...303

- Question: Have the Anunnaki created/genetically upgraded species on other planets? If so, what has been the outcome?...303
- Answer...303
- Question: Page 138 of book one of the three books of Ramadosh mentions that though we are all human beings, we do not come from the same origin. Some were born here on Earth, others were born somewhere else, in some other dimensions and far different spheres. Can you please explain in further detail what do you mean by that, and by us being created according to different specifications?...304
- Answer...304304
- I. Introduction...
- II. First category of humans...305
- Man (Humans) created on Earth from clay...305
- III. Second category of humans...306

- Akama-ra...306
- IV. An'th-Khalka...307
- V. The Earth-made human creatures created from a cell...308
- VI. The space-made human creatures...308
- VII. The Basharma early creatures...308
- VIII. Metabolism created an early human-like form...309
- IX. Bashar category...309
- XI. The Shula with programmed brains...311
- At the time we were created, three things happened to us...313
- a-The Brain Motor...313
- b- The vibrational dimension...314
- c-The Conduit=Health/Youth/ Longevity...314
- XII. The Shula species...316
- XIII. The Emim...316
- XIV. Ezakarerdi, "E-zakar-erdi "Azakar.Ki"...317
- XV. Ezeridim...318
- XVI. Fari-narif "Fari-Hanif"...318
- XVII. The Anunnaki-Ulema from Ashtari...319

Anunnaki-Ulema esoteric and mind-power techniques...321
- Question: What techniques and practices can help us become more spiritual and more open to the 'paranormal' such as seeing auras, ghosts or spirits, seeing into the future etc?...321
- What effect can this awakening have on our lives?...321
- Answer...321
- 1-Gomari "Gumaridu" technique...321

Table of contents

- 2-Gomatirach-Minzari technique...322
- From Ulema Mordechai's Kira'at (Reading)...322
- 3-Gubada-Ari technique...322
- Synopsis of the Theory...323
- 4-Cadari-Rou'yaa technique...324
- 5-Chabariduri technique...324
- 6-Daemat-Afnah technique...324
- 7-Da-Irat technique...325
- 8-Dudurisar technique...326
- 9-Arawadi technique...326
- 10-Baaniradu technique...326
- 11-Baridu technique...327
- 12-Bisho-barkadari "Bukadari" technique...327

On the old way of thinking...329
- Question: A lot of spiritual teachers tell us that the mind with all its conditioning, becomes a barrier to growth and enlightenment.
- When will mankind be able to move on from the old way of thinking to a new paradigm?...329
- Einstein says that "problems cannot be solved by the same level of thinking that created them." What might this new way of thinking look like? Thinking and judging obessively itself may be a large part of the problem...329
- Answer...329

Esoteric/secret calendar of your lucky days and hours...331
- Question: One person who has read your books told me about a technique the Ulema sorcerers used to read the future.

As I understood, it is a calendar of the good days, and the bad days in the life of each one of us. I would be grateful if you could explain to me what it is about and see the calendar. I promise I will use it for a good cause. ..331
- Answer...331
- I. Synopsis of the concept...332
- II. The Ulema-Anunnaki days are...332
- III. The calendar's grids...333
- IV. The use of a language...333
- Grid 1: Calendar of the week...334
- Grid 2: Calendar of your name...335
- Calendar of your lucky hour...335
- Grid 3: Calendar of your lucky hour...336

On different dimensions and multidimensional beings...339
- Question: What dimensions lie beyond the 4th, that we can experience?...339
- Question: Do other beings exist in these dimensions?...341
- Answer...341
- Question: Can we ever contact them, and would there be negative repercussions from doing so?...341
- Answer...341

Miscellaneous...342
Are Earth Governments controlled by aliens?
- Question: Is it true that lots of Earth governments including the U.S. are controlled or ruled by an Alien race called the Reptilians?...342
- Answer...342

Table of contents

Insignia or logo of the Anunnaki...342
- Question: What is the royal insignia or logo of the Anunnaki? The winged disk? Do they use banners or flags like us?...342
- Answer ...342

The Face on Mars...342
- Question: In the Lost Book of Enki (written by Zecharia Sitchin) he wrote that the mysterious face on Mars (which is still unaccepted by NASA) was the Anunnaki Alalu's graveyard. Do you know if it is true?...342
- Answer...342

- **Question: Are Enlil, Enki, Anu etc. still alive?...342**
- Answer...342

On eating meat...343
- Question: Must we stop eating meat for our preparation for 2022 or will we prepare ourselves mentally only? Because I love eating meat!...343
- Answer...343

*** *** ***

Part Three: On Tarot reading

On Divination and Tarot Card Reading

Questions by Salma Tabbah, Amman, Jordan.

Question:
Do the Ulema believe in divination and Tarot card reading?
At the beginning I was skeptical, but after having consulted a Tarot reader, I became a believer. She predicted things nobody knew or heard about. Sometimes her predictions touched on a very personal note. So my question to you is this: Is the Tarot something your people accept? Is it a game or the real thing?- Salma Tabbah.

Note: We encourage the readers to refer to the book "Ulema Anunnaki Tarot. Extraterrestrial Lessons and Techniques to See your Future: The world's most powerful book on the occult and foreseeing your future on Earth and in other dimensions. Published in February 2010.

Answer:
Yes, the Anunnaki-Ulema have used a very unique "Divination" method to explore ultra-dimension. The word divination is not totally correct, but we are going to use it for now, because it is "As close as it gets to the real thing," said Ulema Bukhtiar.
We can also use the word "Oracle", as these words refer to the same thing in essence.
The other term "Ultra-dimension" means a "Surrounding that is not normally and usually detected by scientific or physical means," said Ulema Seif El Din. This ultra-dimension belongs to the realm of many things, including thoughts, perception, extra-sensory feelings (Not caused by anomaly of any sort), and a depot of knowledge that evolves around past, present and future events. One of the aspects of the Ulema's Kira'at deals with Tarot card reading called Bak'ht-Kira'at. The Master taps into a zone that contains lots of information about events to occur in the future.

Part Three: On Tarot reading

The figures and numbers he/she opens up while reading the cards are closely related to that zone called "Da-irat Al-Maaref" (Circumference of Knowledge).

The figures and numbers that appear on the cards guide the Master reader towards a chart that contains and explains all the possible meanings, NOT interpretation.

"But this is not enough, we should not rely only on symbols and numbers, because this could happen in a very ordinary manner, far from the truthful reach of knowledge and discovery…it could fall into the possibility of coincidences. This is why, a reading should be repeated multiple times to detect coincidence and separate superstitions from reality…" explained the Honorable Ulema Ghandar.

Question:
If your answer is yes, then would you please explain the difference between regular Tarot cards and Ulema tarot cards?
Answer:
I will give you a brief explanation.

The Ulema cards are personalized, meaning they are hand-made by you. You do not purchase your Ulema cards from a store. They are not a commercial product. The Master provides you with a set of 50 cards called "Warka". Each card has either a figure or a symbol (Number). The cards are printed on a master-sheet or on several sheets. You cut each card individually, until you have 50 cards.

This constitutes your personal cards deck. Nobody else should touch or use this deck. The Master will instruct you to attach one of your photos to one specific card. You can place your photo on this card and xerox it, and later add it to the deck. This card is extremely important, because the whole deck will rotate around it.

Something else: One of the 50 cards must bear your name. Also, you should give yourself a new surname. Nobody should know about your new name; it should remain secret. What we have so far is this:

a-A set of 50 cards, cut and laminated by you.
b-One of the cards has your photo.

Part Three: On Tarot reading

c-One of the cards has your real name (First name).
d-One of the cards has your new name. (The one you gave yourself)
Now you start to understand why the Ulema cards are called "Personalized".

Question :
OK, would I be able to learn about my future if I use the Ulema Tarot cards?
Answer :
Enough, but not everything. First, you have to remember that if your "Conduit" is not activated, your access to knowledge about your future will be limited.
However, you will be able to learn a lot about some events that are extremely important in your life, and especially about "New happenings or things to happen" that can influence or alter your luck, success, and other vital matters.
The cards will give you some guidance and orientation.
The cards will give you dates and a warning related to each separate event to occur in the future; event(s) detected by your cards.
Something else you should know: If you attach the photo of another person to one of the cards, you could possibly discover lots of things about that person.
However, you will not able to influence his/her mind, or bring a major change to his/her life, unless some criteria are met.

Question:
Is there a particular book on the Anunnaki-Ulema Tarot? If yes, who wrote it? Is it about the past, present or the future?
What did the Ulema say about the future?
Is it already written for us?
Can we change our future?
Answer:
Note: The following answer is taken from our Tarot Book.
Ulema Mordachai ben Zvi said, "Bakht (Ulema Tarot) has been practiced by the Ulema Anunnaki for thousands of years.
It is totally unknown in the Western hemisphere.

Part Three: On Tarot reading

Essentially, Bakht is based upon knowledge received from the early remnants of the Anna.Ki, also called Anu.Na.Ki, an extra-terrestrial race which landed on Earth hundreds of thousands of years ago.
Very few seers and mystics outside the circle of the Ulema Anunnaki penetrated the secrets of the Bakht. They were the elite of the priests of Ra, the early Sinhar Khaldi (Early Chaldean priests/astrologers/astronomers), the Tahar (Early Phoenician Purification priests), and the Rouhaniyiin, known in the West as the alchemists/Kabalists.
In the whole world today, there are no more 700 persons who practice the Bakht, and they are called Ba-khaat or Bakhaati. Two hundred of them are the supreme enlightened masters, called the Mounawariin.
The other five hundred masters are simply called Ulema Anunnaki. The teachers of the Ba-khaat or Bakhaati are called Tahiriim and the Ulema refer to them as the Baal-Shamroutiim.
The earliest manuscript on Bakht appeared in Phoenicia, circa 7,500 B.C., and it was written in Ana'kh. A later version in Anakh-Pro-Ugaritic appeared three thousand years later.
A third version written in the early Phoenician-Byblos script appeared in Byblos and Tyre. There are also two versions in Akkadian and the Old Babylonian language, that are assumed to be lost. Around 65 A.D., a new version in Arabic appeared in the Arabian Peninsula, and Persia, and it was called "Firasa".
Around 685 A.D., a revised edition appeared in Damascus, Syria. It was said that, from this Syrian edition, the hand-written manuscript "Ilmu Al Donia" (Science or Knowledge of the Universe) was derived.
This manuscript included chapters on Arwah (Spirits and non-human entities), Djins, and Afrit.
Around 1365 A.D., a book titled "Shams Al Maaref Al Koubra" appeared in Cairo and Damascus, based upon two books "Al Bakht: Dirasat Al Moustakbal", and "Ilmu Al Donia"."
Maximillien de Lafayette said, "The future is neither concealed, nor hidden, because the future has already happened in a zone or Zamania that exists very close to the zone or sphere of existence, that you already live in.

Part Three: On Tarot reading

In other words, the past, present and future are timelines that exist and run concurrently, called Istimraar."
Does this mean that every event is constantly being repeated indefinitely in different worlds, dimensions and times?
Yes, it is, according to mainstream science and quantum physics – based upon the theory of the "Ever expanding universe." –
And according to the Ulema Anunnaki, people (Humans and other life-forms) live simultaneously on different Woujoud and Zaman.
Most certainly, they might look different, physically and bio-organically, because of the atmospheric and climate conditions, and they could or would act differently –convergent or divergent– according to the level of their awareness and intelligence in different worlds.
Consequently, you can live a past on this Earth and remember very well past events in your life, and in the same time, you remain unaware of your other existences, other pasts and lives in different worlds.
Henceforth, you must learn what has happened or what is currently happening to you, or to your other copies, either on different planets and habitats, or in higher dimensions.
Now, you begin to know that each one of us has infinite copies of ourselves, as well as, many separate and independent past(s).

Knowing the future and revisiting your past in different dimensions and previous lives is a pre-requisite for reading your Bakht Haya.Ti (Linear Future), and Moustakbal Daa-em (Multidimensional Future).
There are some events in your past that greatly influence the course of your life, and part of your future.
The situation gets a little bit tricky, when you are not fully aware of major events, and decisions you have made in your Moustakbal Daa-em, because few of us are capable of visiting our past(s) in different dimensions.

The future in its two forms, linear and multidimensional is what really constitutes your true future.

Part Three: On Tarot reading

However, it is not absolutely necessary to learn about all the phases of your past, and what your Double or your other copies in different time-space zones have done in the past, and/or are currently doing in a zone beyond Earth.

If you believe that life continues after death, then it becomes necessary to learn about your Double, and other bio-organic and etheric copies of yourself that currently exist in other worlds.

On Earth, in this world, we have one single future. The learned Ulema referred to it as Al Maktoob, meaning what was written. This concept has created an intellectual, philosophical and religious controversy, even an outrage, for all those who have rejected the idea that a Supreme Creator has already imposed upon us, a future, the moment we were born; a future that controls our destiny and our life, for ever!

In other words, what it is already written in the front-page of our life, dictates the magnitude, level and development of our future successes, failures, kind of job or profession reserved for us, our health conditions, finances, families, how good or how bad our children will be in the future, sort and amount of joy and pain we will feel in the forthcoming years of our lives, so on...

Others have felt that the Al Maktoob makes us slaves of the Creator, because our destiny has been decided upon, without our knowledge, consent and will.

If this is the case, then our life has no purpose at all, and no matter how hard we try to reach a higher level of spirituality and awareness, we will always fail because, it was written in the book of our future, that we have no choice, no freedom to choose and above all, it was already written, that our efforts in this context were not to bear fruit. Thus, it becomes impossible for any of us to change our future, and/or re-write what it is already written and decided upon, in the book of life and destiny.

Consequently, learning about our Bakht (Future) would not serve any purpose, except to make us feel trapped in this life. This is what many people, and some of the early Gnostics have felt about this unpleasant and horrible scenario. But the Ulema Anunnaki have a different scenario for all of us; a pleasant and a happy one. Humans have retained their freedom of choice, thus, they are accountable for all their actions, deeds, intentions and thoughts.

Part Three: On Tarot reading

They have the right and the freedom to choose, select and carry on their own plans. And in the process of doing so, they remain the masters of their own destiny, and solely responsible for their decisions, and the consequences of these decisions.

Their mental faculties and degree of their creativity are shaped by, and decided upon by many factors, such as the Conduit, the Jabas, and the Fikr.

But their destiny and future remain unconditioned by the DNA, the Conduit and other genetic "ingredients" fashioned by the Anunnaki.

The ethical-moral-spiritual endeavors and aspects of their physical and non-physical structures remain under their personal control.

This part of their future can be learned about and read by using the Bakht.

In addition, humans' present and future decisions and actions, and the consequences of their deeds and intentions could be altered or changed, according to their free will and personal choices.

All these decisions, deeds, intentions, consequences, and effects are part of one single future, which can be changed at will.

But the remaining part of their future which is conditioned by the genetic formula of the Anunnaki cannot be changed, unless the Conduit is fully activated

Reading the Bakht, guides you in this direction, and explains to you what part of your future can be changed, and what part of your future will remain intact.

This, applies exclusively to your future on Earth; your Erdi future.

So, are we trapped in this life?
Are we at the mercy of the Anunnaki?
Is our life, destiny and future already decided upon, by the Anunnaki who created us by using multiple genetic techniques and experiments?
Do we have the power, the choice and the freedom to change our future?
If so, is it the whole future or part of it?

Part Three: On Tarot reading

You will find the answers to these questions while you are reading your Bakht. And step by step, you will learn what is going to happen to you in this life, in the present, in the near future, and in the distant future, simply because your present and future exist simultaneously as you read your Bakht.

In addition, when you consult the Ulema Anunnaki Tarot on different subjects and matters of concern, the cards will tell you what you should do and consider, and what you should avoid. It will become crystal clear, and future events will be displayed right before your eyes.

You have to remember that the Ulema Anunnaki Tarot is a reading of many of your futures; one on Earth, and the others in different zones of times and spaces.

As you progress in this field of Ulema Tarot, and as you begin to learn more about other dimensions, and copies of yourself in other worlds, your mind will start to understand gradually how things work in different dimensions, and particularly how you and part of your multidimensional futures are projected.

*** *** ***

Part Three: On inner bio-rhythm, bad luck, good luck and Anunnaki

On inner bio-rhythm, bad luck, good luck & Anunnaki

Questions asked by Salem Turbi, Tunisia.

Question: Is it true what some mediums have said that some people are conditioned by a bio-rhythm that creates good luck and bad luck?
If so, can we change this rhythm and become luckier, if we were not so lucky in the first place? Was this rhythm created by the Anunnaki when they manipulated our DNA?
Answer:
"Zara-Du", also called "Macari," and "Sabata," is a term for what it is known in Anunnaki-Ulema literature as the "17 Lucky Years of Your Life." Zaradu is very important metaphysical but also "Physical knowledge" that the Anunnaki-Ulema have learned, and kept shrouded in secrecy for thousands of years, fearing that bad/immoral persons might learn and use to it to influence others, and selfishly alter the course of history.
It was revealed to the honorable Ulema that every single human being on planet Earth will have during his/her life, a lucky period extending through 17 consecutive, uninterrupted years.
During those years (Called Mah-Zu-Zah) the doors of luck, fortune and development at many levels will open up, and opportunities for extraordinary success shall be freely given to her/him. This is how the phrase "the 17 Lucky Years of Your Life" came to exist. And for this period of 17 years, there is a calendar, which is well structured, and divided into a sequence of 77 by 7.
This brings us to the Anunnaki-Ulema magical esoteric number of 777, considered to be the Alpha and Omega of all knowledge and "Tana-Wur", which means enlightenment, similar to the Bodhisattva. At one point during these lucky years, a person will acquire two extraordinary faculties:
  1- Rou'h Ya
  2- Firasa (Fi raa-Saa).

Part Three: On inner bio-rhythm, bad luck, good luck and Anunnaki

Ulema-Anunnaki, Alain "Allan" Cardec.

Part Three: On inner bio-rhythm, bad luck, good luck and Anunnaki

These two faculties will positively influence his/her life and guide him/her effortlessly towards reaching the highest level of mental and physical strength, as well success in business and a variety of endeavors.

Examples of these endeavors for instance, are an astonishing power or capability of producing, writing or composing in an exceptionally prolific manner. It also encompasses the ability to learn many languages in next to no time, and read manuscripts written in secret languages, such as the first secret and hidden alphabet (Characters) of the Hindu language. Applied in modern times, reading the secret symbols and alphabets become forecasting events and predicting the rise and fall of world's markets. It was also said, that this 17 year period can alter a DNA sequence, thus preventing accelerated aging, and the deterioration of human cells.

One of the last Anunnaki-Ulema Mounawariin (Enlightened Ones) known to have discovered the secret of the 17 lucky years was Alan Cardec "Allan Cardec" (October 3, 1804- March 31, 1869). Cardec's real name was Hippolyte Léon Denizard Rivail. And his Ulema name was Asha-Kar-Da-Ki. His mentor was the legendary Johann Heinrich Pestalozzi, also known as "Mirdach Kadoshi Sirah" in the Anunnaki-Ulema circle. His incarnated guiding master (Second high level of Anunnaki-Ulema) was Al Zafiru, called Sefiro or Zefiro in mediumship and spiritism literature. In fact, the word or term "Spiritism" was coined by Cardec.

He was the first to use it and explain its application during a contact with a higher entity and other rapports with dead people (Trapped deceased persons) who asked for his help. Sometimes, it was the other way around; Cardec asked for their guidance on matters related to life after death, and the realm of the next life.

Cardec was the father of the French movement of Spiritism, and communications with entities trapped between the next dimension and Earth's boundaries. They are called "Les retenus", meaning those who were trapped in the afterlife dimension, or more precisely, those who were detained. Cardec was buried at the historical French cemetry "Cimetière du Père Lachaise".

Part Three: On inner bio-rhythm, bad luck, good luck and Anunnaki

The inscription on his tomb stele reads: "Naitre, mourir, renaitre encore et progresser sans cesse, telle est la loi." Translated verbatim: "To be born, to die, to be reborn again, and to progress unceasingly, such is the law."

The inner bio-rhthym and the Anunnaki:
Thousands of years ago, before history was recorded, the Anunnaki created Man to meet their needs. They created us as a work-force to take care of the fields, cultivate the land, and bring them food; this is according to the Akkadian/Sumerian clay tablets. It is very clear.
At that time, when the Anunnaki gods and goddesses (Aruru, Mummu, Ea, Ninna, etc.) created the first prototypes of the quasi-human races, Man did not have all the mental faculties we have today. Later on, 13 new faculties were added to his brain. And everything in the brain was wired and functioned according to a cellular rhythm.
We cannot change this rhythm.
But we can improve on it, and ameliorate its functioning, by acquiring new knowledge, developing a stronger memory, reading, writing, listening to intelligent and well-informed people, getting rid of bad habits, and elevating our being to a higher mental/spiritual level, through introspection, meditation, and refraining from hurting others.
Some are born normal, others are born with some mental deficiency, while a few were created as geniuses, like Bach, Mozart, Da Vinci etc., people who astonished us with extraordinary creativity, and unmatched talents.
These talents and mental gifts were already "placed" into their Conduit. Otherwise, how can we explain the astonishing musical compositions of Mozart and other great composers at the age of 4? Yes, we can alter the inner bio-rythm, the Anunnaki installed in us, but we cannot change it completely. The first thing to do is to activate the Conduit. As far as luck (Good and bad) is concerned, the noble in spirit (Mind, or "Soul" if you want) will be given the opportunities and means to learn how to positively reshape future events in his/her life.

Part Three: On inner bio-rhythm, bad luck, good luck and Anunnaki

Unfortunately, there are so many good people in the world who are constantly suffering. And we wonder where is the logic? What is the reason for their suffering? Is it true that good people always finish last? Sadly enough, it happens all the time.
We see hard-working nurses (who save lives) struggling to make a living. We see devoted school teachers unable to pay their bills. We see bloody bastards getting richer and richer, whilst honorable, loving and caring people are being kicked out of their homes!! Where is the justice?
The truth I tell you, is that there is no justice on Earth, despite all the good intentions of so many of us, and despite so many good courts' decisions, and decent laws to maintain law and order. The Ulema taught us that good behavior, a high level of morality, unconditional love, forgiveness and generosity do not guarantee success in life, or secure good luck. Ulema Badri said verbatim: "Your character and good manners are the only things you should keep when you have lost everything in life. To some, this is not enough, for financial security, and some good luck would not hurt.
I agree. So, start developing your brain, activate your Conduit, talk to your inner-self...there you will find the salvation...there you will find a way to change your bad luck into good luck. If your Mind is in harmony with your "Jaba", then, and only then, can you change your inner bio-rhythm, and influence your DNA's metamorphosis."

*** *** ***

Part Three: Ghosts, entities, holographic projections, 40 days period after death

On ghosts, entities, holographic projections, 40 days period after death

Question asked by Ernest B., Sierra Leone.

Question: I know you don't believe in ghost stories, but what about the idea that sometimes people see themselves like a ghost. I read about this in a Celtic story where a prince saw himself getting killed. Is it a hallucination or a prediction? By the way, the prince saw himself like a ghost, and in fact he got killed shortly thereafter. So, seeing ourselves as a ghost, is it an indication that something bad is going to happen to us?
Could it be a holographic projection, like those images projected by aliens to impress or frighten abductees?
Answer:
Zama-ari
Zama-ari refers to an experience where and when a person sees himself or herself as an image or as ghost projected right before his or her eyes. This occurrence is also called "Latabi" in Ana'kh.
In Ulemite, it is referred to as "Canouri" (Ka.Nu.ri). Usually, it is interpreted as an "Announcement of your death."
Those three words, "Zama-ari", "Latabi", and "Canouri" are a term for the experience of encountering or seeing yourself, as a duplicate image of your body. Ulema Al Baydani commented on this.
He said verbatim:
- This is not a good sign.
- Usually the projection of the image of one's body predicts either a fatal event to occur in the very near future, or his/her death within hours or a few days.
- Pets can easily see this image.
- It is not physical, however it appears very clear to the naked eye.
- The image takes the form of a ghost looking at you.

Part Three: Ghosts, entities, holographic projections, 40 days period after death

- The ghost moves like a real person.
- Usually you see confusion and sadness on the face of the ghost.
- This is not hallucination or a trick of your mind.
- It is a holographic projection of an event to occur.
- In other words, your mind (The Supersymetric Mind) can sense and pre-visualize events before they happen. It is like reading a calendar backward; from the end, instead from the very first day of the month.
- It is a rare occurrence, but it happens now and then.

You asked, "Could it be a holographic projection, like those images projected by aliens to impress or frighten abductees?" And the answer is: It is a holographic-mental image or "imprint" produced by your "Supersymetric Mind". But, it is not similar to aliens' holographic projection, because in the aliens' scenario, it is intentional, while in your own experience, it is a "Visual reading" of a future event to happen very soon in your life, at a personal level.

I have never said that I do not believe in ghosts. What I have said is that I do not agree with the definition of a ghost as often given by charlatan mediums and fake channelers. Generally, those people refer to ghosts as the non-physical presence of a deceased person who manifests himself/herself to express a concern, to warn us, to complain about the way he/she was murdered, to solve a mystery, to convey a message to the loved ones left behind, etc. All these interpretations are false.

Many mediums, channelers and psychics are fake. They use the emotional weakness of their "clients" to dupe them and make a buck. This is evident, when they start to ask for more money to reveal further information and messages from the deceased one who appears like a ghost. I do believe that ghosts exist, but they do not manifest themselves, the way it was described by psychics. There are different categories of ghosts.

Some apparitions are real, but they are scarce.

Part Three: Ghosts, entities, holographic projections, 40 days period after death

In 99% of all cases, the apparition is some sort of hallucination. In Ulemite terminology, a ghost is a non-physical imprint of a presence, left on the screen of a metaphysical dimension, very close to real life. I will explain.

Everything in the universe, including people, rocks, plants and living organisms have two dimensions; the one we can see, called physical reality, because we can measure and/or define its dimension, density, limits, colors, shapes, etc., and the other dimension which is called non-physical, because it escapes measurements and normal means to assess and ascertain its physical existence, and properties.

In other words, you body has two dimensions; the physical one which is defined for instance by your height, weight, shape of your face, color of your hair, etc., and the non-physical one, which is a duplicate copy of yourself (the Double), which existed before you were born.

All of us have this duplicate copy. And without knowing it, we (Our mind or whatever you want to call it) constantly project our non-physical image (The duplicate copy of ourselves) wherever we go. This projection is called the non-physical "imprint" of our presence, or ourselves.

When we die, and our body disintegrates, the "imprint" remains intact, and does not disintegrate. So what people see as a ghost, is in fact one of the many "imprints" we have left behind us, after we have died. Yes, there are many imprints corresponding to many moments and times in our lives.

Usually, the imprint we see (As a ghost) is the last imprint we have made while we were alive. But it is very important to remember, that apparitions of ghosts (Projection, imprints, etc.) occur for a very short time, during the 40 days period following the departure of the deceased.

This is applicable, when the deceased has left in peace, and his/her mind has accepted the idea that he/she is dead. Many deceased persons get so confused after their death for many reasons; some still believe that they are alive, and try to reach us in an incomprehensible manner.

Part Three: Ghosts, entities, holographic projections, 40 days period after death

If the deceased person is no longer attached to this world, to materialistic values, to properties he/she once owned, and his/her mind is "clear", then the deceased person will never again project himself/herself as an imprint. He/she is dead, and moves on to a different dimension; the realm of the afterlife.

So the 40 days period after death is very critical. But this period could last for more than 40 days, sometimes for years, when the mind of the deceased is not "clear". This explains the apparition of people who have died centuries ago.

Interestingly enough, when a so-called ghost appears, it is always the same apparition; the ghost is dressed exactly in the same way, does not change outfits, he/she appears in defined areas, always in the same areas, such as a corridor, a balcony, and/or going through walls and doors.

The apparition never changes, because it cannot change, being an imprint. So what we are seeing is not a real person coming back as a ghost, but as one of his/her many imprints he/she has left behind.

Once a deceased has crossed the bridge of the 40 days period, no more apparitions or imprints will occur again. The deceased has left Earth for good, and by now he/she is far far away from us. Thus, it becomes impossible to reach him/her, and all so-called "calling upon the dead", and communications with the dead are false. You are already dead in one dimension, and not born yet in another. You exist somewhere else, and somewhere else you are about to exist.

Yet, you are a living person right here and right now.

How do we explain this? But this is not the most important question. The most important one would be: Could you contact yourself in the other dimension, or would you? And what could you possibly gain from contacting the "Other You" who lives far far away from you? Or would you rather contact the "Other You" in a dimension where you are not born yet, and teach yourself in that dimension what you have already known and learned in another dimension? Yes, this is possible.

If you are not fully convinced, why don't you ask a quantum physics professor, it might reliefve you from your doubt!

Part Three: Living continuously in 3 different time-space zones and Anunnaki

Living continuously in 3 different time-space zones and Anunnaki

Question by Rick D., Michigan.

Question: On the Science Channel, Dr Michio Kaku said the universe is expanding, and there are many universes he called multiverses where the same people live in different time and space zones. Is this something the Ulema can do?

Answer:
Ulema Master Kanazawa lived simultaneously in three different time and space zones. He lived as a real person in three different places at the same time. But the most important part of this phenomenon, is the fact that while he was living around 1896 in Ryu Kyu (Island of Okinawa), he had a family of his own, and he enjoyed a normal life. Around 1939, Master Kanazawa lived in Kyoto, and for a short time he was a special advisor to Emperor Hirohito and the Japanese Imperial Navy.
In this capacity, he advised Japan not to consider any act of aggression against the United States. During the first year of the American-Japanese war, he vanished from the face of the Earth. He reappeared in 1958 in Hawaii, and rendered the most useful services to important scientific communities. The most amazing aspect of these 3 separate lives, is the fact that he has never aged. He remains the same person.
Nothing has changed at the physical level, apparently. But the truth is, Master Kanazawa did change enormously from within, at his sub-structural molecular composition.
On the outside, he looked like a regular human being, like you and me. On the inside, his molecules have changed considerably. This very change in his inner-substance allowed him to traverse time and exist continuously in three different places and three different time-zones. Master Mikami did the very same thing.

Part Three: Anunnaki purification and a new identity

Anunnaki purification and a new identity

Question by Anonymous: You wrote somewhere about Anunnaki purification, and a new identity a young Anunnaki receives after a purification ceremony on Nibiru. What do you mean by purification? Since you do not believe in the existence of SOUL, what are you talking about? Purify what? Dirty laundry? Assuming what you have said is true – I don't believe a bit of it– can you tell me in plain English how does this purification stuff happen and for what purpose?
Answer:
Note: Partially reproduced from my book "Anunnaki and Ulema From 450,000 B.C. to the Present (Volume 4)

The Anunnaki's purification process is called Huina-Ta'h-Ra.
I. Definition
II. Annunaki's purification and its relation to water in Judaism, Essene's sect, and Christianity
III. Anunnaki's "Nif-Malka-Roo'h-Dosh"
IV. Creation of the mental "Conduit"

Note: Ulema de Lafayette has explained the Anunnaki's purification process so many times, and wrote at length about it in two books. We can't reproduce herein everything he has written in the past. But we will give you a synopsis. But before we do this, we have to remind you that the term "Soul" is referred to as "Mind" in Ulemite literature. It is basically the same, but the structural composition of each is very different.

I. Definition:
According to Ulema de Lafayette, and the Book of Ramadosh, it means Anunnaki's student purification ritual before entering the classroom. It is composed of three words:
- **a**-Huina, which means, energy; life.

- **b**-Ta'h, which means purification, or mental cleansing.
- **c**-Ra could mean many things, but in this situation, it is agreed upon that Ra means the "Elevated Being".

II. Annunaki's purification and its relation to water in Judaism, Essene's sect, and Christianity:

All Anunnaki students are required to purify their bodies before starting their course of studies, particularly the first stage, called "Mental Cleansing".

This could have influenced an ancient tradition created by the Jewish scribes, who since earliest times, had to purify their body before adding the name of God into the Torah.

Ulema Naphtali ben Yacob said: "Each student must purify his or her own being "Mind" alone, because the mixing of the impurities might produce a barrier to the proper purification. Incidentally, remember the Essenes, these Judaic sect members of the Second Temple era?

At first, they used the Anunnaki's style of purification, but as time went by, and their numbers grew, they changed into a Mikvah-like, communal purification. A certain similarity can be established with the Christian baptism; it is all the same idea of purity and cleanliness.

The Christians believe that the mind and spirit are indeed cleansed by the baptism. The purification exercise occurs inside a small room, entirely made of shimmering white marble.

In the middle of the room, there is a basin, made out of the same material, and filled with a substance called "Nou-Rah Shams"; an electro-plasma substance that appears like 'liquid-light.'

It actually means, in Anakh, The Liquid of Light.
- **a**-Nou, or Nour, or sometimes Menour, or Menou-Ra, means light.
- **b**-Shams means sun. Nour in Arabic means light.

The Ulema in Egypt, Syria, Iraq and Lebanon use the same word in their opening ceremony. Sometimes, the word Nour becomes Nar, which means fire. This is intentional, because the Ulemas, like the Phoenicians, believed in fire as a symbolic procedure to purify the thoughts.

Part Three: Anunnaki purification and new identity

III. Anunnaki's "Nif-Malka-Roo'h-Dosh":

The Anunnaki's purification does more than purifying the body. The substance Anunnaki use purifies the mind and spirit as well. It's all very pleasant. Every minute you spend in the basin, you will feel lighter, happier, more complete within yourself and sparkling clean.

The second phase of the purification is called "Nif-Malka-Roo'h-Dosh". Nif means mind. Centuries later, it was used by terrestrials as Nifs or Roo'h, meaning Soul or Spirit. Since the Anunnaki did not believe in a 'separate soul,' the mind was the only source of creation and mental development, while humans continued to interpret it as 'Soul.'

Nif, Nifs, Nefes, Nafs, Nefesh mean the same thing in Akkadian, Hittite, Aramaic, Hebrew, Ugaritic, Arabic, Syriac, Turkish, and Anunnaki languages. Malka means kingdom or a higher level of knowledge and mental development.

Humans changed Malka to Malakoot or Malkout, and these words are used in Aramaic, Hebrew, Syriac, Coptic, Arabic, Phoenician and so many other languages.

Roo'h is the highest level of mental achievement.

The Arabs use the same word "Rouh", while the Hebrew word is "Ru'ach". However, the meaning changed in both languages, to represent soul, not "Mind" as originally understood in Anunnaki language.

And "Dosh" means revered or holy.

In Hebrew, it is "Kadosh". After this phase of purification, the Anunnaki student enters a moderately sized room off the classroom. In the room there is a cell, shaped as a transparent cone. The cell floats in the air, approximately twelve centimeters above the floor.

The top of the cell is connected to a beam originating from a grid attached to a ceiling floating in the air; it is totally suspended on its own.

The student steps inside the cone. A door opens and the student enters the contraption. Inside the cone, a clear fog begins to form in the center.

Part Three: Anunnaki purification and new identity

After a short while, the fog's color changes from white to silver-blue in the form of waves, and the student starts to see his/her thoughts registering on a machine serving as an information board and which is posted on the right side of the cell.
These thoughts begin to take physical shape, which is instantly copied to a screen. The screen transforms the thought-forms into a code. Almost instantly, the code is transformed into a sequence of numerical values. The sequences are the genetic formula of the student.
This genetic formula is the "Identity Registration" of the Anunnaki student. In terrestrial terms, you can call it DNA. But it is more than that. It is the level of mental readiness for the next stage.
At this point, the student begins to hear a direction in his/her head, as clear as if someone is talking to him/her directly.
This is the moment when the student has been approached on a telepathic level. The student is instructed to free his/her mind from all thoughts. It is something like what the Japanese call "Koan," or "Kara," a state of "mind nothingness."

IV. Creation of the mental "Conduit":
Then, something starts to happen; rays of various densities and colors surround the student in a cloud. It is tempting to compare it to the aura in terrestrial terms, but this is not the case. It is not an aura, because it is not bio-organic. It is entirely mental. What happens next takes only one minute; this is the most important procedure done for each Anunnaki student on the first day of his/her studies – the creation of the mental "Conduit."
A new identity is created for each Anunnaki student by the development of a new pathway in his or her mind, connecting the student to the rest of the Anunnaki's psyche.
Simultaneously, the cells check with the "other copy" of the mind and body of the Anunnaki student, to make sure that the "Double" and "Other Copy" of the mind and body of the student are totally clean. During this phase, the Anunnaki student temporarily loses his or her memory, for a very short time.
This is how the telepathic faculty is developed, or enhanced in everyone.

Part Three: Anunnaki purification and new identity

It is necessary, to serve the whole community of the Anunnaki. The individual program inside each Anunnaki student is immediately shared with everybody. Incidentally, this is why there is such a big difference between extraterrestrial and human telepathy.

Ulema Rabbi Mordechai said: "On earth, no one ever succeeds in emptying the whole mental content from human cells, like the Anunnaki are so adept at doing, and as such, the Conduit cannot be formed. Lacking the Conduit that is built for each Anunnaki, the human mind is not capable of communication with the extraterrestrials. However, don't think for a moment that there is any kind of invasion of privacy. "

The simplistic idea of any of your friends tapping into your private thoughts does not exist for the Anunnaki. Their telepathy is rather complicated. The Anunnaki have collective intelligence and individual intelligence.

And this is directly connected to two things: the first is the access to the "Community Depot of Knowledge" that any Anunnaki can tap into and update and acquire additional knowledge.

The second is an "Individual Prevention Shield," also referred to as "Personal Privacy." This means that an Anunnaki can switch his direct link to the community on and off, perhaps better defined as his/channel to other Anunnaki.

By establishing the "Screen" or "Filter", an Anunnaki can block others from either communicating with him/her, or simply preventing others from reading his/her personal thoughts. "Filter", "Screen" and "Shield" (Plasmic) are interchangeably used to describe the privacy protection.

In addition, an Anunnaki can program telepathy and set it up on chosen channels, exactly as we turn on our radio set and select the station we wish to listen to.

Telepathy has several frequencies, channels and stations. When the establishment of the Conduit is complete, the student leaves the conical cell, and heads toward the section assigned to him/her at the classroom.

*** *** ***

Part Three: Were dinosaurs created by extraterrestrials?

Were dinosaurs created by extraterrestrials?

Question by Matt Hoxtell, Chicago, Illinois, USA.

Question: Were dinosaurs created by extraterrestrials?
Answer:
Not every life-form on Earth was created by the Anunnaki. It is important to remember that when the first expedition of the Anunnaki landed on Earth, our planet was already populated by an amazing variety of living organisms, animals, quasi-human species, the earliest of human-animal forms, synthesized molecules, substances and biological entities. Many of these life-forms were created from cosmic dust.
Some were the result of photosynthesis, and other groups were produced by bacteria and evolution inertia. Worth mentioning here, is that the Anunnaki had no interest or motivation in creating/altering the creation of pre-existing life-forms that were deemed unnecessary or not very essential for starting and/or carrying on their projects on Earth.
The dinosaurs existed on planet Earth, long before the Anunnaki descended to Earth.
The dinosaurs first appeared about 230 million years ago, and their reign lasted over 100 million years. The Anunnaki arrived to Earth circa 449,000 B.C.

Besides, the Anunnaki(any expedition) did not consider the dinosaurs, or remnants of the dinosaurs and similar reptiles, necessary or useful for their plans for two reasons:
- **a**-They lacked mental/intellectual faculties, necessary for understanding the instructions of the Anunnaki;
- **b**-Their enormous size.

*** *** ***

Part Three: The lost continent of MU's connection with the Anunnaki

The lost continent of MU's connection with the Anunnaki

Question by Ismail Kemal Ciftcioglu, Turkey.

Question: This is the most important question for me. In any of the books I read, I haven't come across any information about the lost continent of MU's connection with the Anunnaki. I assume you know lots of things about it. According to James Churchward's books, MU was even older than Atlantis and home to the human civilization. Humans migrated from MU all over the world. But we know that the Anunnaki were in Mesopotamia. So what about it? What can you tell me about the lost continent of MU?

Answer:
I. Introduction/Mythological backgound:
According to legend and esoteric myth, Mu was a large continent of an advanced civilization. It sank beneath the ocean many thousands of years ago. The story or Myth of Mu appeared for the first time in the 19th century, thanks to the writings of Augustus Le Plongeon (1825-1908), who claimed that the survivors of Mu went to the Americas and established the Mayan Empire.

Then, in the first half of the 20th century, the prolific writer and visionary extraordinaire James Churchward popularized the story of Mu in a series of books he wrote: "The Children of Mu" published in 1931; "The Lost Continent of Mu" published in 1933, and "The Sacred Symbols of Mu", published in 1935.

And in the 1930's, Kamal Atatürk (Baba Kamal) then leader of Turkey, your majestic country, generously funded academic and scientific research on Mu. The great Turkish leader thought that perhaps he would be able to establish a direct link or some sort of connection betweek Turkey and the world's first civilizations that could include the Aztec, and the Maya. Unfortunately, all attempts to prove the existence of MU failed.

Part Three: The lost continent of MU's connection with the Anunnaki

II. Scientific/geological facts:
First of all, you have to remember that the Anunnaki were not only in Mesopotamia.
The first expedition of the Anunnaki to Earth, occurred some 449,000 years ago.
They landed in the Near East (Phoenicia) and explored the territories of Madagascar, Brazil, Central Africa, Turkey (Anatolia) etc., and finally they established their kingdom in Mesopotamia. The continent of MU was already in existence, long, long before the Mesopotamian civilization.
And Atlantis was the bridge between the remnants of Mu, the pre-historic civilization of Crete, Phoenicia(Modern day Lebanon), Ugarit, Arwad, Egypt, Mesopotamia, the lands of the Hittites in Anatolia, and Cyprus.
Mu was established some 14,000 to 20,000 years ago, and its civilization was destroyed some 9,500 to 10,000 years ago, but MU itself did not "sink" under the ocean, as many have claimed, simply because scientifically speaking, continents do not sink; they might shift, drift, and break into two, three or several parts, but this is a very very long geolocial process that takes hundreds of millions of years.
Except for Pangaea, history, archeology, anthropology and oceanography tell us that continents have maintained their original position. Thus, for the continent of MU to change its original position as a continent, or to sink to the bottom of the ocean, these events and changes should have occurred at the time Pangaea shifted some 250 millions years ago, or even during the shift of Pannotia, that was formed on Earth some 600 million years ago, or Rodinia (formed some 1.2 billion years ago) which has totally shifted some 750 million years ago.
Yet once again, geography, natural history, oceanography, anthropology, the study of fossils, and the history of comparative civilizations have not provided any proof that a new shift has ever occurred after those dates.
Thus, the idea that an early advanced civilization existed hundreds of millions of years ago on a vanished continent is pure fantasy, ridiculed by science.

Part Three: The lost continent of MU's connection with the Anunnaki

In conclusion, the civilization of MU must have existed around 14,000 to 20,000 years ago, and during that period, no continent has ever shifted. Therefore, the sinking of MU to the bottom of the ocean is an impossibility.

III. Anunnaki-Ulema views:

Baalbeck, one of the earliest cities/colonies of the Anunnaki on Earth.

Ulema have suggested that MU and Atlantis were one and the same; a community, instead of a continent. This makes it more logical to assume that a migration of a community to another part of the world, including Baalbeck, Tyre, Sidon, Turkey, Anatolia, the Near East/the Middle East could have occurred.
In addition, this migration could also explain the sudden emergence of an advanced civilization that we know little about.
The early community of Mu or Atlantis or both, since they were considered epistemologically and anthropologically the same, had a highly advanced civilization and well-structured societies, "implanted" by an extraterrestrial race.

Part Three: The lost continent of MU's connection with the Anunnaki

And the only extraterrestrial race that left some historical and mythological documents and records on Earth were the Anunnaki. This is the only and most logical link we can attach to the people of MU/Atlantis.

Anunnaki-Ulema Sadek ben Alia Al Bakri stated verbatim: "The Anunnaki had a direct contact with those people, and taught them science, technology, language, and the use of advanced learning techniques and tools. They went to the Near/Middle East and established their new colonies, always under the supervision of the Anunnaki."

Ulema Sharif Al Takki Al Zubyani (1797-1877) stated that Mu did exist some 50,000 years ago according to the Ulemite calendar (14,000-20,000 years in our calendar).

He added that the original name of Mu was Mari, and it was inhabited by people who were very advanced in "Ilm Al Falak", meaning space science. An enormous explosion happened on the continent, caused by the reflection of light and rays emitted by a gigantic "Miraya", which means mirrors, triggered by a huge volcano eruption.

Coincidentally or strangely enough, the Anunnaki and Ulemite literature referred to the Miraya as a galactic tool used to receive and emit cosmic messages, a sort of beam (Possibly atomic or laser), as well as to record and decode events from the past, the present and the future. Al Zubyani added: "Those mirrors were also used as weapons, and if they are not handled properly, they could destroy a whole country."

Those who know Arabic, including the archaic dialect of the Arab Peninsula, and Ana'kh will find out that there is a very close relation (Perhaps linguistically only) between the Name Mari and the Arabic, pre-Islamic word Mir'aat (Mir'-aat and Miraya) which means in both languages (Ana'kh and Arabic) mirror.

Strangely enough, the French word "Miroir" and the English word mirror are derived directly from the Ana'kh (Anunnaki language) Miraya. So here we have a million year old Anunnaki word "Miraya", a 50,000 year old name "Mari", a 7,000 year old Ulemite word "Mirra-ya", and a 5,000 year old Arabic word Miraya! Any connection?

The lost continent of MU's connection with the Anunnaki

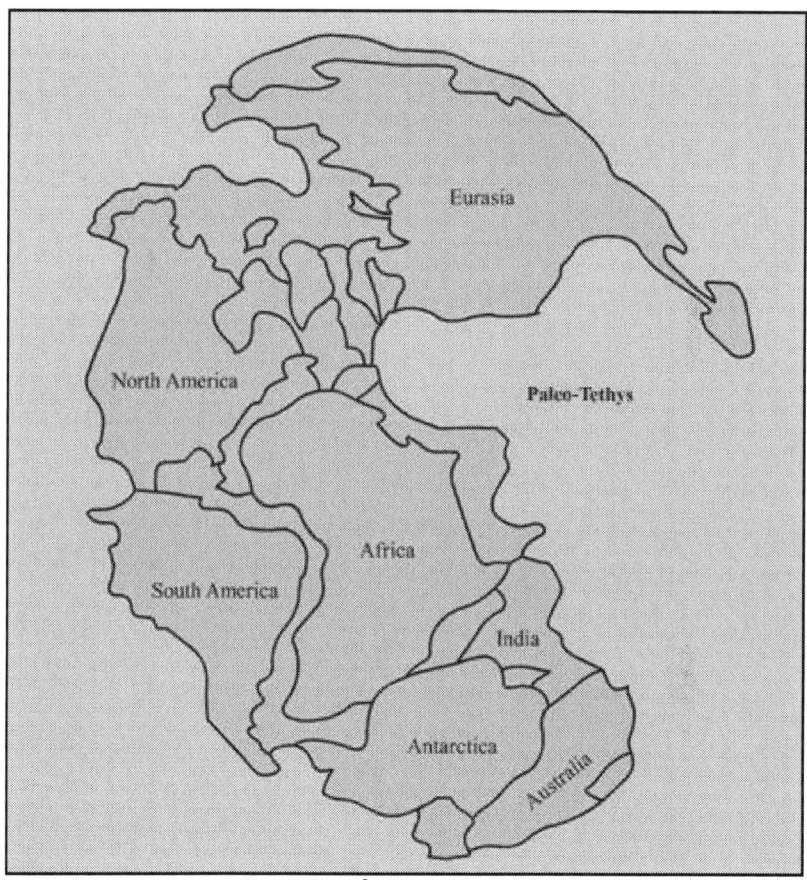

Map of Pangaea.

IV. So, what did we learn from all this?
We have learned the following:
- The continent of MU did not sink to the bottom of the ocean, because scientifically, continents do not sink.

Part Three: The lost continent of MU's connection with the Anunnaki

- 2- Some sort of ecological or geological catastrophe occurred some 9,500 to 10,000 years ago that forced the population of that part of the world to flee and seek refuge somewhere else, probably in the countries I have mentioned earlier. In fact, science has provided evidence of a cosmic catastrophe around 9,500 B.C., and this explains everything.

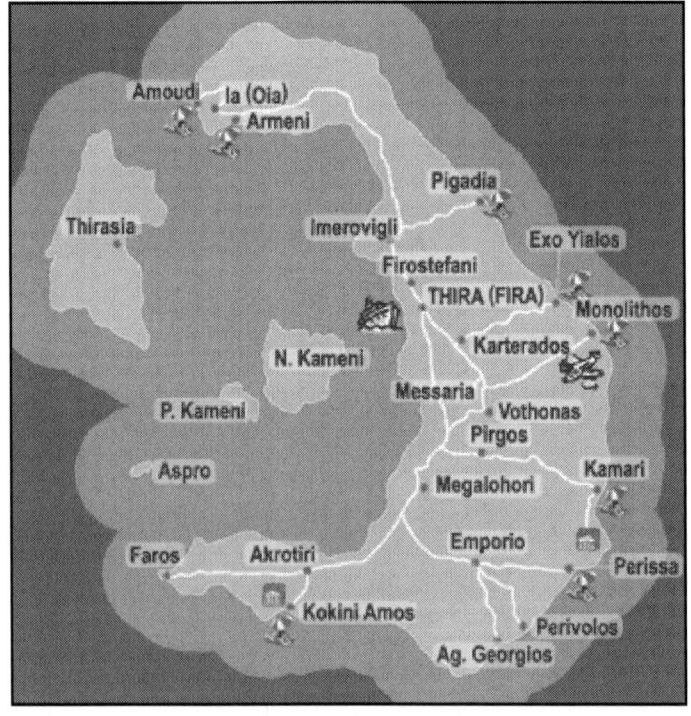

Map of Santorini.
Santorini is a small, circular archipelago of volcanic islands located in the southern Aegean Sea, about 200 km southeast from Greece's mainland.

Part Three: The lost continent of MU's connection with the Anunnaki

- 3- Upon their arrival to new countries, a sudden and new civilization appeared in that part of the world, and that explains the "out of nowhere" origin of human civilization, the birth of language, and the acquired knowledge in so many fields, etc.
- 4- In fact, that society was highly advanced, and most certainly influenced and taught by a super non-human extraterrestrial race. This explains the sudden rise of their civilization, societies, communities and cities, in sharp contrast with other "human societies" which were still living in darkness, ignorance and retarded social conditions.

Map of Crete.

Part Three: The lost continent of MU's connection with the Anunnaki

- 5- This advanced society, the originator of human civilization did exist and live on and around the areas and lands nearby Santorini-Crete, and neighboring islands, where a geological catastrophe, and a huge volcano eruption were proven by science.

*** *** ***

Part Three: Where are the Anunnaki now and why don't they interfere in our planet

Question by Ismail Kemal Ciftcioglu, Turkey.

Where are the Anunnaki now and why don't they interfere in our planet?

Question: Where is the Anunnaki race right now, and why don't they interfere in our planet anymore?
Answer:
The Anunnaki now are where they came from; their own planet, called Nibiru "Ne.Be.Ru", also known as Ashtari. The Anunnaki are part of the "Cosmic Federation of the Seven Galaxies". This is not the so-called federation of lights or cosmic order as claimed by new age ufology. What is so special about the Anunnaki's federation is the different types of alien civilizations and galactic races that have joined, meaning different bio-organic entities, which are totally different from human-like entities, physically, organically, emotionally and mentally.
"Why don't they interfere in our planet anymore?" Humans have very little to offer more advanced galactic civilizations. In reality, the human race has nothing meaningful to offer to the Anunnaki. We are limited in our thoughts, despite the variety and divergence of our philosophical views, inventions, art, the music we compose, the poetry we write, and the magnificent figurines and sculptures we create.
On a cosmic level, all these beauties produced by mankind are very minimal.
In the very early days of humanity's history, the Anunnaki were deeply involved in human affairs, and we know this from reading the Akkadian/Sumerian clay tablets, the Babylonian-Mesopotamian literature as preserved in the legendary library (More than 30,000 tablets) of Ashurbanipal in Nineveh, the Phoenician Cosmogeny, the Book of Ramadosh, etc.
However, the Anunnaki lost interest in us, for many reasons, to name a few:

Part Three: Where are the Anunnaki now and why don't they interfere in our planet

---

1-The Anunnaki's mission-expedition-exploration on planet "Ki", "Ardi" (Earth) was accomplished hundreds of thousands of years ago.

2-The Anunnaki had to return home to take care of their own business. However, they left offspring on Earth, in areas and regions like Turkey, Phoenicia, Sumer, Guatemala, Peru, Mexico, Persia, and Syria.

Their offspring appeared in history's chronologies as legendary kings and queens, and in some cases, as obscure historical figures like Danel, "Danael", "Dnil", a Phoenician-Ugaritic king who was mentioned in the Ras Shamra Texts.

The Anunnaki's offspring had a hard time dealing with humans, because of their greed, violence, betrayals, wars, and their lack of loyalty. In fact, many of the Anunnaki's remnants on Earth were murdered by humans. If you read ancient history books, you will find out that one civilization wipes out other civilizations by invading their territories, and butchering their leaders, and these atrocious acts continue to the present day.

It is quite ironic, we call the Macedonian leader Alexander "the Great"; when he was a man who killed millions of people (families, women, children, elderly) and destroyed some of the greatest civilizations in history.

Equally ironic and shameful is the fact that we depict the Crusaders as the "Saviors of the Faith", when in reality, they were murderers and butchers.

Upon capturing the city of Jerusalem, the Crusaders slaughtered every Muslim infant, woman and man, and wiped out families and communities. And they did it in the name of Jesus, the Pope and Christianity.

The same thing happened again, when the Christian Catholic Conquistadors decimated the Maya, Inca and Aztec civilizations; and when the so-called "Pioneers of the West" annihilated the Native Americans.

And today, history still repeats itself with religious extremists, and superpowers' materialistic and military expansionism.

The Anunnaki have witnessed all these atrocities.

Part Three: Where are the Anunnaki now and why don't they interfere in our planet

Even the notorious "Greys" felt threatened by the human race, because of its nuclear arsenal, and what we are constantly doing to Earth's ecological system/environment. Earth is not a positive and healthy environment or habitat for the Anunnaki, and/ any other highly civilized race.

Sure, the human race produced outstanding people like Madame Curie, Mahatma Gandhi, Mother Theresa, Salah Al Dinn Al Ayoubi, Victor Hugo, Marco Polo, Lamartine, Mary-Magdalena, Buddha Siddhartha, Sophocles, and Chopin, but these wonderful people are a drop in the bucket.

To tell you the truth, if you don't find pleasure in the act of giving, and if you don't forgive others, not only once, but as many times as it takes, maybe fifty times or more if necessary, and as long as our success and respectability on Earth are measured by the weight of our wealth, fame and power, none of the highly advanced communities in the cosmos will find the human race, appealing, meaningful and worthy of any attention.

However, the Anunnaki did not abandon us completely. Thanks to the "Conduit" they have installed in the cells of our brains, they remain in constant touch with us, but only the pure in heart and thoughts will feel it and benefit from it.

*** *** ***

Part Three: **Don't ever underestimate the power of your mind!**

Don't ever underestimate the power of your mind!

Question by anonymous: I can't understand how you could write so many books in such a short time? Do you use some sort of magic or a supernatural power? You know what, some people are spreading rumors that the overwhelming number of your books you wrote were made by a machine and because of this you are a machine.

Answer:
Many, like you, have asked how did I manage to write hundreds of books in a short time, or to be able to speak so many languages, and accomplish multiple tasks simulteneously?
Some have dubbed me superhuman, others have called me nuts, and a few have said that the fact that I have written so many books so in such a short period of time, means that I have got to be a scam. This amuses me a lot, because no supernatural powers or machines are associated with what I do.
I can assure anybody, absolutely anybody can do what I have done, effortlessly if some techniques are learned and utilized.
And these technniques are associated with how you organize your mind. I will try to explain this very simply. Your mind is a wonderful machine composed of Jabas, a collection of pockets or drawers, similar to your computer. When your computer is loaded with temporary internet files, searching, loading and uploading will slow your computer down considerably.
Thus, you have to delete your temporary files, in order to speed up your computer, and have more space on your hard drive. The same thing applies to your mind. When your Jabas are full with old and unnecessay information, your mind slows down; becoming slow in acquiring, storing, organizing, sorting and analyzing new information. In addition to the clearing (Cleaning, emptying) of your Jabas, you must let your Supersymetric mind work on it's own.

Part Three: Don't ever underestimate the power of your mind!

You have to sit, and start talking to yourself. Mind you while you are doing that, your brain is independently listening to you. First of all, you have to convince yourself that you can do it.

Never understimate yourself or your personal powers.

The fact that you do not have – apparently – supernatural powers, does not mean that you cannot accomplish amazing things, even extraordinary deeds by normal standards. Yes you can.! And it is so easy if you start to believe in yourself, in a new and different way.

This opens part of your "Mind Pockets/Jabas." Please refer to the book "The Ulema Anunnaki Forbidden Book of Ramadosh"; as it explains how this can be done.

Basically, your brain is full of junk and storage you do not need. So, as a first step, you have to get rid of this junk. It is easy to do. You start by asking yourself, what did you put in your mind, in the past and now, ten years ago and today?

This exersize is good, simply because you begin to inquire about what you have already learned in your life. It is as if you are probing your own brain, confidentially in the privacy and comfort of your own space .

*** *** ***

Part Three: Scanning brilliant minds to create a "Super-Baby"!

Scanning brilliant minds to create a "Super-Baby"!

Question by Akram Jibril, UAE.

Question: I am not sure who has said aliens can scan our brain and create a new species of babies for their hybrid program. Is it true? Can they do that? And how it is done?

Answer:
Ulema Oppenheimer and Ulema Govinda commented on "Mind Scanning" and duplicating-multiplying brains' potentials:
From their Kira'at, verbatim: Scanning your brain and body to create a new copy of "You" for a new-born baby.
They scan you, mind and body, and place the scan in an "Aetra" mold to recreate you and duplicate you; they can make as many copies as they want. On the top of the "Scan Mold", there is a transparent cover "Kha-Tar" that looks like fiberglass.

As soon as the scan process begins, the Khatar starts to work, meaning, it starts to reshape itself into a human form, the physical form of your body in its miniscule details.

So what we have here, is "you" imprinted three dimensionally on a sheet of a fiberglass. This is the "Physical Scan". What is more facinating, is the "Kha-tra-Fikr", which is the "Mental Scan" of your brains, all your thoughts, feelings, beliefs, memories and intentions.
At the end, they either mix the physical scan with the mental scan to recreate a copy of you, or install your brain into another body (Not Yours), or attached your body to the brain of another scanned person.
Now, imagine if they keep on - indefinitely - duplicating and reduplicating these scans, physically and mentally, how many millions of new hybrid people would be created? More than you can count!!

Part Three: Scanning brilliant minds to create a "Super-Baby"!

In some instances, at birth, some of them have already implanted scanned brains into the brain/mind of new born babies. The baby is 2 hours old, but his/her memory is 50 years old.

The new born's mind is almost virgin and clean like a dry sponge, but with their genetic manipulation, they can feed this "virgin mind" with the contents of brilliant minds they have scanned for hundreds of years.
So what we have here is a superbaby, an infant who is more intelligent than all the geniuses on Earth, combined!

*** *** ***

Part Three: Is the Ulema group administered by men or women?

Is the Ulema-Anunnaki group administered by men or a matriarch woman?

Question by Rita Montiel, Madrid, Spain.

Question: Is the Ulema-Anunnaki group administered by men or a matriarch woman as I have heard?

Answer:
No, the Ulema are not exclusively all men. In fact, the head of one Ma'had (Center/Institute) is Umdasturia; a magnificent woman. And her name is quite interesting and revealing.
Those who know Turkish, Arabic, Farsi, and some ancient Middle Eastern languages will be able to know what her name means. Well, Um means mother, and Dasturia means the law, or the constitution of the Ulema's assembly.
By the way, the assembly is called Majlas. In the eye of Baal Shamroot and Ameliku (the great supreme Sinhars of the Anunnaki), even though men and women are equal, women remain far more superior to men.

Women are the first and exclusive source of Man's life and existence in the known universe. Women are the first cell and the first molecule of the life of all men. The earliest Akkadian-Babylonian- Sumerian tablets tell us that the early women on Earth, the offspring of the Anunnaki and Igigi did not need men's sperm to fertilize their eggs and give birth to babies.

Women-goddesses were self-reproductive, and could give birth to babies without having intercourse with a man. But they lost this capability, by constantly interbreeding with Earth's men and continuously engaging in sexual acts with Earth's "creatures". According to the Akkadian-Sumerian tablets, at the beginning of time, the second most powerful person in the universe was a woman goddess - creator of the universe, and of men.

Part Three: Is the Ulema group administered by men or women?

She was called Tiamat. But Tiamat was dethroned and killed by a male god known as Marduk. The male scribes and the kings needed to restore the "Authority of Man" over everything, thus they created the myth of Marduk and justified the reason for his killing Tiamat.

Marduk fighting the dragon Tiamat.

Marduk fighting the dragon Tiamat, and putting an end to her major influence on the affairs of the universe, the state and Man. By doing so, Marduk became the absolute and most powerful god of the Anunnaki, the Igigi, and Babylon.

Part Three: Is the Ulema group administered by men or women?

Marduk chasing and fighting Tiamat.

Eventually, Marduk will slaughter Tiamat, and from parts of her body, Marduk will create the universe, according to the Akkadian-Babylonian tablets.

*** *** ***

Part Three: Relation between our Mind, body and cellular memory?

The relationship between our mind, body and cellular memory?

Question by Tony Rossi, Bocan Raton, Florida.

Question: What is the relationship between our mind, body and cellular memory?

Answer:
"Do you think you are seeing yourself as a physical reality when you in a mirror? Think again. Some highly evolved people extend to the outside perimeter of their physical body..." said Ulema Li.
Ulema ben Yacob stated: "You too, can do this...you can transcend the physical boundaries of your body. There are two presences/substances that made you what and who you are:
- **a**-You as a person;
- **b**-You as a human being.

The human being is the physical form of yourself.
The "Person" is what constitutes everything about yourself.
There are lots of things (Matter and Mind) about you that are somewhere you are not aware of. Part of you exists in a tree, in a river, in a thought, in a memory cell, in a beautiful song, in a dream, in another country, and way beyond; in dimensions that most recently were elaborated on, by quantum physics' leading thinkers and pioneers.
You have to find out everything that is part of you, in order to reach extraordinary standards of intelligence, and unmatched success at multiple levels.
Part of your "Extraordinary Intelligence" rotates around cellular memory.
Do you know where your cellular memory is?
Is it in your physical body, or in your psyche?
Is it in you "The Person", or in you the "Human Entity"?
And why is cellular memory so important to be concerned about?

Part Three: Relation between our Mind, body and cellular memory?

It is important, because that memory is everything you have experienced and learned from, as well as the stimulus and conditioner of your judgment, analysis and the understanding of the world you live in.
But it is not perfect because it is not complete.
You have to tap into both segments of yourself, the physical body that takes you from your home to your office, and the "Person" that transports you from a limited physical sphere of knowledge to the ultimate and highest zone of awareness, that is so close to you, close to your physical body.
There, you will find the ultimate truth about yourself, how much information and knowledge you have stored within you before you were born, after you were born, and what you are going to be once you are no longer here.
You are too important to be confined in 150 pounds, 190 pounds, 200 pounds, 5 feet, or 6 feet 11. You are much bigger and denser than you think. So tap into the missing part of yourself. It is so enjoyable, so remunerating, so profitable, and so powerful.
Visit yourself iin other dimensions, rediscover the zone you that are not fully aware of exists. It belongs to you, and to you alone.
Once there, you will reinforce your physical and mental powers and energies.
The denser the body of your other person is, the healthier you become. That other person you may call whatever you want: a guardian, an angel, an etheric presence, your double. All are the very same thing. People who have succeeded in blending with the other part of themselves that extends beyond and outside their physical mass of muscles, feet, hands and lungs, have accomplished extraordinary things.
You too can do it. It just requires a certain degree of belief, practice and determination.

Where is this other part of me, you might ask?
It is so close to your physical body, and wherever you go, it goes with you, it does not follow you, but accompany you. You have to make a deal with it.

Part Three: Relation between our Mind, body and cellular memory?

You have to reach some sort of agreement with it.
An agreement to chat together, to meet somewhere, and go from there.
If you don't converse with your own mind, you will never work out/exercize the mental muscles in your brain, and if you do not increase the size and strength of your mental muscles, your intellect will shrink.

Note: In the "Ulema Anunnaki Forbidden Book of Ramadosh", Maximillien de Lafayette and Germain Lumiere provided some techniques that could enable you to do so, and reach your other "Etheric Zone". Please refer to the book.

*** *** ***

Part Three: Anunnaki-Phoenician Chavad-nitrin & the immortality of gods

Anunnaki-Phoenician Chavad-nitrin and the immortality of the gods

Question by Georges Haddad, Michigan.

Question: I am originally from Byblos (Jbeil) in Lebanon, and we Lebanese are descendants of the Crusaders who learned some of the secrets of the Anunnaki in Lebanon and Jerusalem. I have heard that my ancestors the Phoenicians have used a product similar to athletes' steroids. This product I was told was also used by the Egyptian Pharaohs. Could you please tell me more about it? Many thanks.

Roman pillars leading up to the temple of Balaat Gebal, in Byblos, Phoenicia, where the Chavad-nitrin was used by the priests of Baal.

Part Three: Anunnaki-Phoenician Chavad-nitrin & the immortality of gods

God Osiris.

Part Three: Anunnaki-Phoenician Chavad-nitrin & the immortality of gods

Answer:
Correct, that product was called "Chavad-nitrin", after an ancient Phoenician embalming process, learned from Byblos and Arwad Anunnaki remnants, using Mah'rit (Maha-reet), a secret substance considered to be humanity's first formula for steroids, mixed with barks from the cedars of Phoenicia. It was frequently used by athletes in Ugarit, Amrit, and Arwad.

Ruins of the ancient city of Ugarit.

From Chavad-nitrin, derived the Greek word Natron or Natrin, a substance used in the embalming process.
Because of the reported physical endurance and legendary longevity it produced, the Egyptians equated the words Neter, Netjer and Netjet with the immortality of the gods.

Part Three: Anunnaki-Phoenician Chavad-nitrin & the immortality of gods

According to Egyptian tradition, the first human being to be mummified was the god Osiris, whose body floated down the Nile in a wooden casket, and washed ashore at Byblos (Your hometown) in Phoenicia.
For this reason, Byblos was a sacred region to Osiris, to his cult, and to the Egyptians. This explains the reason why the Egyptians have called Byblos the land of the god Osiris; Ta Netjer.

*** *** ***

Part Three: Hidden entrances to other worlds/dimensions, here on Earth

Hidden entrances to other worlds and dimensions, right here on Earth

Question by Isabelle Franchot, and Emile Farkas, Beverly Hills, California.

Question: Do UFOs and extraterrestrials use galactic entrances and space-time corridors to enter and exit our world? And how many are there? Are they visible to the naked eye?

Answer:
There are several unseen, hidden, and undetectable entrances to three different dimensions beyond ours:
 a- Entrance(s) to the after-life (After death);
 b- Entrances to the fourth dimension;
 c- Entrance(s) to the parallel dimension (Ba'ab)

Each dimension (Zone) is a totally different world in structure, substance, composition, and boundaries. Some are extremely close to us. Closer than you might think.
I will explain:

a-Entrance to the after-life:
This is called life after death. And it is exactly what you might think. The realm of deceased people. Only dead people enter this zone, and they never return. The Babylonians called it "The Land of no Return".
It was mentioned in their epics. In some passages, it was called Kur in Akkadian. On their way into that dimension, deceased people encounter all sorts of entities, benevolent and malevolent. This is not my personal theory. I did not invent such a story. This was mentioned thousands of years ago in the Egyptian Book of the Dead, in the Tibetan "Bardo Todol", and many other texts from various ancient cultures.

Part Three: Hidden entrances to other worlds/dimensions, here on Earth

---

b-Entrance to the fourth dimension:

This is a zone that a person can enter in two manners, mentally and physically.
This zone could have entrances everywhere; in your bedroom, in a valley, in a building corridor, absolutely everywhere and anywhere. And this includes the oceans, the bottom of the sea, in thin air, and right inside your home doors. Many people have been sucked-up, absorbed by its "Pulling Force" (Magnetic field) in a split second. Once they are attracted or pulled in by these entrances, they zoom inside the entrance at incredible speed. For incomprehensible reasons, these entrances could open up and close at anytime, any moment. And as soon as a person or an object is swallowed up by the current (Flux-Influx) of those entrances, the entrance shut's its opening (Overture) in on itself.
Those kinds of entrances are situated everywhere in our world. There is vast literature on people, vehicles, animals who have vanished into thin air, in a split second.
Highly advanced alien races know exactly where the locations of these entrances are, as well as their currents and times of opening and closing. They have used these entrances as corridors and passages for millions of years.
Many of their spaceships have navigated through these channels. Some Ulema have explained the passages of these entrances as a net of time and space bending on itself, and thus reducing distances and time between points and destinations.
Sometimes, UFOs sharp angular turns and zigzag pattern indicate where these entrances are located in the skies. This is why Ulema have said that UFOS do not fly, they jump. Meaning, they jump from one pocket to another.
In other words, these pockets are nothing more than entrances to a higher dimension; the fourth dimension.
I am absolutely sure that several scientists working on classified outer-space programs (sponsored by some governments) have already worked on projects related to fourth dimensional entrances. Some might have succeeded. And I will rest my case here, and keep my mouth shut!

Part Three: Hidden entrances to other worlds/dimensions, here on Earth

It was reported in close circles, that a couple living somewhere in the United States had a nightmarish experience, when the nanny of their two lovely children vanished into thin air, in a fraction of a second in their kitchen, while opening a can of concentrated milk; never to be found again.

The military police were called in to investigate. Two days later, the "case was closed" and the couple were order to evacuate their home. You have every right to doubt my words.

To an alert mind, these sorts of stories are science fiction. From the bottom of my heart, I do not wish to see you in a similar situation, because this could happen to all of us.

A highly regarded scientist told me once that the disappearance of the nanny was never considered a "closed case". He said that a few hours after this tragic and frightening experience happened, one parapsychologist and one quantum physics expert were taken to the couple's home to conduct further investigations.

They searched the whole house, and after three laborious hours, found the entrance to the fourth dimension, located on the right side of the kitchen sink. They sealed the kitchen area, and encircled the entrance "Door" of the threatening dimension with colored fiberglass sheets. From these types of openings, entities, substances, other life-forms, gravity and reverse-gravity can also leak into our world from that fourth dimension.

3-Entrance to the parallel dimension:
I will not elaborate on this dimension, because I have written on this subject ad infinitum in many of my previous books. But worth mentioning here, is that parallel dimensions are not the product of fantasy or science fiction. Some of the world's most admired scientists and professors teaching quantum physics have already explained what a parallel dimension is, and/ or how multiple dimensions work.

According to their most recent findings and theories, there are 11 known parallel dimensions in the universe.

*** *** ***

Part Three: Paranormal mirrors and extraterrestrials

Paranormal mirrors and extraterrestrials:
Mirrors that remember their previous owners.

Question by Fabio T., Rome, Italy

Question: I read a small article on a mysterious antique mirror that caused the death of an owner, because as it was explained in the articles, the mirrors had a vengeful memory against it's owner. There are people who believe that the mirrors had an extraterrestrial origin and were contaminated by aliens.
Logically, they said the contamination killed people. What is your personal opinion?

Answer:
Coincidentally, I wrote an entry on your question in my last book. Apparently you did not read it. I will avoid asking you to refer to the book, fearing that some might think I am using this new book to sell a previous one. So, I am going to repeat here and briefly, some of the most important points.

I. Introduction
II. The story
III. Italian philosopher Tommaso Campanella's explanation
IV. Paris Academy of Science
V. Parapsychology
VI. Psychology and metalogic
VII. Extraterrestrial influence

I. Introduction:
This is one of the most striking and mind-twisting stories in the annals of the black arts, extraterrestrial studies, parapsychology, and alien phenomena.
It is part parapsychological, biological, and part alien.

Part Three: Paranormal mirror and extraterrestrials

The subject was discussed by members of prestigious French academies of science, noted historians, and most recently, a learned group of Anunnaki-Ulema.

II. The story:
This bizarre event took place in France in 1997, and it was described by Del senso delle cose, so it is not my fabrication (As noted by Del senso delle cose):
Antique dealers addressed journalists with a request to warn the collectors of antiques not to buy the mirror, which had the inscription Louis Arpo 1743 on the frame. They said that the mirror had killed almost 38 people during the long history of its existence.
Antique dealers decided to address the media, as the mirror had disappeared. It was found missing when a criminal law professor asked to take photographs of the mirror, to show them at his lectures. "The mirror was kept at a police station after it had killed two people in 1910. However, someone penetrated their storage facilities and stole several things, including the mirror.
We think that the thief will try sell it, that is why we are trying to provide as much information as possible about the mirror to warn potential customers of the danger," a spokesman for the French association of antique collectors said.
The mentioned mirror provoked a cerebral hemorrhage for the people that were looking into it. Some people believed that the mirror was reflecting rays of light in a specific way, whereas other believed that it happened because of the mirror's negative energy that it had stored for hundreds of years.
There were some people, who thought that the mirror was a window another world. There is no common opinion about the antique mirror, but people still try to explain the reason for the mysterious deaths that it had caused.

III. Tommaso Campanella's explanation:
A mirror is like a magnet, thus it is capable of attracting poisonous evaporations and accumulate them on its surface. Italian philosopher Tommaso Campanella (1568-1639) had a rather scary theory about this.

Part Three: Paranormal mirror and extraterrestrials

He stated: "Old women, who do not have warm blood in their veins, who have horrible smell coming out of their mouth and eyes, find that their mirrors become blurred, because moisture drops of their heavy breath stick to the clear cold glass. If their saliva drops on fabric, the fabric decays.
If a child sleeps with an old woman, its days will become shorter and her days will become longer, and the child will die."

IV. Paris Academy of Science:
French scientists discussed the same question a hundred years later. A document of the Paris Academy of Science, dated 1739, stated: "When an old woman approaches a clear mirror and spends a lot of time in front of it, a mirror absorbs a lot of her bad juices. The chemical analysis showed the juices to be very poisonous." Some researchers use this property of mirrors to explain a superstition, which says that one should not come up to a mirror during an ailment.
Poisonous substances that a sick person breathes out stay on the glass of a mirror and then evaporate, causing damage to the health of people who inhale the poisonous air.

V. Parapsychology:
Researchers stated that it was not the chemical sediment of the Louis Arpo mirror that had killed its owners. Poisonous substances on a mirror can be washed away with water very easily.
The mirror has certainly been washed many times. However, a mirror might save some information - it would not be insane to suppose that a mirror has memory. A mirror in a house witnesses all events that happen there.
A mirror reflects dramas and tragedies, stupid and funny things, it reflects beauty and ugliness. At times, people wish a mirror could show episodes that it used to reflect years ago, to playback the past.
A. Vulis wrote in his book Literary Mirrors: "A mirror is always the present, without the past and without the future.

Part Three: Paranormal mirror and extraterrestrials

A mirror is the incarnation of amnesia. It is a streaming moment that disappears forever once it has been reflected."
It is really very hard to believe that a mirror is like a video camera, but it is not excluded that mirrors are capable of remembering something. Visual images are not likely, but it is possible that a mirror can "remember" peculiar features of its owner, like other things can.

VI. Psychology and metalogic:
Doctor Hans Berendt from Israel conducted an interesting experiment with a woman, who had extraordinary sensory abilities.
He asked her to explain the feelings that she experienced from unknown objects inside two identical boxes. The woman said that she had felt a strange feeling of a push from one box, but the thing in the other box was completely different. She said, there was something ancient about it, a dilapidated amphitheatre with huge ancient amphoras. When the doctor opened the boxes, the woman found windowpane pieces in one of them and ancient Roman coins that archaeologists had found in Bethlehem.
Glass fragments in the first box were taken from a window that was broken from a powerful blast in Jerusalem that had killed dozens of people. If all things have certain memory properties, a mirror is no exception, especially when it comes to mirrors with silvery amalgams, because silver is the metal of strong informational capacity.
One should assume that a mirror can radiate the information that it has saved before. This radiation might affect a human being. One should be very careful before hanging an old mirror in a room.
It might be filled with negative energy. An old mirror with a rich history often causes strange dreams full of bizarre images; it might evoke unusual desires, inexplicable fears and so on.
Most likely, a mirror remembers the condition, emotions and feelings that a human being had. Most likely, a mirror keeps the information, and remembers not images, but the meaning of them. This meaning might affect the mind of a new owner.

Part Three: Paranormal mirror and extraterrestrials

VII. Extraterrestrial influence:
An Anunnaki-Ulema stated that "everything in the universe has memory, including matter. Thus we have spatial memory, metal memory (memory metal), time memory, emotional memory, parallel memory, multidimensional memory, and so on. All objects retain a depot of events and vibes that have occurred around them. Some of the depot's contents is of a positive nature, while other parts of the contents are of a negative nature. If an object is of extraterrestrial origin, it could radiate vibes that fatally affect the mind.
Health will deteriorate, and death becomes imminent." A type of mirror reported in Anunnaki-Ulema literature is called the Miraya, a very sophisticated tool allegedly used by the Anunnaki to monitor time and space, and the activities of other extraterrestrial races. The Miraya can be deadly if used by humans.
Another type of mirror is called a Mnaizar (small Minzar), a sort of table-magnifier made out of plasma-energy, that Ulema-Anunnaki use to track events and produce supernatural phenomena such as teleportation, and metals' transmutation.
The Mnaizar is a highly sophisticated instrument originally developed by the Anunnaki while they inhabited Earth. The Ulema have several copies of these mirrors.
Ulema W. Li stated that it is very possible that the French mirror is some sort of version of the Mnaizar. It retains memory, and even projects a holographic calendar of future events. Humans who gaze at this sort of mirror will expose themselves to great danger. The Mnaizar emits undetected fatal radiation."

*** *** ***

Part Three: Anunnaki type of civilization

Anunnaki type of civilization

Questions by Reverend Nancy Santos.

Question: What type of civilization are the Anunnaki at this moment in time? A Type One, Two, Three, or other civilization? According to Professor Michio Kaku, a theoretical physicist from New York University, a Type One is a civilization is one that gets there energy from all planets. Type Two Civilization is a (Stellar) getting energy from their, Mother Sun only! Type Three Civilization gets their Energy from all the suns in our universe and the next.
Answer:
You don't need to classify the Anunnaki in any category. On Earth, we love to classify people, categorize subjects, create lists; list of the year's best in this or that, list of the worst in this and that, the list of the best dressed stars, the list of the worst dressed stars, David Letterman's list of 10, and so on. This is how human minds work: Classification, rating, grades, etc.

In the immensity of the universe, the galactic mind works differently, and we will talk one day about the "Galactic Mind", the "Universal Mind", the "Supersymetric Mind", etc.
It is necessary sometimes to classify a subject, a topic, a product, or even – in this case, as you have asked– a type of civilization, in order to understand what level of accomplishment such and such a civilization has reached. This is necessary, especially when a civilization is new, and/or when a civilization is going through multiple phases/stages of development. This does not apply to the Anunnaki and other highly developed galactic civilizations, simply because the human mind cannot fully understand the extremely high and extraordinary standards/levels of technology and science of civilizations which are millions, perhaps billions of years ahead of us.
The classification given by Dr. Kaku is wonderful, and appeals to many of us. Our mind can understand it, or at least cope with it.

Part Three: Anunnaki type of civilization

In the cosmos, galactic civilizations evolve differently, and have nothing to do with "Getting energy from their, Mother Sun", or getting "energy from all planets."
In our Solar system, we have one sun. In other galactic systems, some planets have more than one sun, and more than one moon. So we cannot, and should not define and classify alien civilizations, by why and how they get their energies; from the sun or other sources.
However, and according to Ulema Bader El-din, Berkov, and Oppenheimer, the Anunnaki civilization has reached its ultimate level some 30,000.000 years ago.
It is difficult to define "Ultimate level", because we do not understand all the advancement levels of alien communities. We do not know who they are. Where they are? How many are they in the universe?

*** *** ***

Part Three: Anunnaki immaturity, emotional control, jealousy, sin?

Anunnaki immaturity, emotional control, jealousy, sin?

Questions by Reverend Nancy Santos.

Question: Have the Anunnaki matured away from their immaturity in emotional control, past stories of jealousy, power, etc., sin?
Answer:
On what base(s) or ground, have you created this opinion of yours? How did you know about Anunnaki's maturity or immaturity? Jealousy, sin, etc.? The only and very few authentic and authoritative references (Historical, chronological, linguistic, religious, epistemological, etymological, artistic, archeological, anthropological, and of course cosmological) on the Anunnaki are found in:

- **1-The Akkadian clay tablets texts:**

The Akkadian clay tablets texts, (Nineveh Library of Ashur-ba-Nipal) which millions of readers in the West cannot read. And almost 99% of those who read about ufology and related topics have based their opinions about the Anunnaki (and also other aliens as well), on personal interpretations of very crafty authors with fabulous and phantasmagorical theories that defy logic and common sense.
Unless you know Akkadian, Old Babylonian, Ugaritic, Hittite, Assyrian, and Phoenician languages, you cannot form any opinion on the Anunnaki. However, you can shape a pretty clear idea about the Anunnaki, by reading the works and translations of the early Assyriologists and eminent linguists, who deciphered and translated the Akkadian cuneiform tablets in the 19th and early 20th centuries. Unfortunately, very few readers in the West are interested in these literary and academic publications, because they are not fun – or so they think!

Part Three: Anunnaki immaturity, emotional control, jealousy, sin?

They would rather prefer to read paperback books, and stories by contemporary authors who have managed to somehow mesmerize the public with fabulous stories and extraordinary interpretations, which is why their books have become bestsellers, whilst the serious and well-researched books on the history and civilization of Mesopotamia, Babylon, Sumer, Assyria, Chaldea, Akkad, Ugarit, and Anunnaki are largely ignored and forgotten under a heavy layer of dust in college libraries, and in the archives of rarely visited museums.
But I have some good news for you.
In many works by archeologists, historians, linguists and museum curators (From the early 1810 to the mid 20th century), you can find translations of Akkadian and Old Babylonian texts, referring to how and why the Sumerians depicted the Anunnaki as they did. Please read the serious books written by acclaimed scholars, and not the third rate novels, commercial essays, paperbacks, and idiotic blogs on the Internet!!
In those translations by academicians and noted historians, you will find plenty of stories about the emotions, feelings, and the way of life of the Anunnaki, as depicted by Babylonian scribes and writers in the Akkadian language, and proto-Babylonian. These stories encompass all sorts of dramas and soap operas, like gods raping women, Anunnaki Sinhars (Leaders) fighting each other, an Anunnaki god who planned the destruction of the human race; Anunnaki goddesses with extreme anger and legendary jealousy, so on. But bear in mind, those Anunnaki stories came from the mouth of fabulous story-tellers in Sumer. And this was intentional on their part.
They wanted to portray the Anunnaki as divine-human, so at least they could share some common and similar traits with them. The Greeks did the very same thing.
Some of their deities were jealous, ferocious, malicious and yes, some were rapists and sexual predators!!
Something else you should remember:
The Anunnaki who descended to Earth (Sumer, Phoenicia, Turkey) are quite different from the Anunnaki who were, and still are in Nibiru!

Part Three: Anunnaki immaturity, emotional control, jealousy, sin?

Earth's Anunnaki had to look in some way, somehow not very much different from humans, otherwise the Babylonians would have not tried to identify and associate their legendary kings with the Anunnaki kings.

- **2-The Bible:**

Lafayette said, "I will be brief. The Old Testament offered contradicting, convergent and divergent portrayals of the Anunnaki, usually referred to as Rephaim, Anakim, Nephilim, B'nai Elohim, so on.
Don't count on these Biblical accounts. The early Hebrew scribes borrowed their major Biblical stories from the myths and religions of Babylon, Ugarit, Amrit and Phoenicia.

As a matter of fact, Yahweh was Baal-El, the Ugaritic-Phoenician god. And almost all the powerful traits and virtues of Enki and Ea were transferred to the attributes of Jehovah (Yahweh, the god of the Israelites), even Daniel was copied from the Phoenician myth of Danel (Ugarit).
This is a fact.
You can read several translations of this myth as well as numerous Ugaritic texts referring to the early prototypes and characteristics of Yahweh found in the depiction of the Ugaritic deities. Having said that, bear in mind that the Biblical depiction of the Anunnaki in various forms and names is not accurate. In fact, they are hostile, and there are reasons for doing so.
Firstly, Abraham and Moses desperately wanted to establish an identity for their people.
In ancient times, a nation was usually associated with its deities. If their god was strong and all mighty, then they become a powerful and rightful nation.
If, however, you have a bad/weak god, you end up with a bad/weak nation. Secondly, the early Israelites feared the expansion of the Phoenician cults. They were a direct threat to Yahweh, their own god.

Part Three: Anunnaki immaturity, emotional control, jealousy, sin?

The Israelite prophets waged hysterical wars against the gods of Tyre, Sidon, Byblos, Arwad, Ugarit and Amrit.
Consequently, they had to assassinate the character of all other gods, and portray Yahweh as the only, the mightiest and most righteous god of all. Therefore, what you have read in the Bible about the sin, the anger, the jealousy, the vices of the Anunnaki, were written by scribes who had to defend their own interests, authority, the pride of their nation, their raison d'etre, and the status/importance/legitimacy of their god, and above all, to justify the reasons for conquering the lands of their neighbors, and building their new cities on territories taken away from their legitimate owners.
Yes, the Bible is the most colorful propaganda literature in the world."

3- Phoenician and Anatolian texts and archeological finds:
You can learn a lot about the Anunnaki from studying slabs, texts, obelisks and cylinder seals found in Turkey, Arwad, Malta, Cyprus, Ugarit, Amrit, Phoenicia, Armenia (Urartu, Cilicia), Byblos, Batroun, Sidon, Afkah, Amchit and Tyre in Lebanon (Ancient Phoenicia). In addition, there are several myths and poems in Phoenician and Ugaritic that tell us about the traits and characteristics of the Anunnaki.
Worth mentioning here is that none of these archeological finds indicate what you have stated: "Anunnaki immaturity, jealousy, control, etc." On the contrary, the Anatolian and Phoenician texts and slabs offered us a different picture of the Anunnaki, in sharp contrast to the Hebrew depiction of the Anunnaki.
Before passing judgment on the Anunnaki, we should first refer to historical sources, and above all to original texts written in Akkadian/Sumerian, Babylonian and Phoenician.
What you read on the Internet (Usually written by ignorant red necks, self-proclaimed channelers and psychics, and people totally unfamiliar with Middle Eastern and Near Eastern languages) is pure fabrication.
Stick to the historical and linguistic facts!

Anunnaki management skills

Questions by Reverend Nancy Santos.

Question: Have they learned to manage their emotions and improve their management skills?
Answer:
What kind of management skills are you talking about?
Do you think Anunnaki have or need to have IBM, Kentucky Fried Chicken, Video Professor, E-Harmony, and E-bay on Nibiru, to properly improve corporation and management skills?

- The Anunnaki created the human race.
- The Anunnaki conquered the frontiers of time and space.
- The Anunnaki penetrated the depth and infinity of the universe.
- The Anunnaki's longevity exceeds 450,000 years.
- The Anunnaki conquered the fastest speed in the known cosmos, faster than the speed of light.

Well, my dear Nancy, all of the above require lots of management skills.
They already have great management skills.
Oh yes! They got it millions of years ago!!

*** *** ***

Part Three: The Anunnaki's God: A critical God?

The Anunnaki's God: A critical God?

Question by Reverend Nancy Santos.

Question: Are the Anunnaki a Critical God?
No forgiveness, and no exceptions as in an eye for an eye and a tooth for a tooth?
Answer:
The Anunnaki do not have a God.
The God we know (Judeo-Christian-Muslim God) was invented by an Iraqi man called Abraham (Real name Av-Ram, and he was born in Ur in Mesopotamia, modern day Iraq.) And this God called Yahweh or Jehovah by the Hebrews was in fact a replica of the Anunnaki Ea-Enki lords, and later on embellished with a divine caricature borrowed from the Ugaritic-Phoenician pagan god Baal, El.
The concept of God, or one God was reinforced by Moses; a god he met in the bushes! Quite a rendez-vous!
The same God he had a chat with on Mount Sinai, where he received the 10 Commandments! The truth I tell you, Yahweh was modeled after the Anunnaki lords who descended on Iraq, and the Phoenician Baal (Ba'al Hadadd) of Tyre and Ugarit.
Besides, Moses did not need to go all the way up to the top of the mountain to get his Commandments.
They were already available to him in Egypt, while he served as a chief advisor and a military commander to the Pharaoh. The 10 Commandments were in fact 613 Commandments. Almost 80% of these Hebraic Commandments were taken from the Egyptian scriptures and the Egyptian Book of the Dead!!
Some 50 years ago, German and French archeologists found the Famous "Byblos Building Inscriptions" which specifically contained the name of Yahweh as Yaw, and Ya-weh (Phoenician pronunciation) centuries before Moses announced to his people the name of their Hebrew God.
God was created by Man.

Part Three: The Anunnaki's God: A critical God?

However, the Anunnaki have A Maha-Sinhar, also called Gala-Amroot, and Baalshamrout, which means a great lord. He/she is in charge. He is both female and male, the creator/creatrice of all intelligent life-forms on Earth.

On Nibiru and in the galactic infinity, the Maha-Sinhar is a merciful lord. Her/his wisdom is based upon a complete understanding of Donia (The world; the universe). Her/his truth is founded in science; a positive and "friendly" science.

"No exceptions as in an eye for an eye and a tooth for a tooth?" as you have stated, is an alarming truth, because it is part of early Man's literature. Yes, Nancy, you are right this time, if you associate this phrase with the God we have learned about from the Israelites.

Some of the Anunnaki so-called gods who descended to Earth (Sumer/Assyria) displayed anger, vengeance et al, as depicted by scribes on planet Earth. This primordial depiction gave birth to the character, persona and traits of the Hebrew God who become the God of the Christians and the Muslims.

But...but NOT to the early Gnostic Christians (The Real and first Christians), for they understood that the Judaic God was a vicious, vengeful and aggressive villain-god!

The Anunnaki's God on Earth was a "Critical God" as you have correctly stated.

The Anunnaki so-called God on Nibiru is just the opposite!

This is not a personal attack on Judaism and Christianity and/or Islam. My favorite mentors/teachers were Mordachai ben Zvi and N. ben Yacob. I was raised as a Roman-Catholic and as a Jew. And I have served the Vatican and the Jewish community and media in several roles and capacities.

As to my affiliation with Islam, (I am not a Muslim) I have studied the Koran and Arabic literature for more than 55 years, and I have taught Islamic literature and language for decades, in addition to which I have studied the Sharia, the Fukh, and Islamic laws and procedures for a very long time, and appeared before Islamic courts as an attorney at law; a tradition I became very fond of!

Part Three: Benevolent and malevolent Anunnaki gods

Benevolent and malevolent Anunnaki gods

Question by Reverend Nancy Santos.

Question: Is there a benevolent and a malevolent faction of Anunnaki Gods?
Answer:
Not in their homeland, and not on their planet!
On Earth, yes!
And on Earth in ancient times, not today.
Ancient stories and inscriptions on clay tablets found in Iraq revealed a great deal of violence, aggression, and malevolence of the Anunnaki gods.

- **a**-The Epic of Gilgamesh,
- **b**-the Descent of Ishtar to Kurnugi (Hell),
- **c**-The Enuma Elish,
- **d**-The exploits of Marduk,
- **e**-The Akkadian epic of creation,
- **f**-The story of the fight between Tiamat and Marduk,
- **g**-The struggle between the Anunnaki lords, Ea, Enki, Anu,
- **h**-The story of the revolt of the Igigi,
- **i**-The story of the rape of an Anunnaki goddess by an Anunnaki god/king,
- **j**-The story of the genetic creation of the first Man by slaughtering an Igigi god,
- **k**-The poems and literature of Babylon (Ishtar, Inanna, Eabani, Enkidu, etc.)

All have revealed the good and bad aspects of the Anunnaki gods on Earth, as written by the Babylonian scribes. But these stories are pure literature, myths, legends, and tales, and exclusively related to Earth's Anunnaki. The truth of these events can only be found within the manuscripts/scrolls of the Anunnaki-Ulema.

Part Three: Clairvoyance (Telepathic communication/vision) between members of the same family

Clairvoyance (Telepathic communication/vision) between members of the same family

Question from his Eminence, Archbishop Frédéric Burcklé von Aarburg. Brussels, Belgium.

Question: Y a-t-il une voyance entre les membres d'une meme famille? (Ce que disent les Mormons). Je pense que nous sommes des récepteurs d'ondes, peut etre plus fortes émanant d'une famille. Mon grand père paternel est décédé au milieu d'une haine familiale énorme, la principale raison en était que notre famille étant Alsacienne, mon grand père se trouva du coté de l'occupant, alors que mon père fut dans la résistance.
Je résidais à l'époque entre Bruxelles et Amsterdam; Je décidais de faire dire une messe pour mon grand père 6 mois après son déces; Bien sur je fis en sorte de calculer quel jour je serais présent pour la dite messe à Bruxelles;
Il se fit que je ne pouvais etre à Bruxelles le jour de la messe; Le soir j'ai téléphoné à Paris et mon père m'a déclaré: Figure toi que je ne sais pourquoi aujourd'hui mes pas m'ont porté à telle Eglise (il n'allait jamais plus à l'Eglise) à 18heures (heure de la messe prévue à Bruxelles) et j'ai prié et allumé un cierge pour mon père (mon grand père)
Il se trouve donc que, ce qui est logique, il fit le devoir que je lui avait mentalement suggéré (c'est mon interprétation)

Translation in brief: Is there clairvoyance (Telepathic communication/vision) between members of the same family?

Answer:
Science has split interpretations on the subject. However, such telepathic communication does occur quite often, especially between siblings and members of the same family, who share a strong affectionate bondage.
This telepathic phenomenon is usually reinforced in cases, when two members of the same family are deeply concerned with one

Part Three: Clairvoyance (Telepathic communication/vision) between members of the same family

subject and/or a situation that tie(s) them very closely to each other; such occurrences are manifested in cases of death, imminent threat, accentuated anxiety, fear, a deep concern, and an urgent need to reach other.
Clairvoyance rapport and/or mental suggestion can be taught.
It is a matter of:

a-Rapport:
- 1-Determination of two persons or more who wish to contact each other,
- 2-Concentration on the same subject or object,
- 3- Parties' agreeing on contacting each other at a specific time,
- 4-Parties willingness to be patient;
- 5-One party to act as a recipient (A receiver),
- 6-Another party to act as an emitter (Sender) of the message.
- 7-The locale is very important. The parties involved should not be distracted.

b-Message:
The message should be:
- 1-Clear and precise,
- 2-Brief,
- 3-Totally mental, meaning no words are pronounced, no phrases are used. The message is transmitted as a mental image/wave. (Ondulation; ondes)
- 4-Suggested by a single person directed toward one single person. No mass communication is to be considered.
- 5-The sender (Emitter) must be younger than the recipient, except when a message is sent by a female sender, such as mother and sister, NOT a wife or a girlfriend.

"Yes, I agree with you, Your Eminence, your mental suggestion and transmission of your message were effective..." said Ulema de Lafayette.

Part Three: Anunnaki's creation of early humans & Earth original species

On the Anunnaki's creation of early humans and Earth original species

Questions by Angelique Marquise, New York, New York.

Question: Were the quasi-humans (lifeforms) the Anunnaki encountered (when they first came to earth) a natural product of evolution, or genetically manipulated by the Igigi / prior ET?

Answer:
Anunnaki-Ulema records show that Earth was inhabited by 47 different kinds of human species. The book "Ilmu Al Donia" (Knowledge of the Universe or the World) indicates 36 intelligent life-forms, as ten were considered animal-human/bestial humans. Many species existed on Earth, long before the Anunnaki landed on Earth.

Some were the result of:

- **a**-Photo-synthesis;
- **b**-Metabolism;
- **c**-Molecular metamorphosis;
- **d**-Cosmic dust;
- **e**-Ma'iya, meaning verbatim "Aquatic fertilization". In other words, a blend of photo-synthesis and maritime bacteria;
- **f**-Etc, etc

As you can see, some of these species were bio-organic causes and effects. Consequently, a large number of these species were the development of natural elements found on Earth, or "imported" from other celestial bodies, stars, planets, comets, cosmic dust, collisions between spatial molecules, clay found in asteroids, etc...

Part Three: Anunnaki's creation of early humans & Earth original species

So, when the Anunnaki, Igigi, the Lyrans and other extraterrestrial races landed on Earth, this planet already had a large variety of quasi-human forms.

Some of these quasi-human life-forms were captured by the Anunnaki while exploring Central Africa, Brazil, Madagascar and other regions of the planet.
They conducted several genetic operations on these life-forms, but their experiments failed miserably. Simply put, they gave up.
Then, they decided to use the genes or DNA of one of the Igigi gods (Egeshu) and mixed the extract with elements from the Earth, such as Tourba, Tourab (Dirt, Clay, etc.)
This was written in the Akkadian clay tablets, known to Western readers as the Sumerian tablets. What is not totally known to many is the fact, that Igigi also attempted to create humans, and of course they failed, because they are not geneticists like the Anunnaki. They were expert mineralogists, topographers and agriculture/irrigation experts.

Question: Have we ever found skeletons and bones of them and what do we call them? (Australopithecus, Afarensis, Homo habilis, Erectus, Cro-magnon?)
Answer:
All of the above, of course, not taking into consideration a proper chronology. What you have listed are science and anthropological terms.
In Anunnaki Ulemite literature, they are called differently. Names like:
- 1-Baha'em
- 2-Adamath
- 3-Adamu
- 4-Zakkar
- 5-Jens
- 6-Behemoth
- 7-So on. The list is endless.

Part Three: All human beings do not come from the same origin

All human beings do not come from the same origin

Questions by Angelique Marquise, New York, New York.

Question: Have the Anunnaki created/genetically upgraded species on other planets?
If so, what has been the outcome?
Answer:
No, the Anunnaki did not create or upgrade species on other planets.

Question: Page 138 of book one of the three books of Ramadosh mentions that though we are all human beings, we do not come from the same origin.
Some were born here on Earth, others were born somewhere else, in some other dimensions and far different spheres.
Can you please explain in further detail what do you mean by that, and by us being created according to different specifications?
Answer:

- I. Introduction
- II. First category of humans
- Man (Humans) created on Earth from clay
- III. Second category of humans
- IV. An'th-Khalka
- V. The Earth-made human creatures created from a cell
- VI. The space-made human creatures
- VII. The Basharma early creatures
- VIII. Metabolism and the oceans-made human creatures
- IX. Bashar category
- X. An-Nafar Jinmarkah humans

Part Three: All human beings do not come from the same origin

- XI. The Shula
- Humans with programmed brains
- At the time we were created, three things happened to us
- a-The Brain Motor
- b- The vibrational dimension
- c- The Conduit=Health/Youth/Longevity
- XII. The Shula species
- XIII. The Emim
- XIV. Ezakarerdi, "E-zakar-erdi "Azakar.Ki"
- XV. Ezeridim
- XVI. Fari-narif "Fari-Hanif"
- XVII. The Anunnaki-Ulema from Ashtari.

*** *** ***

Answers by Ulema Maximillien de Lafayette
Note: Excerpts from his writings/Kiraat:

I. Introduction:
According to Maximillien de Lafayette , The Earth was populated with 47 different quasi-human life-forms, but other scholars have stated that 36 different intelligent life-forms inhabited the Earth.
There is a big difference between quasi-humans and intelligent life-forms. And this distinction explains the difference in the origin of the human race(s), and the creation of Man according to different specifications. I will try to explain, but it is quite complicated. There are numerous tales about the creation of Man, emanating from various cultures, civilizations and periods. The Bible told us, that Man was created by God. Almost all religions claimed a divine source for the creation of Man on Earth. However, the Gnostics believe that Man, Earth and the Universe we know were created by an "Evil God", and there is nothing divine or holy in his attributes.

Part Three: All human beings do not come from the same origin

The leading concept Angelique, is that "god" or "the gods" used clay from Earth to fashion Man.
Of course, the methods and processes of creation are not similar, but the material used in the creation process is almost the same. This is of course, related exclusively to humans who were created on Earth; more precisely on dry land. It does also apply to humans who were created elsewhere, or life-forms which were created from other substances, and we will talk about this. Later on, we will briefly approach different concepts and methods of creation throughout the ages, and the phases of development of human civilizations. But before we do that, let's bring out the concept of creating man from clay on Earth, because it is almost universal.

II. First category of humans:
Man (Humans) created on Earth from clay.
Before we begin Angelique, please allow me to add this note on the Assyrian word Dadmi, and the Arabic word Adam, and the Ana'kh/Ulemite words Chaii, and Chaiturabi because they are essential.
Chaii means human life. In the Book of Rama-Dosh, the scribes put strong emphasis on the expression "human being life", to bring to the attention of the adept, the origin of life and mankind on Earth, vis-à-vis other living "super" beings in the cosmos.
The Ana'kh word Chaii appeared in various passages of the book, but the most important instance is when the word appeared as "Chaiturabi", thus shedding light on the creation of man from clay. From the Ana'kh Chaii, the Hebrew word Chay or Chai (Pronounced like Jose in Spanish) was derived, which means life. Chaiturabi means lively clay. It is composed of two words:
- **a**-Chai (Life);
- **b**-Turabi (Dirt; dust; earth; soil; clay.)

From Turabi, derived the ancient Arabic word Turab, which means exactly the same thing.

Part Three: All human beings do not come from the same origin

From the Ana'kh Chai, as you already know, came the Hebrew word Chay or Chai which means life. In the first edition of the Aramaic/Arabic Bible, we found this sentence: "Anta min al turab, wa ila turan ta'hoodou." Translated verbatim: "You are *(anta)* from *(min)* dirt *(turab)*, and *(wa)* to *(ila)* dirt *(turab)* you shall return *(ta'houdou)*.

The general meaning of Chaiturabi is the genetic creation of the Adama species (First humans; primitive beings; human prototypes...) by the Anunnaki, and in-vitro fertilization by Ninti, Enki, and other goddesses in a laboratory called a "Chimiti". This creation was mentioned in Sumerian, Akkadian, and Assyrian texts.

The idea or concept of the creation of mankind from clay is universal, and appeared in many mythologies, cosmogenies, and religions such as that of the Ugaritic, Phoenician, Babylonian, Chaldean, Mesopotamian, Assyrian, Sumerian, Ana'kh, Ulemite, Greek, African, Aztec, Mongolian, Egyptian, Islamic, and Christian religions.

Dadmim "Admi", "Adamai", "Adami": Ana'kh-Ulemite words which mean the human race; people on Earth; mankind. In Arabic, it is Adami, which means man. From Dadmin and Admi, derived the Assyrian Dadmi, which means mankind and people. From Adami, came the name Adam.

III. Second category of humans:
Akama-ra:
According to the Ulema, the Akama-ra were the first beings who were allowed by the Anunnaki (Enki and Inanna) to date the "Women of Light", who were quarantined on earth in what is today the Arab Peninsular and Bahrain.

M. de Lafayette explained the meaning of "Bahrain": In Arabic, Baha means one sea, and Bahrain means two seas. The Akama-ra were genetically created by the Anunnaki on their home planet of Ashtari (Nibiru), and were transported to planet earth on Anunnaki's spaceships, called Merkabahs.

Part Three: All human beings do not come from the same origin

IV. An'th-Khalka:
Creation of the first humans, and different categories of human beings:
Composed of two words:
- **a**-An'th, which means race; people.
- **b**-Khalka, which means creation; birth.

From An'th, is derived the Arabic word Ounth, which means people, humans, human race. And from Khalka, is derived the Arabic word Khalika, which means creation of the human beings.
Excerpts from Ulema's Kira'at (Reading):
Mankind was not created by one single Sumerian god. More than one Anunnaki participated in the creation of mankind.
And contrary to common belief, the Anunnaki were not the first extraterrestrials and gods to create a human from clay. Many other deities from different pantheons also created man from clay. For instance, Khnum "Kneph" (Meaning: To build, to unify in Egyptian) was one of the oldest Egyptian gods who created mankind from clay on a potter's wheel. Khnum became a variation of Ptah.
The Anunnaki first landed in Phoenicia, where they established their first colonies, and short thereafter, they created their most elaborate medical center on the Island of Arwad, then a Phoenician territory. However, the Anunnaki ameliorated their genetic creations, and upgraded early human forms and primitive humans in their laboratories in Sumer.
The Sumerian texts, and their translations in western languages, gave more exposure to the Anunnaki of Sumer than to the other and equally powerful Anunnaki of Phoenicia and Central Africa.
The Sumerian texts include various versions of the creation of mankind by a multitude of Anunnaki gods and goddesses. Some passages in the Sumerian texts refer to different creators, as well as to multiple genetic experiments.
There is no reference to one singular genetic creation of the early human races, or a solid certainty to the fact that mankind was genetically created by one single god. In fact, a multitude of gods and goddesses created the human race, as it exists today in its final form.

Part Three: All human beings do not come from the same origin

V. The Earth-made human creatures created from a cell:

The early quasi-human beings were created from a single cell.

The Ulema said that the Anunnaki's matrix mentioned earth-made quasi human creatures who originated from single cell organisms. Those creatures were an organism that looked like bacteria. And the primordial bacterium was in fact, the very first life-form on planet earth. These appeared as tiny mini-microscopic organisms that used chemical energy (chemosynthesis). They did not need the sun to grow and develop via photosynthesis.

In fact, these early organisms existed long before photosynthesis developed on planet earth.

This explains the reason for their deformity, and horrific dysmorphic features (Dysmorphism).

Those creatures were Earth-made, and first appeared in Australia, Brazil, and Madagascar, but not in Africa. They were not created by any "God".

VI. The space-made human creatures:

Some of the very early human races (The genes, DNA) were originally created in space. Their life started within the clay found inside comets. The amazing aspect of this explanation is the fact that only recently, leading scientists and university professors in the United Kingdom have stated, that in fact, the inside of comets contains gluey material identical to heated clay.

Once this comet clay is mixed with earth's water, its creates cells, molecules and membranes. In other words: LIFE. Thus, these humans or life-forms were not created by a "God".

VII. The Basharma early creatures:

Metabolism and the ocean-made human creatures:

The Anunnaki's matrix also revealed the existence and origin of early human-like creatures who lived at the bottom of the oceans. The Ulema explained that one of the earliest life-forms on planet earth began at the very bottom of the oceans, where metabolism originated.

Part Three: All human beings do not come from the same origin

VIII. Metabolism created an early human-like form:
Those creatures had a human skull, two eyes without retina, two legs and four long arms, but no nose, no ears, and no hair on their bodies.
They were called the Basharma'h. (Bashar means human race, and Ma'h means water.) Later on in history, these two words were added to several ancient Near and Middle Eastern languages; Mem in Hebrew, Mayim in ancient Aramaic; Ma' or Maay in Arabic, etc...

IX. Bashar category:
According to the Ulema, Bashar (Human beings) appeared on planet earth in a multitude of forms and shapes.

Excerpt from their Kira'at (Reading):
On planet earth existed many different human races for millions of years. Some are known to us, while many others are totally unknown because they have vanished without leaving a trace.
The truth is that they have left many traces, but we did not discover them yet.
In the near future, we will discover some of their remains, and a new chapter on the history of mankind will be written.
However, in 2003, the skeletons of four vanished early forms of humans (who did not look like humans) were discovered by English archeologists and anthropologists, but were shrouded in secrecy, and their discoveries were never made public for many reasons. These skeletons were about 8ft to 9ft tall, possessed a thin long tail, and their remains were discovered in England, Germany, Africa and Palestine/ what is today known as Israel.
Two leading and extremely powerful Catholic theologians were behind the cover-up. Some of those early quasi-human forms were 10 feet in height, and others less than 2 feet, and looked like hobbits.
Those species were created by various extraterrestrial races. The Anunnaki did not take part in the creation process of these very tall and very small quasi-humans.
The extraterrestrials created them on planet earth.

Part Three: All human beings do not come from the same origin

But there are other early human beings who were created in space, and on other planets, and like the very small and very tall species, who were not part of the evolutionary process of the modern human beings.

In total, 36 (Some say 46) different human and quasi-human species lived on planet earth in many regions of the globe. And none of them were created by the God we know and worship. After all, they did not look like humans, and if we have to believe that humans were created in the image of God, as Judaism, Christianity and Islam tell us, then, most certainly those early 36 different species who looked like ferocious beasts, were not made in the image of God.

Because they were created in many regions of planet earth, and interbred around the globe, new horrifying species populated the planet. So the "out-of-Africa" theory is entirely wrong. Humanity did neither start in, nor expand from Africa. All those species died out after very short lifespans, as they did not have installed in their brains, the Anunnaki's Conduit.

X. An-Nafar Jinmarkah humans:

An-Nafar Jinmarkah is the name for the humans who walked on three legs, supposedly created by non-terrestrial geneticists who have visited earth some 450,000 years ago.

Some ufologists suggest that they were genetically created by the Igigi. Some authors have claimed that the Igigi have created a very primitive form of human beings, lacking intelligence and mobility. The Igigi considered the early quasi-humans to be not much more than machines with limited mental faculties, and those early forms of humans looked like apes.

The earth was extremely cold at that time (between ice ages), and the Igigi had to cover the human bodies with lots of hair to protect them from the elements. It took the quasi-human race thousands of years to evolve into an early human form, and even then not totally human, still looking like apes.

Some of them had bizarre skulls and facial bones. The Igigi actually experimented a bit with the early human-forms.

Part Three: All human beings do not come from the same origin

First, they created the "Nafar Jinmarkah" meaning 'individual on three legs.' They consisted of a very strong physical body but it lacked agility. These bodies were created to carry heavy loads. The purpose of three was to support heavy loads that they could lift and carry. Later on, the Igigi worked on a new human form that consisted of a body with only two legs, in order to bring speed and better agility. Yet, early humans remained terrifying, looking nothing like the Biblical descriptions. The Igigi tried several times. And each time, they faced a problem in designing the human skull. Early Igigi creators did not want to put brains inside the skull so the human-like forms would not think. These early human-forms were the world's first biological robots.

XI. The Shula with programmed brains:
Humans with programmed brains.
From the Secret Doctrine of the Ulema.
According to M. de Lafayette, the Ulema said that the many and different categories of early humans were not (All of them) mentioned in the Akkadian tablets. Those "human creatures" mentioned in the Babylonian epics were intentionally selected by the Babylonian scribes, and authors of Mesopotamian myths for specific reasons. One of the early intelligent human races were the Shula. They were different from all the other species, because they had a well-developed brain, which was programmed by the Anunnaki. This race was experimented upon in Arwad. The Shula were about 5ft 1 to 5ft 4 on average, on the chubby side in stature, and more resourceful than we are today, as they had larger brains.

In one of his fascinating Kira'ats, Ulema ben Zvi said:
- **1-**You can reprogram yourself and adjust your genes. The Anunnaki, and the sages of Melkart taught the enlightened ones, and the righteous ones how to do it.
- **2-**Your body is a biological machine, like so many other machines here on Earth, in the universe, and beyond.

Part Three: All human beings do not come from the same origin

- 3-Some machines run on fuel, others on atomic energy...your body is very special, and a great mystery, because it runs on a substance known only to very few people in the world.

Is it your blood?
Is it the oxygen you breathe in the air?
Is it your soul?
Is it the mind of God?
Is it your essence, your Chi, your DNA, or all of the above? Or perhaps something we cannot touch, we cannot see, we cannot measure, and consequently we cannot understand, or be sure of?

- 4-You were taught that the human body is created from a male's semen and a female's eggs. That is very true. But this semen and these eggs must have "something" extraordinary, something non-physical to allow a physical human body to perform physical and non-physical acts such as writing poetry, epics, music, symphonies, and love letters, to measure light, to read others' thoughts, to communicate telepathically, to fall in love, to think about new ideas, and possibly to escape the laws of physics. This very special and extraordinary "something" is somewhere...not necessarily in the semen and the eggs...
- 5-Although, we are all human beings, the truth is, we did not all come from the same origin. Some were born here on earth, others were born elsewhere...in other dimensions and far distant spheres. And yet, we have many things in common, because we were created by the same Khalek (Creator,) and his assistants.
- 6-We are not an assembly-line product. We are not like automobiles, all manufactured and assembled exactly the same way, by the same plant.
- 7-This is why each one of us is different. And this difference exists, because each one of us was created in a different plant, according to different specifications, and a very distinct genetic-programming process.

Part Three: All human beings do not come from the same origin

- **8**-Those who created us know these specifications and what went into our creation, thus, they can reprogram us, alter our properties, give us a new form, new faculties, and reduce or increase our life span.

At the time we were created, three things happened to us:
- **9**-At the time we were created (designed, produced, manufactured, etc.), three things happened to us, and are directly related to (a) intelligence, (b) luck/success in life, and (c) health/youth/longevity.

a-The Brain Motor:
A brain was designed and instantly tested.
The brain was created before the body took shape and form.
And in this brain, all faculties were installed.
A copy or blueprint of the brain (Mind) was duplicated and stored in an etheric (fourth) dimension aka "ED" (This is the best way we can describe this dimension for now). This ED is similar to a cosmic net that consists of trillions and millions of trillions of canals, stations, terminals and channels, all connected together, yet functioning separately according to very specific frequencies and vibrations.
Once these faculties are installed and begin to function, no matter at what rate or level, they become a permanent and final fixture of our thinking process, i.e. intelligence, logic, creativity, etc.
However, these faculties will get better and better by constant learning and acquiring new knowledge.
This is only possible, if the Conduit (Installed by the An. Na. Ki or other non-terrestrial geneticists-creators in your brain's cells) has more room for improvement.
The capacity of the Conduit is usually detected at an early age, between 3 and 5.
Many of the greatest geniuses on earth manifested the Conduit's capacity and potentials during this short and early period of time.

Part Three: All human beings do not come from the same origin

b- The vibrational dimension:
Creation of a place for the vibrations of our mind.
Nothing in the physical and non-physical dimensions exists, continues to exist, and functions, without vibrations and frequencies. When these rays (Vibrations and frequencies) get damaged or cease to radiate or emanate, the organism stops functioning.
In other words, the brain (Mind) as a motor dies out instantly. When our creators designed this motor during the first stage of manufacturing us, they carefully tested and measured the frequencies and vibrations of the brain, and adjusted the level of its creativity.
At this very moment, they created a space for this creativity, called the vibrational dimension.
Now, if these vibrations resonate in synchronization with the vibrations of the canals and channels of the cosmic net, the person who has these kind of vibrations will be a very luck y person, but not necessarily a righteous one. In other words, either you were born lucky, or unlucky, and you are going to stay lucky or unlucky for the rest of your life, and there is nothing you can do to change your luck.

However, Master Li said: "It is not totally the case...although you have no control over your destiny and luck, your Conduit will be able to ameliorate your chances if it is activated by your Double. The sad part of this story is that many of us either do not believe in a Double, or do not accept the idea that a Conduit does in fact exist in our brains' cells."

c-The Conduit=Health/Youth/Longevity:
Those who have read my books are now familiar with the concept of the Conduit. For those who didn't, here is a brief description of the nature of the Conduit.
Basically, the Conduit is a depot of everything that is YOU; intelligence, emotions, feelings, attributes, qualities, talents, health, dreams, physiognomy, ability to learn many languages, creativity, endurance, and yes, your future as well.

Part Three: All human beings do not come from the same origin

At the time you were born, a Conduit was installed in the cells of your brain. If the Conduit has been activated, then everything you touch will turn into gold, all your deeds will become honorable, and you will be destined for greatness. If the Conduit remains inactive, you will lead a normal life, nothing spectacular about it, and continue to live a very ordinary life like all the others.
A miniscule, infinitely small part of the Conduit deals with health, youth, and longevity. And this very small part has been already programmed by those who created you. You can't deprogram it. You can't find it. And you can't reach it. It is way beyond your reach and comprehension. So let's leave it at that for now.

In the Conduit, your life-span has been formulated and its length and/or continuity has been decided upon genetically. Some people will die young, others will live for 100 years.
Some people will grow up to be very tall and physically strong, despite malnutrition/a good diet, while many others will stay short, fat, or weak despite their healthy life style, good diet, and impeccable hygiene.

Physicians and scientists are so quick to say: It is in the genes! And they stop there! But one thing they don't know for sure is what or who created those genes, and according to what guidelines, specifications and creation process?
They don't know.
Well, the Ulema do know, because they have learned it from their teachers the An.Na.Ki.
You can't control longevity, youth and your life-span by deprogramming their genetic codes, because first of all, you don't know where to find these sequences, secondly, you have no control over the Conduit, and lastly, you don't know how much to add to, or subtract from, the genetic codes.
If you do, if you know for a fact, how to prolong the vibrations of these sequences and how much "stuff" to add to the Conduit, then, and only then, will you be able to control your life-span.

Part Three: All human beings do not come from the same origin

Ulema Marash said: "It is like filling up your automobile gas tank. The more fuel you put in your tank, the more miles your car will run.
The difference, is that at the gas station, you are in control, because you can decide how much gas you want to buy. But when it comes to being young and living forever, firstly, you don't know where the youth station (in comparison to the gas station) is, and secondly, you are not in control of your Conduit (in comparison to your car)." "The good news", said Ulema Albakr is that a Conduit can be activated and/or reactivated if training and orientation programs are completed.

XII. The Shula species:
The Shula were human beings with a high degree of enlightenment. Those are the ones who distinguish themselves with prolific work, exemplary generosity, unconditional love and compassion, and above all, a unique sense of creativity. Some Ulema call them "Ana'a Alnour", the children of light. However, they are not the Mounawariin "The Enlightened Ones", or the "Ascended Masters". One of their characteristics and traits is the Fik'r, which means the faculty of using their brain to accomplish what others thought impossible, and because of the astonishing speed of their productivity.
Their programmed brain uses the "Jaba", which enable them to accomplish many tasks instantly and simultaneously. This has disturbed many people, and led them to question the veracity and authenticity of their work. It appears to them be too fast, too fascinating and too extraordinary to be true.
But Ulema Yazid explained, "Many can accomplish the very same things, if they reprogram the "Zaka", meaning the sequence of intelligentsia flux (one of the sequences of the Conduit).

XIII. The Emim: Ana'kh/Sumerian/Hebrew.
Name given to the children of Anak. The Bible referred to them as the offspring of the giants and the women of earth. They are the corrupted offspring of the Anakim.
Here are some excerpts from the Bible:

Part Three: All human beings do not come from the same origin

- Jos: 11:21: "And at that time came Joshua, and cut off the Anakim from the mountains, from Hebron, from Debir, from Anab, and from all the mountains of Judah, and from all the mountains of Israel: Joshua destroyed them utterly with their cities."
- Jos: 11:22: "There was none of the Anakim left in the land of the children of Israel: only in Gaza, in Gath, and in Ashdod, there remained..."
- Jos: 14:12: "Now therefore give me this mountain, whereof the Lord spoke in that day; for thou heardest in that day how the Anakim were there, and that the cities were great and fenced: if so be the Lord will be with me, then I shall be able to drive them out, as the Lord said."
- Jos: 14:15: "And the name of Hebron before was Kirjatharba; which Arba was a great man among the Anakim. And the land had rest from war."

The Ulema called them "B'nai Rouch", meaning the offspring or children of the light, who were capable of extraordinary deeds.

XIV. Ezakarerdi, "E-zakar-erdi "Azakar.Ki":
Term for the "Inhabitants of Earth" as named by the Anunnaki, and mentioned in the Ulemite language in the "Book of Rama-Dosh." Oppositely, extraterrestrials are called Ezakarfalki. "Inhabitants of Heaven or Sky".
The term or phrase "Inhabitants of Earth" refers only to humans, because animals and sea creatures are called Ezbahaiim-erdi. Ezakarerdi is composed of three words:

- **1**-E (Pronounced Eeh or Ea) means first.
- **2**-Zakar: This is the Akkadian/Sumerian name given to Adam by Enki. The same word is still in use today in Arabic, and it means male. In Arabic, the female is called: Ountha (Oonsa).

The word "Zakar" means:

Part Three: All human beings do not come from the same origin

- **a**-A male, and sometime a stud.
- **b**-To remember.

In Hebrew, "Zakar" also means:
- **a**-To remember (Qal in Hebrew).
- **b**-Be thought of (Niphal in Hebrew).
- **c**-Make remembrance (Hiphil in Hebrew).

3-Erdi means planet Earth. Erdi was transformed by scribes into Ki in the Akkadian, Sumerian and Babylonian epics.

From Erd, derived:
- **a**-The Sumerian Ersetu and Erdsetu,
- **b**-The Arabic Ard,
- **c**-The Hebrew Eretz.

All sharing the same meaning: Earth; land.
Thus the word Ezakarerdi means verbatim: The first man (Or Created one) of Earth or the first man on Earth, or simply, the Earth-Man. In other words, the first terrestrial human.

The Ezakarerdi was considered the final product of human geneology.

XV. Ezeridim:
Term for entities or super-beings from the future.
The Ezeredim were not created by the Anunnaki.
In Ufology and paranormal terminologies, they are called chrononauts, a word derived from the Greek Kronos, which means time, and "nauts" referring to space travelers, or simply voyagers.

XVI. Fari-narif "Fari-Hanif":
Or simply Ra-Nif.
A term for categorizing different forms of spirits, and non-physical entities.

Part Three: All human beings do not come from the same origin

The Anunnaki referred to many different forms, shapes and ratings of entities, known to the human race as "Spirits" and "Souls". From "Ra" and "Ra-Nif" are derived the Semitic words Rouh, Rafesh, Nefes, Nefs, Roach, and Ruach, meaning the soul in Arabic, Aramaic and Hebrew.

"The truth is they are neither spirits, nor are they messengers of God, but a projection of a higher level of goodness and intelligence...and those who (after their physical death on earth) enter a higher dimension, would meet the angels in the Fourth dimension as meta-plasmic presences, emanating beauty and goodness, but they are not divine spirits or pure souls..." added Ulema Bakri.

XVII. The Anunnaki-Ulema from Ashtari:
Some of the Anunnaki Ulema on Earth today, were created on Ashtari in human form, gestated in the Anunnaki light tube via the same process as Anbar Anati's daughter, then brought to Earth either as children (who would then join the Ulema Mahad school), or would arrive on earth as adult Masters.

The lower level of Ulema (third and fourth level) would be created via an "immaculate conception" process wherein the mother (who was genetically created by the Anunnaki and brought to Earth for the purpose of being a vessel to give birth to these Ulema babies) carries the baby within her for only a period of three months – enough to give him/her human attributes and properties.

At three months of pregnancy, the mother is taken to a clinic found within the Mahad to deliver the baby. The baby is taken from within her by an apparatus that "sucks the light molecules of the baby" into a large test-tube where the baby continues to develop and grow. The baby will be nourished with a form of liquid light for an additional three months, at which point it is fully developed and has gained more human properties, attributes, organs etc.

As soon as the baby is delivered from the light tube, it is placed in the care of one of the Masters, who then becomes his/her tutor and guardian for life.

Part Three: All human beings do not come from the same origin

The infant remains in the care of the Master at the Mahad for a period of three years, at which point his/her conduit is opened, and his/her brain is rewired, according to decisions made by the chosen enlightened master, as to what role the child will play on Earth, in the future.

Thus his/her talents and special abilities are decided upon in infancy, by his/her personal master. At the age of three, the master then places the child with a carefully screened and chosen adoptive family.

The male children created this way are called the "Beninourim", which means the son of the light. The female children are called the "Bnatnourim", which means the daughters of the light. (As usual, outsiders and conspiracy theorists, and people with wild imaginations will rush to call them Reptilians, Shapeshifters, children of the Illuminati etc, intentionally implanted within our societies to influence governments and take over the world!!)

However, the purest form of Ulema known as "Tahiriin" (The Pure) who are the first level, and "Mounawariin" (The Enlightened Master) who are the second level, also have etheric as well as physical/human forms. These are the human beings from other dimensions, and far different spheres, that are here on Earth.

*** *** ***

Part Three: Anunnaki-Ulema esoteric and mind-power techniques

Anunnaki-Ulema esoteric and mind-power techniques

Questions by Steven Morello

Question: What techniques and practices can help us become more spiritual and more open to the 'paranormal' such as seeing auras, ghosts or spirits, seeing into the future etc?
What effect can this awakening have on our lives?

Answer:
In the "Book of Ramadosh", I wrote about 13 Anunnaki-Ulema techniques to achieve what you are looking for. Full details on how to use these techniques step-by-step are outlined and itemized in the book.
Here is a summary/synopsis of the definition of the techniques:

1-Gomari "Gumaridu" technique:
A term referring to an Anunnaki-Ulema technique capable of manipulating time. It is also called the "Net Technique".
Ulema Rabbi Mordachai said: "Human beings treat time as if it were linear. Day follows day, year follows year, and task follows task. The Anunnaki Ulema, however, have long ago learned how to treat time nonlinearly, and thus be able to accomplish more in their lives."

Ulema Rabbi Mordechai talking to his student Germain Lumiere, who visited with him in Budapest, where he resided for some years, "It would be beneficial if you could manipulate time in such a way as to be faster than normal people, and this is what we are going to do in the forthcoming exercise (Gomari)..."

Part Three: Anunnaki-Ulema esoteric and mind-power techniques

2-Gomatirach-Minzari "Gomu-Minzaar" technique:
Known also as the "Mirror to Alternate Realities."
Rabbi Mordechai said: "Building and using the Minzar is risky. However, if the student reads the instructions carefully and does not deviate from them, it should be a reasonably safe procedure. If you choose to try it, this may be one of the most important lessons you will ever learn, since the benefits, both physical and spiritual, are without equal."

Note: From Ulema Rabbi Mordechai's Kira'at (Reading)

"Those who are familiar with the concept of the Anunnaki's Miraya would notice a resemblance in the way these tools are used. However, one should realize that we are not pretending to use the kind of cosmic monitor that is connected, through the Akashic Libraries on Nibiru, to the Akashic Record itself.

It is beyond our scope to even conceive how such a tool had ever been created. Nor are we attempting to recreate the kind of Minzar that is used by the Anunnaki-Ulema, enlightened beings whose Conduit has been opened.
Most of us possess a Conduit that has not been opened, and the Minzar we recommend is fitted to our level of advancement. Nevertheless, working with the Minzar will open doors that will astound and amaze any student.
You will be using the techniques to create an alternate reality that will allow you to do things you have never imagined are possible."

3-Gubada-Ari technique:
The Triangle Of Life Technique.
Term referring to the Anunnaki-Ulema "Triangle of Life", and how to apply the value of the "Triangle" shape to health, success, and peace of mind. Most importantly, it shows you how to find the healthiest spots and luckiest areas on earth, including private places and countries, and take advantage of this.

Part Three: Anunnaki-Ulema esoteric and mind-power techniques

Ulema Rabbi Mordechai explained the concept, importance, and practical use. He said (Verbatim): "How this technique will enhance your life:
With the help of the triangle, you will able to find the perfect areas on earth where your health, success, and peace of mind will be at their optimum. You can work it on a large scale and find out the best countries to live in, or on a small scale, which would give you the best neighbourhoods in your own city or county."

Synopsis of the Theory:

- There are lines of energy spinning around the world. In this exercise, we will concentrate on the lines that are revealed by the use of the triangle.
- The energy flows in currents, both negative and positive, mostly underground, traversing the globe.
- Those who live above the positive lines, will have good health, success, and peace of mind. Those who live above the negative lines, will have bad health, lack of success, and will experience mind turmoil.
- The meaning of life is based on the fact that life is, in itself, a triangle.
- One corner of the triangle represents health.
- The second represents success.
- The third represents peace of mind.
- You find meaning by placing the triangle you are about to draw, on the world.
- The student might ask, where do I put the triangle? How do I choose the right location? The answer is, you put the triangle wherever you are.
- The student might ask "what if I change locations?" The answer is, this technique is working within the dictates of the moment.
- Wherever you are, the triangle follows. Change it as many times in life as you need. It always works.

Part Three: Anunnaki-Ulema esoteric and mind-power techniques

4-Cadari-Rou'yaa technique:
Reading the Aura.
Name or term for a secret technique developed by the Anunnaki-Ulema, centuries ago, that enabled them to read the thoughts, intentions, and feelings of others.

It is composed of two words:
- **a**-Cadari, which means a grid; a plasma-screen.
- **b**-Rou'yaa, which means vision; perception.

Cadari-Rou'yaa is also a method to diagnose health, and prevent health problems from occurring in the present, and in the future, by reading and interpreting the rays and radiations, a human body diffuses on a regular basis. In the West, it is called reading of the aura.

5-Chabariduri technique:
Remote viewing.
Name of an Anunnaki-Ulema technique/exercise to develop the faculty of remote viewing.
The Ulema taught their students the art and science of remote viewing, in order to improve their knowledge, enrich their awareness, and widen their perception of life, not to spy on others, as it is the case in the West.

6-Daemat-Afnah technique:
How to Stay and Look 37 Permanently.
Term for longevity, and halting the process of aging.

It is composed of two words:
- **a**-Daemat, which means longevity.
- **b**-Afnah, which means many things, including health, fecundity, and longevity.

According to the Anunnaki-Ulema, we are not programmed to age.

Part Three: Anunnaki-Ulema esoteric and mind-power techniques

7-Da-Irat technique:
Name for Anunnaki's "Circle Technique"

Da-Irat is known to the Enlightened Ones and Ulema adepts, as the "Circle Technique" (Da-Ira-Maaref), which means the circle of knowledge.

This technique eliminates stress, through one's self-energy. In other words, it is an Ulema technique used to energize one's mind and body, and to eliminate worries, that are preventing an individual from functioning properly everywhere, including the office, home, social gatherings, etc.
In the western world, zillions of techniques to reduce stress and counter bad vibes were proposed. And many of those techniques work very well.

The following will explain the Ulema's techniques that were in practice for thousands of years, in the Near and Middle East.
No physical exercise is required. It is purely mental, although some of the steps might look esoteric or spiritual in nature.

These techniques were developed by the early Ulema and members of the "Fish Circle", a brotherhood of the ancient island of Arwad, where allegedly, remnants of the An.na.Ki (Anunnaki) lived, and developed the Mah-Rit in sophisticated genetic labs.

The Da-Irat Technique (The Circle Technique) as used by the Fish Circle Brotherhood:

Terminology:
- 1-In Ulemite, it is called Da-Irat (Circle; sphere).
- 2-In Ana'kh, it is called Arac-ta.
- 3-In Phoenician, it is called Teth-Ra. Teth is circle or good thing. Ra is creative energy or first source of life.

Part Three: Anunnaki-Ulema esoteric and mind-power techniques

8-Dudurisar technique:
Name for the act or ability to rethink and examine past events in your life, change them, and in doing so, create for yourself a new life and new opportunities.
To a certain degree, and in a sense, it is like revisiting your past, and changing unpleasant events, decisions, choices, and related matters that put you where you are today.

9-Arawadi technique:
A term for the supernatural power or faculty that allows the initiated ones, to halt or send away difficulties, problems and mishaps into another time and another place, thus freeing themselves from worries, anxiety and fear.
It is a very complex concept that touches metaphysics, esoterism and quantum physics. Ulema Stephanos Lambrakis said that it is very possible to get rid of current problems by "transposing" them into a different time frame.
He added that "all of us live in two separate dimensions so close to us.
One we know and we call it our physical reality, the other is the adjacent dimension that surrounds our physical world.
Enlightened ones visit that dimension quite frequently.
It is a matter of a deep concentration, and perseverance. In fact, it is possible to enter that parallel dimension and leave there all your troubles, and return to your physical world free of worries and problems."

10-Baaniradu technique:
Baaniradu is the Anunnaki-Ulema term for the healing touch technique. It was first used by the priests of Melkart in Ancient Phoenicia, Ugarit and Arwad.
It is extremely important to bear in mind, that this technique does not in any shape or form, replace any scientific and medical treatment(s). Baaniradu has not been fully explored and used in the West.

Part Three: Anunnaki-Ulema esoteric and mind-power techniques

11-Baridu technique:
Baridu is the Anunnaki-Ulema term for the act of zooming into an astral body or a Double. We have used the expression "Astral body", because of the Western readers' familiarity with what it basically represents. This representation is not the depiction usually used by the Ulema, but it is close enough, to use it in this work.

12-Bisho-barkadari "Bukadari" technique:
Bisho-barkadari "Bukadari" is the Anunnaki-Ulema term for the technique used in blocking bad vibes that negatively affect human beings.

It is composed of two words:
- **a**-Bisho, which means bad; negative.
- **b**-Barkadari, which means flames; rays, vibes; beams.

13-Etc...

*** *** ***

Part Three: On the old way of thinking

On the old way of thinking

Questions by Steven Morello

Question: A lot of spiritual teachers tell us that the mind with all its conditioning, becomes a barrier to growth and enlightenment. When will mankind be able to move on from the old way of thinking to a new paradigm?
Einstein says that "problems cannot be solved by the same level of thinking that created them."
What might this new way of thinking look like? Thinking and judging obessively itself may be a large part of the problem.

Answer:
Sometimes, the answer is right before your eyes. Have you ever heard of this expression: Think outside the box?
The box can block the flux of creative ideas. The mind is like a parachute, it works better when open, as my dear friend Laura Lebron once said. And try to leave your mind open, like the door of a Zen shrine. You are correct when you said the mind is "a barrier to growth and enlightenment." But only for the rigid mind. Do not fight the wind if you are an old oak tree. A shrub is safer. Do not reject new, unorthodox and unconventional ideas, because they are contrary to your beliefs, or because your mind cannot understand them or accept them.

Take a different attitude and ask yourself with humility and absolute honesty: "What if?" That's correct, what if they were the right ideas and you were wrong? Do not doubt anybody, do not contradict anybody until your truth is stronger than theirs. And the truth should not be subjective, but based upon solid ground and verifiable facts! Yes, the mind can destroy morality and goodness, if it is not well nourished and properly managed.

*** *** ***

Part Three: Esoteric/secret calendar of your lucky days and hours

Esoteric/secret calendar of your lucky days and hours

Question by Ray Mantoya.

Question: One person who has read your books told me about a technique the Ulema sorcerers used to read the future. As I understood, it is a calendar of the good days, and the bad days in the life of each one of us. I would be grateful if you could explain to me what it is about and see the calendar. I promise I will use it for a good cause. Thank you.

*** *** ***

> Note: **Sorcerers?**
> The Ulema are not sorcerers. They are men of spirituality and science. I will gladly reproduce the article I wrote years ago, but promise me that you will educate yourself on matters related to the honorable Ulema.

Answer:
This esoteric practice is called Hamnika-mekhakeh- ilmu.
It is complicated, and it requires a lot of patience and diligence. But it is worth the effort.
The technique of using the Hamnika-mekhakeh.
I. Synopsis of the concept
II. Ulema-Anunnaki days are
III. The calendars' grids
IV. The use of a language
V. The preparation and use of the grids

Part Three: Hamnika-mekhakeh- ilmu (Cont'd)

I. Synopsis of the concept:
Humans follow certain calendars. The most common one is the Gregorian calendar, which is a reflection of the Christian faith. It is younger than the Muslim calendar, which in turn, is younger than the Jewish calendar. All of these are considerably younger than the Anunnaki calendar, which is the only one used by the Anunnaki-Ulema.
The Anunnaki-Ulema reject the idea that the week consists of seven days. Their week consists of four days, corresponding to certain days of our week. These are the only days to use in this technique, and the other three days in our week should not be calculated upon.

II. The Ulema-Anunnaki days are:
- Day 1: Thilta (Tuesday)
- Day 2: Araba (Wednesday)
- Day 3: Jema (Friday)
- Day 4: Saba (Saturday).

The importance of these days is in the relationship between the person and the hours in each day. Using the calendar of the Anunnaki-Ulema, each person can find the luckiest hour of his or her week, according to the Book of Ramadosh (Rama-Dosh). Ulema Rabbi Mordachai said: "You might feel that one hour a week is not sufficient for anyone's needs. It might also not improve your luck at work if it occurs, say, at two o'clock in the morning each Saturday.
This predicament can be easily resolved by performing another technique, Time Manipulation, on that exact hour. The time that will be added to your life under such circumstances will be as lucky as the original hour, and your chances of success will be vastly improved."
The Anunnaki-Ulema teachers highly recommend performing a combination of techniques, since each enhances the other considerably.

Part Three: Hamnika-mekhakeh- ilmu (Cont'd)

III. The calendar's grids:
A couple of questions might arise as you work with this technique. First, do all people with the same number of letters in their name, share a lucky hour?
Yes, indeed they would. There are only sixteen grid lines to represent millions of people. And this leads to an interesting discovery. The numbers of letters in people's names represent a certain harmony that exists between them. For example, if you wish to approach people in high places for a favor, finding out that he or she shares the same number of letters and the lucky hour will enhance your chances. Always send your request to him or her during the lucky hour, either by calling on the phone, using your e-mail, or placing a written letter in the mailbox.

IV. The use of a language:
Another question is the issue of languages. What if your name is written with four letters in America, where you live, but with five letters in your native language? The answer is simple.
Always use your native language, the language that you were first aware of your name in, in your grid. It will be much more accurate and certainly more powerful. An important fact to add to this, is that this technique is simple, but it can be enhanced in many ways by subtle variations.
Adding those variations extends the knowledge of how time and space is related to luck and success, and how to fine tune the process. But even in this straightforward version, the technique is incredibly powerful, so much so that it may change your life completely, and always for the better.

> **Tip:** If any added numbers are higher than one digit, always add the numbers and use the result. For example, if instead of 3+1+1+1= 6 you will find yourself with, say, 4+7+7+7=25, add 2+5 and use the result, namely 7. If you have 40+41+42+43=126, add 1+2+6=9.

Part Three: Hamnika-mekhakeh- ilmu (Cont'd)

V. The preparation and use of the grids:
The first step is to prepare a grid of sixteen squares, like the one below.

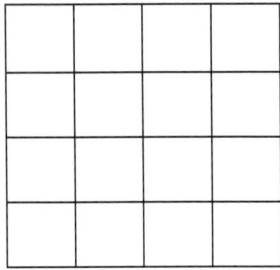

In the next step, you will establish the calendar of the week, by writing them in this specific order.

Grid 1: Calendar of the Week

Day 1	Day 2	Day 3	Day 4
Day 2	Day 3	Day 4	Day 1
Day 3	Day 4	Day 1	Day 2
Day 4	Day 1	Day 2	Day 3

- **1**-In the next step, you will establish the calendar of your name. Let's say your name is Suzan.
- **2**-You will write your name in the squares, but you must write from right to left, the way they did in many ancient languages, including Ana'kh.
- **3**-Then, you follow, still from right to left, with the number of the days, 1, 2, 3, 4.

Part Three: Hamnika-mekhakeh- ilmu (Cont'd)

Grid 2: Calendar of Your Name

A	Z	U	S
3	2	1	N
Z	U	S	4
2	1	N	A

*** *** ***

Calendar of your lucky hour

- **1**-In the next step, you will establish the calendar of your lucky hour.
- **2**-Look at the two squares above.
- **3**-Try to find the one square that has the same number in both drawings.
- **4**-When you compare each square, you will see that the second square in the last row has the #1 in it.
- **5**-Fill in the number of the days in the first row, the way it appeared in the first grid. (Tues, Wed, Fri, Sat)

Therefore, Suzan's lucky hour will occur during the second day. (If more than one square presents the same number, add the numbers.)

*** *** ***

Part Three: Hamnika-mekhakeh- ilmu (Cont'd)

Grid 3: Calendar of your lucky hour

Day 1	Day 2	Day 3	Day 4
	1		

*** *** ***

In the next step, we shall start our calculations.

- **1**-Keep the first row as is.
- **2**-fill the rest of the grid with the number 1.
- **3**-In each column, you will now subtract the three #1 's from the day in the first row. 1-1-1-1= -2; 2-1-1-1= -1; 3-1-1-1= 0; 4-1-1-1 = 1

Grid 4

Day 1	Day 2	Day 3	Day 4
1	1	1	1
1	1	1	1
1	1	1	1
-2	-1	0	1

Part Three: Hamnika-mekhakeh- ilmu (Cont'd)

- **4**-We will now add the number we have calculated. (-2) + (-1) + 0 + 1 = (-2)
- **5**-We continue our calculations by using the number we have achieved, -2, as a filler in the grid below, in three rows under the basic days row on top.
- **6**-Then, we will calculate the values of the columns the way we have done in the previous grid.

Grid 5

Day 1	Day 2	Day 3	Day 4
-2	-2	-2	-2
-2	-2	-2	-2
-2	-2	-2	-2
-5	-4	-3	-2

- **7**-We will add these numbers: (-5) + (-4) + (-3) + (-2) = -14
- **8**-We will combine the individual numbers comprising the number fourteen by adding them: 1+ 4 = 5
- **9**-We will add these two numbers. (-14) + 5 = -9

*** *** ***

In the next step:
- **1**-Return to the first grid, displaying the calendar of the week.
- **2**-Starting on the second row, count the squares, going from right to left, nine times.
- **3**-You will reach Day 3.

Part Three: Hamnika-mekhakeh- ilmu (Cont'd)

- **4**-This establishes that your lucky hour will occur on Friday, the third day of the Anunnaki week.
- **5**-To establish the hour, go back to Grid 4, and look at the row that expresses Day 3.
- **6**-Add the numbers: $3 + 1 + 1 + 1 = 6$
- **7**-Calculate: $(-9) - (+6) = -3$
- **8**-To establish the hour within the 24 hours of each day, subtract $24 - 3 = 21$.
  21 is 9 P.M.

Therefore, Suzan's luckiest hour of the week occurs at nine o'clock in the evening of each Friday.

*** *** ***

Part Three: On different dimensions and multidimensional beings

On different dimensions and multidimensional beings

Questions by Steven Morello

Question: What dimensions lie beyond the 4th, that we can experience?

Answer:
According to quantum physics, there are eleven dimensions. Up to a few years ago, scientists believed in only 7 dimensions.
And do not forget that the theorist and eminent scientist who advanced the theory of the 11 dimensions had been ridiculed by peers for 11 years! And unfortunately, he also lost one of his teaching positions.
But finally and thankfully he has recently been vindicated.
Yes sir, they ridiculed him and disgraced him for years!
According to the Ulema, there exist far more than 11 dimensions.
Steven, I have already answered this question in another section of this book. Never mind, I am glad to give you more information and accommodate your question.
Quantum physics pioneers compared the multiple dimensions of the universe (Multiverse) to strings. And quite correctly added, that the universe was created by collisions of membranes (M theory). And this collision is continuing as we speak. Thus, they concluded that the universe is expanding. Well, the Catholic priest and scientist, Christian Lemaitre said the very same thing 90 years ago.
Einstein reviewed his theory and commented: "Your math is correct, but your physics are lousy!" Einstein was wrong.

Centuries ago, the Ulema have stated (As I have mentioned in my previous books) that the known universe was created by several collisions of bubbles.

Part Three: On different dimensions and multidimensional beings

In 1961, when I reported this to several scientists and some of my colleagues (authors), they laughed at me and at the Ulema! I didn't mind, because I laughed too.

There is an enormous difference between traditional science, avant-garde quantum physics and Ulema science-metaphysics-metalogic.
The Ulema views are based upon science and knowledge gained from the Anunnaki. What they have learned from the Anunnaki Sinhars, remains incomprehensible to most of us. But I can assure you that a few extraordinary scientists strongly believe in the astronomy and cosmogeny of the Anunnaki, and honestly admitted that our mind is incapable of understanding the Anunnaki's highly advanced science and technology.

The Anunnaki saw our universe before we were born. And they witnessed the birth of many stars, planets and galaxies!
According to Ulemite literature, the Anunnaki told the Ulema that there are several "Layers" and "Outer-Dimensions" beyond the boundaries of planet Earth. Some are purely mental, others are physical. And even in the "Mental Sphere" you will find multiple spheres and zones, which are extra or para-mental. This applies also to the physical planes, membranes or branes as coined in quantum physics.
Most recently, quantum physics theorists began to admit that within each and every separate molecule, each brane, and each universe, there are multiple universes. But they don't know for sure how these intra-universes were created in one single universe or molecule. Some have advanced the theory, that the inner universe of a global universe (One single molecule) was created by an "Implosion".
Ironically, this is what the Ulema have said centuries ago. We can conclude from the statements of the Ulema, that there are zillions of universes and dimensions beyond our physical world, and these universes are increasing in number, size and mobility. And some are running away from us and from the very fabric of the universe.

Part Three: On different dimensions and multidimensional beings

This is very convenient to quantum physics pioneers, because it strengthens their theory of "The universe is expanding."

Question: Do other beings exist in these dimensions?
Answer:
Absolutely. According to quantum physics pioneers and leading theorists in the field, (led by Dr. Michio Kaku) there are even copies of ourselves in other worlds. On the Science Channel in the United States, Dr. Kaku stated that in some universes, Elvis Presley is still alive, Napoleon won the war, and you were never born. I am pleased and relieved that such a fantastic statement came directly from the mouth of an eminent and highly respected scientist. Just imagine if I had said that to people who hate my guts... how they would react, and how gossipy and vicious would the blogs be, posted on cheap websites on the Internet to ridicule and discredit me.

There is vast literature on this subject, part of it written by eminent scientists, and several other parts produced by New Age ufology writers and "Psychics to the Stars". Take your pick. Some researchers have reported to me, that at least two governments have already catalogued the different categories of aliens and non-alien entities living in different universes.

Question: Can we ever contact them, and would there be negative repercussions from doing so?

Answer:
Dr. Stephen Hawking said: "It would a very bad idea!"

*** *** ***

Part Three: Miscellaneous

Are Earth Governments controlled by aliens?

Questions by Ismail Kemal Ciftcioglu, Turkey.

Question: Is it true that lots of Earth governments including the U.S. are controlled or ruled by an Alien race called the Reptilians?

Answer:
No! This is my personal opinion. But I know for sure that no government on Earth is under the control or influence of any reptilian race. Some governments (No more than 3) have joint programs with aliens (Non-humans), but they do not belong to the reptilian race.

Question: What is the royal insignia or logo of the Anunnaki? The winged disk? Do they use banners or flags like us?

Answer:
They have several logos and symbols such as:
a-Winged disc.
b-The Triangle (Delta)
c-The rosette, also called the mushroom.
d-A tree of life inside a circle.

Question: In the Lost book of Enki, Zecharia Sitchin wrote that the mysterious face on Mars (which is still unaccepted by NASA) was Anunnaki Alalu's graveyard. Do you know if this is true?
Answer:
I don't comment on others people's books, nor do I pass judgement or give an opinion, and I most certainly do not criticize their beliefs and work.

Question: Are Enlil, Enki, Anu etc. still alive?
No reason(s) to believe otherwise. Their life-span could exceed 445,000 years.

Part Three: Miscellaneous

On eating meat.
Question: Must we stop eating meat for our preparation for 2022 or will we prepare ourselves mentally only? Because I love eating meat!
Answer:
I don't want the beef industry to come after me. A piece of friendly advice: Do not hurt anybody, do not speak evil, do not cause any suffering to anyone, and do not kill animals.

***   ***   ***

INDEX

A

Abductees, 127,157,235
Abduction, 53
   by the Grays, 117
Abolishing
   Fossil fuels, 91
   Governments, 91
Adjacent
   Parallel dimensions, 202
   to Earth, 200
   to our world, 202
Adon, 116
Adonai, 116
Adonis, 116
Adoon, 116
Advanced
   Military weapons systems from aliens, 119
   Spatial weapons-missiles systems, 117,119
Afghanistan, 97
Afrit, 224
Agenda of the Greys, 53,54
Air Force, 117
   Fields, 71
Akkadian/Sumerian clay tablets, 232
Aktion, 56
Al Annaki, 6
Al Maktoob, 226
Al Zafiru, 231
Alaska, 56

Alchemists/Kabalists, 224
Aleph, 58
Alien
   Asphyxiation effect, 130
   Entities living in different universes, 341
   Frogmen, 187,188
   Held underground at Andrews Air Force Base, 119
   Images projected by, 235
   Living quarters, 68
   Races programs, 54
   Reverse engineering, 104
   Scratchy voice, 68
   Technology, 53,67,137
   Threat, 136
   Treaties with the United States, 70
All-That-Is, 89
Alphabet
   Anunnaki, 58
   Arabic, 58
   Aramaic, 58
   Hebrew, 58
   Phoenician, 58
Alteration of
   DNA sequence, 231
   Laws of physics on Earth, 97
Amalika, 6
Ambar Anati, 50,51,59
Amchit, 56
America, Grays bases in, 97

American
  Military bases, 98
  Military scientists, 50,189
Americans, 97
  Hiding truth from, 119
Amrit, 56
An-Hayya'h, 173,174
An.Na Kim, 6
Anakh-Pro-Ugaritic, 224
Ana'kh, the Anunnaki
  language, 5,6
Anaki, 5
Anakim, 5,6
Ananaki, 6
Anatolia, 6
Andrews Air Force Base, 119
Angel Gabriel, 171
Animals, 81,84
  Mutilation, 53
Annihilated, ninety percent of
  Earth's human population
  will be, 196
Annihilation, tool of, 87,205
Annodoti, 6
Announcement of your death,
  235
Anomaly of stargates, 203
Anti-Ba'ab, 105
Anti-radar emissions, 198
Antioch, 56
Anu, 6,342
Anu.ki, 6
Anu. Ki.ram, 6
Anunna, 5
Anunnaki
  Ba'abs, 83,85,86,103,131
  Bubble, 81,86
  Contact with the, 52
  Council, 72,73,75,76
  Created in the image of the,
  75,77
  Date of the return of the, 9
  Deserted their research on
  Earth, 77
  Evolutionary process,
  fostered by the, 76
  Guides for humans, 82
  High Council, 205
  Indications of the return of
  the, 9
  Interest in human affairs, 54
  Landing spots of the, 55,56,
  105
  Landing terminal of the, 50,
  55
  Language of the, 6
  Logo of the, 104
  Miraya, 85,86
  Other names of the, 5
  Programmed us, 53
  Remnants of the, 111
  Return of the, 5,49,50,54,55,
  57,59,73,117,197
  Return protocol, 203
  Scientists on Nibiru, 74
  Signs of the return of the,
  204
  Space-center of the, 109
  Spaceships, 103
  Stronger than humans, 63
  Technology, 91
  Tool of annihilation, 87
  Triangle of the, 56
  Ulema manuscripts, 55
  Ulema Ramadosh Society,
  345
Anunnaku, 6
Anuramkim, 5,6
Anuramkir, 6
Ape-like humanoids, 86
Apsu, 169
Aquatic plasma corridors, 187
Arabian Peninsula, 224
Arabic, 6

Arabs, 6,55
Aramaic Syriac, 6
Araya, 149
Archuleta Mesa, 65
Ard, 6
Area 51, 137
Arizona, 50,56,67
Arizona, 56
Armenians, 6
Arrival of the "Four
  Horsemen", 204
Aruru, 232
Arwad, 56, 105
  Early inhabitants of, 6
Arwadians, 5
Arwah, 224
Ascended Masters, 7
Ascension, 116
Asha-Kar-Da-Ki, 231
Ashtari, 59,76
Ashuric (Assyrian-Chaldean), 6
Assyrian, 6,7
Astronomy, 49
Atmospheric shield network, 197
Atomic number of 6, 104
Atomic/thermonuclear
  weapons, 193
Aura research, 70
Aurora, 189
AUTEC, 501,88

B

Ba'abs, 83,85,86,103,116,131, 194
  Anti, 105
  In Chicago, 201,202
  Multidimensional, 101
  of Liberation, 103
  Over Madison Square
    Garden, 203
Baal-Shamroutiim, 224
Baalbeck, 56,105,109,110
Baalshamroot Ram, 148
Babel, Tower of, 115
Babylon, 172
Babylonian-Sumerian account
  of Creation, 172
Bach, 232
Bak'ht-Kira'at, 221
Ba-khaat, 224
Bakht, 223,224
Bakhaati, 224
Bakht Haya.Ti, 225
Bases
  American military, 98
  Grays in America, 97
  Secret, 104
  Underwater Russian, 187
Basra, 56
Bayt al-Zahab, 55
Beams of light, 87
Belgian incident, 189
Bhutto, Benazir, 193
Bijjeh, 56
Bio-organic copies of yourself
  in other worlds, 226
Bio-psychological makeup of
  human nature, 149
Bio-rhythm that creates good
  luck and bad luck, 229
Biological, living forms,
  creating 75
Biosystem of the earth, 96
Black liquid, mixed with light
  and electricity, 87
Black Projects, 104,118
Bodhisattva, 229
Body contamination, 51
Boeing, 95
Book of Dirasat Al

347

Clash, 93
Stage, 87
Financial elite, 72
Fi raa-Saa, 229
Firasa, 224,229
First
   Element used by the Anunnaki to genetically create the early human race, 104
   Prototypes of the quasi-human races, 232
Fort Knox, 90
Fossil fuels, abolishing, 91
Fostered the evolutionary process, 76
Four Horsemen, arrival of the 204
Four Seasons Hotel, 60,117
Freedom of choice, 226,227
Freemasonry, 111
French scientists, 189
Frogmen
   Alien, 187,188
   Russian, 187
Future, 221,223,224225,,227, 228
   Linear, 225
   Multidimensional, 225

G

Gabala, 56
Galactic
   Enterprises, 54
   Federation/Council, 194
   Mind of the extraterrestrials, 197
   Lab tubes, 186
Gargoyles, 68

Gates
   Celestial, 116
   Stars, 83
Geilenkirchen, 56
Genes, 53,179
Genetic, 68
   Experiments, 53
   Laboratories, 98,104,117
   Laboratories of Zeta Reticuli, 117
Genetically, 53,104
Georgetown, 60,117
Ghaffurian, Dr. Mary Ann, 346
Ghost, 235,236,237,238
Gibborim, 6
God, 6,89,103,131
God-Particle/Higgs Boson, 194
Government, 71,74,179
   United States, 74
   Will be abolished, 91
Grand Central Station in downtown Chicago, 201,203
Gravity, 96
Greeks, 6
Greys (Grays), 50,51,61,63,64, 65,67,68,70,71,74,77,93,95, 99,103
   Abduction of humans by, 117
   Affiliation with the, 93,97
   Agenda of the, 53,150
   Bases in America, 97
   Claustrophobia, 128
   DNA, 77,79,80,81,103
   Domination of earth and the human race by the, 174
   Experimentation with manipulation of the nervous system, 69
   Extinction, 177
   Eye identification system, 69
   Habitat of the, 189
   Interbreeding program with

humans, 176
Liberation from the contamination and control of the, 103,104
Manipulation, 67
Material of the Anunnaki, 76
Second meeting with the in1954, 128
Shape-shifted, 61,69,70,71
Spacecraft crashed in Roswell, 119
Storage units of fully grown creatures and tissues, 69
Work center of the, 189
Gyumri, 56

H

Habiru, 6
Harvest tissues, 68
Hawking, Stephen William, 184,341
Hawwa, 171
Hayat, 171
Hayya'h, 171, see An-Hayyah
Heaven, 6
Hebrew, 5,6
Heretz, 6
Higgs Boson, God Particle, 194
High Council on Nibiru, 64,72,73
Higher dimensions, 225
Hind and Sindh, 55
Hinduism, 149
Hiram, tomb of, 111
History channel's show "UFO Hunters", 203
Hittites, 6
Holographic
　Mental image, 236
　Pictures, 62,132
　Projection, 235,236
Honolulu, 56
Hook, Phoenician, 116
Hot spots on Earth, 105
Human race, 52,54
　Abduction, 53
　Anunnaki guides for, 82
　Aura research, 70
　Cleansing of, 197
　Contaminating the, 51
　Deformed, 68
　Evacuation plan by the Anunnaki, 201
　Excess, 90
　Freedom of choice, 226,227
　Non-, 224
　Races, quasi, 232
　Rendezvous with the Anunnaki, 105
　Specimens, 179
Humanity, 50,59,74,77,86
　Control over, 70
Humanoids, ape-like 86
Hybrids, 61,67,71,131,156,157,178,179,180
Hydrogen particles around our solar system, 147,
Hyksos, 5,6
Hypnosis, 70

I

Igigi, 54,150
Images
　(Duplicate) of your body, 235
　Mental-holographic, 236
　Projected by aliens, 235
Implosion, universe created by

Plants, 86
Plasma aquatic corridors, 187
Plasmic belt, 97
Poitiers, Germaine, 346
Polar magnetism, change of, 97
Population, 93
   Will be annihilated by ninety percent, 196
Prague, 56
President of the United States, 64,119,123
Previous lives, 225
Pre-visualizing events before they happen, 236
Priests of Ra, 224
Professions, elimination of, 91, 92
Progeria, 96,176,177,178
Programmed by the Anunnaki, 53
Programs by the alien races, 54
Project Plato, 127
Project Sigma, 127
Prophet Mohammad, 171
Protocol,
   Extraterrestrials, 129, 191
   Of the return of the Anunnaki, 203
Pro-Ugaritic-Anakh, 224
Psychic
   Phenomena, 70
   Powers, 70
Puerto Rico, 50,56
Punjab, 55
Purification Phoenician priests, 224
Purified Ones, 7

Q

Quantum physics, 203,225,339
Quasi-human races, first prototypes of the , 232
Quran, 171

R

Ra, priests of, 224
Ram, 6
Religious
   Belief systems, 51
   Dogma with "intelligent design", 204
Remnants of the Anunnaki, 111
Rendezvous of the human race with the Anunnaki, 105
Reptilian, 194
   Look, 68
   Race, 70
Return
   Of the Anunnaki to Earth, 5,9,49,50,51,54,55,57, 59,73, 117
   Protocol of the Anunnaki, 197,203
   Signs of the Anunnaki, 204
Reverse engineering, 104,118
Rhythm, cellular 232
Rituals, secret, 116
Rosette, logo and symbol, 342
Roswell crash, 62
Rou'h Ya, 229
Rouhaniyiin, 224
Russia, 74,97
Russian(s), 117
   Extraterrestrial operation, 188
   Military scientists, 189
   Underwater base, 187

S

Sabata, 229
Saint Petersburg, 56
Satellites which harness cosmic Energy, 200
Scanning
  Device, 52
  Particular areas in the United States for several military strategic reasons, 197
Science Channel, 341
Screen/monitor, cosmic 194
Second meeting with the Grays in 1954, 128
Secret
  Code of the year 2022, 105
  Military bases, 54,104
  Rituals of the Phoenician, 116
Sefiro, 231
Scmites, 5
Separate pasts, 225
Sequence of 77 by 7, 229
Shabka, 198
Shape-shifted, Grays, 61,69,70, 71
Shemesh, 76
Sidon, 56
Signs that people will see in the skies the day before the Anunnaki return, 204
SMS, 189
Sinhar, 5
Sinhar Inannaschamra, 89,93, 158, 172,176
Sinhar Khaldi, 224
Sitchin, Z, 49
Sixth dimension, 105

Social order to be established by the Anunnaki, 149
Social Security system, 90
Societies, 51
Sol, 76
Sons of God, 6
Sour, 113
Space
  Center of the Anunnaki, 109
  Geometrical value of, 104
  Outer, 103
Space-time, 195,198
Space-time-zones, copies of ourselves in different, 226
Spacecraft of Grays crashed in Roswell, 119
Spaceships, 88,103
Spatial/terrestrial base, 54
Special beams of light, 87
Specimens of human, 179
Spheres,
  Mental, 340
  Para-mental, 340
Spirit in the Phoenician language, 104
Spinning Mobile Satellite, 189
Spiritism, 231
Spirits, 224
Stairway to heaven, 116
Stargate(s) 83,98,103
  Anomaly, 203
  In New York City 203
  Over Chicago, 201,202,203
Star Wars program, 97,98
State of Multan, 55
Storage units of fully grown creatures and tissues, 69
Sumer, 172
Sumerians, 49
Sun, 76
  Eclipse, 86
Supersymetric mind, 236

Imprint produced by, 236
Supreme
  Court, 91
  Creator, 226
Surviving Gray, 119
Swirling streams, 87
Syria, 224
Syriac-Aramaic, 6

T

Tahar, 224
Tahiriim, 7,224
Tana-Wur, 229

Tarot, 221,222,223,228
Tayarah, Farid, 56
Technology,
  Alien 53,67,118
  Anunnaki, 91
Telepathically transferred to Nibiru, 76
Terrestrial
  Orbit, 54
  Spatial base, 54
Territorial ambitions, 53
Terror, 71
Tesla, Nikola, 194,195
Texas, 56
Theory of the "Ever expanding universe", 225
Thermonuclear/atomic weapons, 193
Thursday, December 1st, 2022, 9
Tiglath Pileser, 7
Time(s),
  Different, 225
  Space, 195,198,202
  Space depository, 194

Space pocket, 198
Space zones, copies of ourselves in different, 226
Tiamat, 169
Tomb of Hiram, 111
Tool of annihilation, 87,205
Tower of Babel, 115
Trapani, 56
Trapped
  Deceased persons, 231
  In this life, 227
Treaties signed with aliens, 70,117
Tree of life inside a circle, logo and symbol, 342
Triangle
  Delta sign, 104,342
  Of the Anunnaki, 56
Triangular number, 104
Trilithon of Baalbeck, 109,110
Turkish, 6
Tyre, 56,105,111,112,113,224

U

UFO, 133,135,136,204
UFO Hunters, History channel's show, 203
Ugaritic, 6
  Proto-Anakh, 224
Ulema, 6,50,105
Ulema Al Baydani, 235
Ulema-Anunnaki, 7
Ulema Bukhtiar, 221
Ulema Ghandar, 222
Ulema Mordachai ben Zvi, 223,346,
Ulema Seif El Din, 221
  Manuscripts, 55
  Underground genetic

laboratories in America, 98
Ultra-dimension, 221
Underwater, 54
  Base, Russian, 187
Unification numerical code for the Anunnaki, 105
United States, 50,52,60,94,97, 104
  Air Force, 130, 189
  Allowed abductions, 117
  Department of Energy, 130
  Extraterrestrial protocol, 191
  Genetic laboratories in the, 104,117
  Government, 74
  Military, 73
  Military scientists, 53
  President of the, 64,123
  Protocol on extraterrestrials, 129
  Publications on extraterrestrial invasions, 132
  Treaties with aliens, 70
Universe(s),
  Global, 340
  Inner, 340
  Intra, 340
  Multiple, 103
  Single, 340
  Theory of the "Ever expanding universe", 225, 341
Ur, 56,115
  Enki Ziggurat in, 196
Ur Nammu, 115
Urdu, 6
USOs, 204

V

Vatican, 131
Vav, 116
Vegetarian diet, 84
Vehicles of the Gray aliens jointly operated with the military, 204
Ventura, Jesse "The Body", 190
Vera Cruz, 56
Vimanas, 149
Visiting our past(s) in different dimensions, 225

W

Warka, 222
Washington, D.C., 51,56,60,117
Watchers, the, 6
Water, 6
Waves of cold lava, 87
Waw, Phoenician, 105,116
Wednesday, November 30th, 2022, 9
White House, the, 96,97,100, 118
Winged disc, logo and symbol, 342
Work center of the Grays, 189
World(s)
  Copies of yourself in other, 226,
  Different, 225
  Economy, 131
  End of the, 198
  Etheric and bio-organic Lives in different, 225
  Parallel dimensions adjacent to our, 202
Woujoud, 225

X

Xenotransplantation, 134

Y

Y, 116
Year 685 A.D., 224
Year 1365, 224
Year 1947, Grays' spacecraft crashed in Roswell, 119
Year 2012, 49,51
Year 2021, 97,204
Year, 2022, 49,51,56,57,58,59, 82,105,147,148,149,186, 196, 201,202
  Coding and decoding the significance of the Year 2022,103
  Energy systems of the Anunnaki, after, 200
Year 2085, 49,51
10,000 years ago, 149
65,000 years ago, 53, 172,173
450,000 years ago, 149

Z

Zafta, 198
Zama-ari,235
Zaman, 225
Zamania, 224
Zara-Du, 229
Zefiro, 231
Zeta Reticuli, 76, 117,124
Ziggurat
  Of Enki in Ur, 196
  Of Nippur, 113
Zikr, 5
Zinar, 155
Zone(s)
  Beyond Earth, 226
  Mental, 340
  Of times and spaces, Different, 228
  Para-mental, 3

NOTES

NOTES

Printed in Great Britain
by Amazon